MW00388217

AIR FRYER

COOKBOOK #2019

600 Best Recipes for Whole Family:

(Bonus) 30 Day Quick and Easy Air Fryer Recipes Meal Plan: Ultimate Cookbook for Beginners

SUSAN CLIFFORD

TABLE OF CONTENTS

DESCRIPTION

The air fryer is a simple tool that will use the air and the heat around it to help you to cook up, or fry your foods. You will be able to get the great taste and crunch that you love from some of your favorite restaurants, but since you are using the fraction of the oil, or no oil at all, you will be able to enjoy these foods without all of the guilt that comes with it.

You aren't limited to just some snacks or the regular things that you would think go with your fried foods, you will be able to use this on any of the meals that your family usually enjoys. Most of your favorite meals will work great inside of the air fryer and you are going to be impressed by what all you can make in a short amount of time.

What are you waiting for? Grab your bag and start shopping for a happy and fulfilling meal!

Happy Cooking!!

INTRODUCTION

The air fryer is not only for making French fries. It can do much more. From perfectly roasted veggie dinners to deliciously spicy beans burgers or breakfast muffins, the air fryer can handle themall.

Whatever you can cook for 40 minutes or less in an oven, on a stovetop, or in a deep fryer can be cooked in an air fryer. This appliance is suitable for any meal that has to be fried, baked, grilled or roasted. It is however not designed for steaming vegetables or for frying ingredients that have to be fried with a batter.

The 600 recipes in this guide provide you with more than enough variety of recipes for making the most of your air fryer.

BREAKFAST

01. Bacon and Tomato Breakfast

Preparation Time:40 Minutes

Servings: 6

Ingredients:

- 1 lb. white bread; cubed
- 1 lb. smoked bacon; cooked and chopped.
- 1/4 cup olive oil
- 2 tbsp. chives; chopped
- 1/2 lb. Monterey jack; shredded
- 2 tbsp. stock
- 1 yellow onion; chopped
- 28 oz. canned tomatoes; chopped.
- 1/2 tsp. red pepper; crushed
- 1/2 lb. cheddar; shredded
- Salt and black pepper to the taste
- 8 eggs; whisked

Directions:

1. Add the oil to your air fryer and heat it up at 350 degrees F.
2. Add bread, bacon, onion, tomatoes, red pepper and stock and stir.
3. Add eggs, cheddar and Monterey jack and cook everything for 20 minutes. Divide among plates; sprinkle chives and serve.

Nutrition information:Calories: 231; Fat: 5; Fiber: 7; Carbs: 12; Protein: 4

02. Yummy Hash

Preparation Time:25 Minutes

Servings: 6

Ingredients:

- 16 oz. hash browns
- 1/4 cup olive oil
- 1/2 tsp. paprika
- 1/2 tsp. garlic powder
- 1 egg; whisked
- 2 tbsp. chives; chopped
- 1 cup cheddar; shredded
- Salt and black pepper to the taste

Directions:

1. Add oil to your air fryer; heat it up at 350 °F and add hash browns.
2. Also add paprika, garlic powder, salt, pepper and egg; toss and cook for 15 minutes. Add cheddar and chives, toss; divide among plates and serve.

Nutrition information:Calories: 213; Fat: 7; Fiber: 8; Carbs: 12; Protein: 4

03. Quick Turkey Burrito

Preparation Time:20 Minutes

Servings: 2

Ingredients:

- 4 slices turkey breast already cooked
- 1/2 red bell pepper; sliced
- 2 eggs
- 1/8 cup mozzarella cheese; grated

- 1 small avocado; peeled; pitted and sliced
- 2 tbsp. salsa
- Salt and black pepper to the taste
- Tortillas for serving

Directions:

1. In a bowl; whisk eggs with salt and pepper to the taste, pour them in a pan and place it in the air fryer's basket.
2. Cook at 400 °F, for 5 minutes; take pan out of the fryer and transfer eggs to a plate.
3. Arrange tortillas on a working surface, divide eggs on them; also divide turkey meat, bell pepper, cheese, salsa and avocado.
4. Roll your burritos and place them in your air fryer after you've lined it with some tin foil. Heat up the burritos at 300 °F, for 3 minutes; divide them on plates and serve.

Nutrition information:Calories: 349; Fat: 23; Fiber: 11; Carbs: 20; Protein: 21

04. Simple Breakfast

Preparation Time:23 Minutes

Servings: 4

Ingredients:

- 7 oz. baby spinach
- 8 chestnuts mushrooms; halved
- 8 tomatoes; halved
- 1 garlic clove; minced
- 4 eggs
- 4 chipolatas
- 4 bacon slices; chopped.
- Salt and black pepper to the taste
- Cooking spray

Directions:

1. Grease a cooking pan with the oil and add tomatoes, garlic and mushrooms.
2. Add bacon and chipolatas, also add spinach and crack eggs at the end.
3. Season with salt and pepper; place pan in the cooking basket of your air fryer and cook for 13 minutes at 350 degrees F. Divide among plates and serve for breakfast.

Nutrition information:Calories: 312; Fat: 6; Fiber: 8; Carbs: 15; Protein: 5

05. Biscuits Casserole Delight

Preparation Time:25 Minutes

Servings: 8

Ingredients:

- 12 oz. biscuits; quartered
- 3 tbsp. flour
- 1/2 lb. sausage; chopped.
- 2 ½ cups milk
- A pinch of salt and black pepper
- Cooking spray

Directions:

1. Grease your air fryer with cooking spray and heat it over 350 degrees F.
2. Add biscuits on the bottom and mix with sausage.
3. Add flour, milk, salt and pepper; toss a bit and cook for 15 minutes. Divide among plates and serve for breakfast.

Nutrition information:Calories: 321; Fat:

4; Fiber: 7; Carbs: 12; Protein: 5

06. Baked Eggs

Preparation Time:30 Minutes

Servings: 4

Ingredients:

- 4 eggs
- 1 lb. baby spinach; torn
- 4 tbsp. milk
- 1 tbsp. olive oil
- 7 oz. ham; chopped.
- Cooking spray
- Salt and black pepper to the taste

Directions:

1. Heat up a pan with the oil over medium heat; add baby spinach, stir cook for a couple of minutes and take off heat.
2. Grease 4 ramekins with cooking spray and divide baby spinach and ham in each.
3. Crack an egg in each ramekin, also divide milk, season with salt and pepper; place ramekins in preheated air fryer at 350 °F and bake for 20 minutes. Serve baked eggs for breakfast.

Nutrition information:Calories: 321; Fat: 6; Fiber: 8; Carbs: 15; Protein: 12

07. Eggs, Sausage and Cheese Mix

Preparation Time:30 Minutes

Servings: 4

Ingredients:

- 10 oz. sausages; cooked and crumbled
- 8 eggs; whisked
- 1 cup milk
- 1 cup cheddar cheese; shredded
- 1 cup mozzarella cheese; shredded
- Salt and black pepper to the taste
- Cooking spray

Directions:

1. In a bowl; mix sausages with cheese, mozzarella, eggs, milk, salt and pepper and whisk well.
2. Heat up your air fryer at 380 degrees F; spray cooking oil, add eggs and sausage mix and cook for 20 minutes. Divide among plates and serve.

Nutrition information:Calories: 320; Fat: 6; Fiber: 8; Carbs: 12; Protein: 5

08. Special Hash Browns

Preparation Time:30 Minutes

Servings: 6

Ingredients:

- 2 lbs. hash browns
- 1 cup whole milk
- 1 cup cheddar cheese; shredded
- 6 green onions; chopped
- 8 bacon slices; chopped
- 6 eggs
- 9 oz. cream cheese
- 1 yellow onion; chopped
- Salt and black pepper to the taste
- Cooking spray

Directions:

1. Heat up your air fryer at 350 °F and grease it with cooking spray.
2. In a bowl; mix eggs with milk, cream cheese, cheddar cheese, bacon, onion, salt and pepper and whisk well.
3. Add hash browns to your air fryer; add eggs mix over them and cook for 20 minutes. Divide among plates and serve.

Nutrition information:Calories: 261; Fat: 6; Fiber: 9; Carbs: 8; Protein: 12

09. Mixed Bell Peppers Frittata

Preparation Time:30 Minutes

Servings: 4

Ingredients:

- 1/2 lbs. chicken sausage; casings removed and chopped.
- 1 sweet onion; chopped
- 1 red bell pepper; chopped
- 2 tbsp. olive oil
- 1 orange bell pepper; chopped
- 1 green bell pepper; chopped
- 8 eggs; whisked
- 1/2 cup mozzarella cheese; shredded
- 2 tsp. oregano; chopped
- Salt and black pepper to the taste

Directions:

1. Add 1 tbsp. oil to your air fryer; add sausage, heat up at 320 °F and brown for 1 minute.
2. Add the rest of the oil, onion, red bell pepper, orange and green one; stir and cook for 2 minutes more.
3. Add oregano, salt, pepper and eggs; stir and cook for 15 minutes. Add mozzarella, leave frittata aside for a few minutes; divide among plates and serve.

Nutrition information:Calories: 212; Fat: 4; Fiber: 6; Carbs: 8; Protein: 12

10. Yummy Creamy Eggs

Preparation Time:22 Minutes

Servings: 4

Ingredients:

- 4 eggs
- 2 tsp. butter; soft
- 2 ham slices
- 3 tbsp. parmesan; grated
- 2 tsp. chives; chopped
- 2 tbsp. heavy cream
- Salt and black pepper to the taste
- A pinch of smoked paprika

Directions:

1. Grease your air fryer's pan with the butter; line it with the ham and add it to your air fryer's basket.
2. In a bowl; mix 1 egg with heavy cream, salt and pepper, whisk well and add over ham.
3. Crack the rest of the eggs in the pan, sprinkle parmesan and cook your mix for 12 minutes at 320 degrees F. Sprinkle paprika and chives all over; divide among plates and serve for breakfast.

Nutrition information:Calories: 263; Fat: 5; Fiber: 8; Carbs: 12; Protein: 5

11. Healthy Asparagus Frittata

Preparation Time:15 Minutes

Servings: 2

Ingredients:

- 4 eggs; whisked
- 2 tbsp. parmesan; grated
- 4 tbsp. milk
- 10 asparagus tips; steamed
- Salt and black pepper to the taste
- Cooking spray

Directions:

1. In a bowl; mix eggs with parmesan, milk, salt and pepper and whisk well.
2. Heat up your air fryer at 400 °F and grease with cooking spray.
3. Add asparagus, add eggs mix; toss a bit and cook for 5 minutes. Divide frittata on plates and serve for breakfast.

Nutrition information:Calories: 312; Fat: 5; Fiber: 8; Carbs: 14; Protein: 2

12. Potato Frittata

Preparation Time:30 Minutes

Servings: 6

Ingredients:

- 6 oz. jarred roasted red bell peppers; chopped.
- 12 eggs; whisked
- 2 tbsp. chives; chopped.
- 16 potato wedges
- 6 tbsp. ricotta cheese
- 1/2 cup parmesan; grated
- 3 garlic cloves; minced
- 2 tbsp. parsley; chopped.
- Salt and black pepper to the taste
- Cooking spray

Directions:

1. In a bowl; mix eggs with red peppers, garlic, parsley, salt, pepper and ricotta and whisk well.
2. Heat up your air fryer at 300 °F and grease it with cooking spray.
3. Add half of the potato wedges on the bottom and sprinkle half of the parmesan all over.
4. Add half of the egg mix; add the rest of the potatoes and the rest of the parmesan.
5. Add the rest of the eggs mix; sprinkle chives and cook for 20 minutes. Divide among plates and serve for breakfast.

Nutrition information:Calories: 312; Fat: 6; Fiber: 9; Carbs: 16; Protein: 5

13. Smoked Sausage Breakfast

Preparation Time:40 Minutes

Servings: 4

Ingredients:

- 1 ½ lbs. smoked sausage; chopped and browned
- A pinch of salt and black pepper
- 1 ½ cups grits
- 1 ½ tsp. thyme; chopped.
- 1/4 tsp. garlic powder
- 4 ½ cups water
- 16 oz. cheddar cheese; shredded

- 1 cup milk
- Cooking spray
- 4 eggs; whisked

Directions:

1. Put the water in a pot; bring to a boil over medium heat, add grits, stir and cover, cook for 5 minutes and take off heat.
2. Add cheese, stir until it melts and mix with milk, thyme, salt, pepper, garlic powder and eggs and whisk really well.
3. Heat up your air fryer at 300 degrees F; grease with cooking spray and add browned sausage.
4. Add grits mix; spread and cook for 25 minutes. Divide among plates and serve for breakfast.

Nutrition information:Calories: 321; Fat: 6; Fiber: 7; Carbs: 17; Protein: 4

14. Yummy Tofu Scramble

Preparation Time:35 Minutes

Servings: 4

Ingredients:

- 2 tbsp. soy sauce
- 1 tofu block; cubed
- 1 tsp. turmeric; ground
- 1/2 tsp. garlic powder
- 2½ cup red potatoes; cubed
- 1/2 cup yellow onion; chopped.
- 2 tbsp. extra virgin olive oil
- 4 cups broccoli florets
- 1/2 tsp. onion powder
- Salt and black pepper to the taste

Directions:

1. Mix tofu with 1 tbsp. oil, salt, pepper, soy sauce, garlic powder, onion powder, turmeric and onion in a bowl; stir and leave aside.
2. In a separate bowl; combine potatoes with the rest of the oil, a pinch of salt and pepper and toss to coat.
3. Put potatoes in your air fryer at 350 °F and bake for 15 minutes; shaking once.
4. Add tofu and its marinade to your air fryer and bake for 15 minutes.
5. Add broccoli to the fryer and cook everything for 5 minutes more. Serve right away.

Nutrition information:Calories: 140; Fat: 4; Fiber: 3; Carbs: 10; Protein: 14

15. Rice, Almonds Pudding

Preparation Time:13 Minutes

Servings: 4

Ingredients:

- 1 cup brown rice
- 1/2 cup coconut chips
- 1 cup milk
- 2 cups water
- 1/2 cup maple syrup
- 1/4 cup raisins
- 1/4 cup almonds
- A pinch of cinnamon powder

Directions:

1. Put the rice in a pan that fits your air fryer, add the water, heat up on the stove over medium high heat; cook

until rice is soft and drain.

2. Add milk, coconut chips, almonds, raisins, cinnamon and maple syrup; stir well, introduce in your air fryer and cook at 360 °F, for 8 minutes. Divide rice pudding in bowls and serve.

Nutrition information:Calories: 251; Fat: 6; Fiber: 8; Carbs: 39; Protein: 12

16. Pesto Breakfast Toast

Preparation time: 5 minutes

Cooking time: 8 minutes

Servings: 3

Ingredients:

- 6 bread slices
- 5 tablespoons butter, melted
- 3 garlic cloves, minced
- 6 teaspoons basil and tomato pesto
- 1 cup mozzarella cheese, grated

Directions:

1. Arrange bread slices on a working surface.
2. In a bowl, mix the butter, pesto, and garlic, and spread on each bread slice.
3. Place them in your air fryer's basket, sprinkle the cheese on top, and cook at 350 degrees F for 8 minutes.
4. Serve right away.

Nutrition information:calories 187, fat 6, fiber 6, carbs 13, protein 5

17. Sausage Omelet

Preparation time: 5 minutes

Cooking time: 11 minutes

Servings: 2

Ingredients:

- 1 sausage link, sliced
- 2 eggs, whisked
- 4 cherry tomatoes, halved
- 1 tablespoon cilantro, chopped
- 1 tablespoon olive oil
- 1 tablespoon cheddar cheese, grated
- Salt and black pepper to taste

Directions:

1. Put the tomatoes and sausage in the air fryer's basket and cook at 360 degrees F for 5 minutes.
2. Take a pan that fits your air fryer, grease it with the oil, and then transfer the tomatoes and sausage to the pan.
3. In a bowl, mix all remaining ingredients and stir.
4. Pour this over the sausage and tomato mixture, spread, and place the pan in the air fryer; cook at 360 degrees F for 6 minutes more.
5. Serve immediately and enjoy.

Nutrition information: calories 270, fat 14, fiber 3, carbs 23, protein 16

18. Polenta Cakes

Preparation time: 10 minutes

Cooking time: 25 minutes

Servings: 4

Ingredients:

- 1 cup cornmeal
- 3 cups water
- Salt and black pepper to taste
- 1 tablespoon butter, softened
- ¼ cup potato starch
- A drizzle of vegetable oil
- Maple syrup for serving

Directions:

1. Put the water in a pot, heat up over medium heat, add the cornmeal, whisk, and cook for 10 minutes.
2. Add the butter, whisk well again, then take off the heat and allow to cool down.
3. Take spoonfuls of polenta and shape into balls; flatten them, dredge in potato starch, and place them on a lined baking sheet that fits your air fryer. Drizzle with oil.
4. Place the baking sheet in the fryer and cook at 380 degrees F for 15 minutes, flipping them halfway.
5. Serve with maple syrup drizzled on top.

Nutrition information:calories 170, fat 2, fiber 2, carbs 12, protein 4

19. Vanilla Toast

Preparation time: 5 minutes

Cooking time: 5 minutes

Servings: 6

Ingredients:

- 1 stick butter, softened
- 12 bread slices
- ½ cup brown sugar
- 2 teaspoons vanilla extract

Directions:

1. In a bowl, mix the butter, sugar, and vanilla; stir.
2. Spread mixture over bread slices, put them in your air fryer, and cook at 400 degrees F for 5 minutes.
3. Serve immediately and enjoy.

Nutrition information:calories 170, fat 6, fiber 5, carbs 11, protein 2

20. Chili and Parsley Soufflé

Preparation time: 5 minutes

Cooking time: 9 minutes

Servings: 3

Ingredients:

- 3 eggs
- 2 tablespoons heavy cream
- 1 red chili pepper, chopped
- 2 tablespoons parsley, finely chopped
- Salt and white pepper to taste

Directions:

1. In a bowl, mix all ingredients, whisk, and pour into 3 ramekins.
2. Place ramekins in your air fryer's basket and cook at 400 degrees F for 9 minutes.
3. Serve the soufflés immediately and enjoy!

Nutrition information:calories 200, fat 6, fiber 1, carbs 11, protein 3

21. Air Fried Mushroom Mix

Preparation time: 5 minutes

Cooking time: 20 minutes

Servings: 4

Ingredients:

- 8 white mushrooms, sliced
- 1 garlic clove, minced
- 8 cherry tomatoes, halved
- 4 slices bacon, chopped
- 7 ounces spinach, torn
- A drizzle of olive oil
- 4 eggs
- Salt and black pepper to taste

Directions:

1. In a pan greased with oil and that fits your air fryer, mix all ingredients except for the spinach; stir.
2. Put the pan in your air fryer and cook at 400 degrees F for 15 minutes.
3. Add the spinach, toss, and cook for 5 minutes more.
4. Divide between plates and serve.

Nutrition information:calories 160, fat 2, fiber 5, carbs 12, protein 9

22. Parmesan Breakfast Muffins

Preparation time: 5 minutes

Cooking time: 15 minutes

Servings: 4

Ingredients:

- 2 eggs
- 2 tablespoons olive oil
- 3 ounces almond milk
- 1 tablespoon baking powder
- 4 ounces white flour
- A splash of Worcestershire sauce
- 2 ounces parmesan cheese, grated

Directions:

1. In a bowl, mix the eggs with 1 tablespoon of the oil, milk, baking powder, flour, Worcestershire sauce, and the parmesan; stir well.
2. Grease a muffin pan that fits your air fryer with the remaining 1 tablespoon of oil, divide the cheesy mix evenly, and place the pan in the air fryer.
3. 3.Cook at 320 degrees F for 15 minutes.
4. 4.Enjoy.

Nutrition information:calories 190, fat 12, fiber 2, carbs 11, protein 5

23. Tomato and Eggs Mix

Preparation time: 5 minutes

Cooking time: 30 minutes

Servings: 2

Ingredients:

- 2 eggs
- ½ cup cheddar cheese, shredded
- 2 tablespoons red onion, chopped
- A pinch of salt and black pepper
- ¼ cup milk
- ½ cup tomatoes, chopped

Directions:

1. In a bowl, mix all ingredients except for the cheese; stir well.
2. Pour mixture into a pan that fits your air fryer, sprinkle the cheese on top, and place the pan in the fryer.
3. Cook at 350 degrees F for 30 minutes.
4. Divide the mix between plates, serve, and enjoy!

Nutrition information:calories 210, fat 4, fiber 2, carbs 12, protein 9

24. Italian Eggplant Sandwich

Preparation time: 30 minutes

Cooking time: 25 minutes

Servings: 2

Ingredients:

- 1 eggplant, sliced
- 2 teaspoons parsley, chopped
- Salt and black pepper to taste
- ½ cup panko breadcrumbs
- ½ teaspoon garlic powder
- 2 tablespoons coconut milk
- ½ teaspoon Italian seasoning
- 4 bread slices
- 1 tablespoon avocado oil + a drizzle
- ½ cup mayonnaise
- ¾ cup tomato paste
- 2 tablespoons cheddar cheese, grated
- 2 cups mozzarella cheese, grated
- 2 tablespoons fresh basil, chopped

Directions:

1. Season eggplant slices with salt and pepper and set aside for 30 minutes. Then pat them dry them and brush with mayo and milk.
2. In a bowl, combine the parsley, breadcrumbs, Italian seasoning, garlic powder, salt, and black pepper; stir.
3. Next, dip the eggplant slices in this mix, and place them on a lined baking sheet; drizzle with oil.
4. Place the baking sheet in your air fryer's basket and cook at 400 degrees F for 15 minutes, flipping the eggplant slices halfway.
5. Brush the bread slices with the remaining 1 tablespoon of the oil. Then arrange 2 of them on a working surface, and add cheddar, mozzarella, baked eggplant slices, tomato paste, and basil; top with the other 2 bread slices.
6. Grill sandwiches on your grill for 10 minutes, serve immediately, and enjoy.

Nutrition information:calories 251, fat 11, fiber 4, carbs 8, protein 7

25. Corn Pudding

Preparation time: 10 minutes

Cooking time: 1 hour and 15 minutes

Servings: 6

Ingredients:

- 4 bacon slices, cooked and chopped
- 1 tablespoon olive oil
- 2 cups corn
- ½ cup green bell pepper, chopped
- 1 yellow onion, chopped
- ¼ cup celery, chopped
- 1 teaspoon thyme, chopped

- 2 teaspoons garlic, grated
- Salt and black pepper
- ½ cup heavy cream
- 1½ cups whole milk
- 3 eggs
- 3 cups bread, cubed
- 3 tablespoons parmesan cheese, grated
- 1 cup cheddar cheese, grated

Directions:

1. Heat up the oil in a pan over medium heat.
2. Add the corn, celery, onion, bell pepper, salt, pepper, garlic, and thyme to the pan; stir, sauté for 15 minutes, and transfer to a bowl.
3. To the same bowl, add the bacon, milk, cream, eggs, salt, pepper, bread, and the cheddar cheese. Stir well, then pour into a casserole dish that fits your air fryer.
4. Place the dish in the fryer and cook at 350 degrees F for 30 minutes.
5. Sprinkle the pudding with parmesan cheese, and cook for 30 minutes more.
6. Slice, divide between plates, and serve.

26. Long Beans Omelet

Preparation time: 10 minutes

Cooking time: 10 minutes

Servings: 3

Ingredients:

- ½ teaspoon soy sauce
- 1 tablespoon olive oil
- 3 eggs, whisked
- A pinch of salt and black pepper
- 4 garlic cloves, minced
- 4 long beans, trimmed and sliced

Directions:

1. In a bowl, mix eggs with a pinch of salt, black pepper and soy sauce and whisk well.
2. Heat up your air fryer at 320 degrees F, add oil and garlic, stir and brown for 1 minute.
3. Add long beans and eggs mix, spread and cook for 10 minutes.
4. Divide omelet on plates and serve for breakfast.
5. Enjoy!

Nutrition information:calories 200, fat 3, fiber 7, carbs 9, protein 3

27. French Beans and Egg Breakfast Mix

Preparation time: 10 minutes

Cooking time: 10 minutes

Servings: 3

Ingredients:

- 2 eggs, whisked
- ½ teaspoon soy sauce
- 1 tablespoon olive oil
- 4 garlic cloves, minced
- 3 ounces French beans, trimmed and sliced diagonally
- Salt and white pepper to the taste

Directions:

1. In a bowl, mix eggs with soy sauce,

salt and pepper and whisk well.
2. Heat up your air fryer at 320 degrees F, add oil and heat it up as well.
3. Add garlic and brown for 1 minute.
4. Add French beans and egg mix, toss and cook for 10 minutes.
5. Divide among plates and serve for breakfast.
6. Enjoy!

Nutrition information:calories 182, fat 3, fiber 6, carbs 8, protein 3

28. Breakfast Doughnuts

Preparation time: 10 minutes

Cooking time: 18 minutes

Servings: 6

Ingredients:

- 4 tablespoons butter, soft
- 1 and ½ teaspoon baking powder
- 2 an ¼ cups white flour
- ½ cup sugar
- 1/3 cup caster sugar
- 1 teaspoon cinnamon powder
- 2 egg yolks
- ½ cup sour cream

Directions:

1. In a bowl, mix 2 tablespoons butter with simple sugar and egg yolks and whisk well.
2. Add half of the sour cream and stir.
3. In another bowls, mix flour with baking powder, stir and also add to eggs mix.
4. Stir well until you obtain a dough, transfer it to a floured working surface, roll it out and cut big circles with smaller ones in the middle.
5. Brush doughnuts with the rest of the butter, heat up your air fryer at 360 degrees F, place doughnuts inside and cook them for 8 minutes.
6. In a bowl, mix cinnamon with caster sugar and stir.
7. Arrange doughnuts on plates and dip them in cinnamon and sugar before serving.
8. Enjoy!

Nutrition information:calories 182, fat 3, fiber 7, carbs 8, protein 3

29. Creamy Breakfast Tofu

Preparation time: 15 minutes

Cooking time: 20 minutes

Servings: 4

Ingredients:

- 1 block firm tofu, pressed and cubed
- 1 teaspoon rice vinegar
- 2 tablespoons soy sauce
- 2 teaspoons sesame oil
- 1 tablespoon potato starch
- 1 cup Greek yogurt

Directions:

1. In a bowl, mix tofu cubes with vinegar, soy sauce and oil, toss, and leave aside for 15 minutes.
2. Dip tofu cubes in potato starch, toss, transfer to your air fryer, heat up at 370 degrees F and cook for 20 minutes shaking halfway.
3. Divide into bowls and serve for breakfast with some Greek yogurt on

the side.

4. Enjoy!

Nutrition information:calories 110, fat 4, fiber 5, carbs 8, protein 4

30. Veggie Burritos

Preparation time: 10 minutes

Cooking time: 10 minutes

Servings: 4

Ingredients:

- 2 tablespoons cashew butter
- 2 tablespoons tamari
- 2 tablespoons water
- 2 tablespoons liquid smoke
- 4 rice papers
- ½ cup sweet potatoes, steamed and cubed
- ½ small broccoli head, florets separated and steamed
- 7 asparagus stalks
- 8 roasted red peppers, chopped
- A handful kale, chopped

Directions:

1. In a bowl, mix cashew butter with water, tamari and liquid smoke and whisk well.
2. Wet rice papers and arrange them on a working surface.
3. Divide sweet potatoes, broccoli, asparagus, red peppers and kale, wrap burritos and dip each in cashew mix.
4. Arrange burritos in your air fryer and cook them at 350 degrees F for 10 minutes.
5. Divide veggie burritos on plates d serve.
6. Enjoy !

Nutrition information:calories 172, fat 4, fiber 7, carbs 8, protein 3

31. Breakfast Fish Tacos

Preparation time: 10 minutes

Cooking time: 13 minutes

Servings: 4

Ingredients:

- 4 big tortillas
- 1 red bell pepper, chopped
- 1 yellow onion, chopped
- 1 cup corn
- 4 white fish fillets, skinless and boneless
- ½ cup salsa
- A handful mixed romaine lettuce, spinach and radicchio
- 4 tablespoon parmesan, grated

Directions:

1. Put fish fillets in your air fryer and cook at 350 degrees F for 6 minutes.
2. Meanwhile, heat up a pan over medium high heat, add bell pepper, onion and corn, stir and cook for 1-2 minutes.
3. Arrange tortillas on a working surface, divide fish fillets, spread salsa over them, divide mixed veggies and mixed greens and spread parmesan on each at the end.
4. Roll your tacos, place them in preheated air fryer and cook at 350 degrees F for 6 minutes more.

5. Divide fish tacos on plates and serve for breakfast.
6. Enjoy!

Nutrition information:calories 200, fat 3, fiber 7, carbs 9, protein 5

32. Garlic Potatoes with Bacon

Preparation time: 10 minutes

Cooking time: 20 minutes

Servings: 4

Ingredients:

- 4 potatoes, peeled and cut into medium cubes
- 6 garlic cloves, minced
- 4 bacon slices, chopped
- 2 rosemary springs, chopped
- 1 tablespoon olive oil
- Salt and black pepper to the taste
- 2 eggs, whisked

Directions:

1. In your air fryer's pan, mix oil with potatoes, garlic, bacon, rosemary, salt, pepper and eggs and whisk.
2. Cook potatoes at 400 degrees F for 20 minutes, divide everything on plates and serve for breakfast.
3. Enjoy!

Nutrition information:calories 211, fat 3, fiber 5, carbs 8, protein 5

34. Spinach Breakfast Parcels

Preparation time: 10 minutes

Cooking time: 4 minutes

Servings: 2

Ingredients:

- 4 sheets filo pastry
- 1 pound baby spinach leaves, roughly chopped
- ½ pound ricotta cheese
- 2 tablespoons pine nuts
- 1 eggs, whisked
- Zest from 1 lemon, grated
- Greek yogurt for serving
- Salt and black pepper to the taste

Directions:

1. In a bowl, mix spinach with cheese, egg, lemon zest, salt, pepper and pine nuts and stir.
2. Arrange filo sheets on a working surface, divide spinach mix, fold diagonally to shape your parcels and place them in your preheated air fryer at 400 degrees F.
3. Bake parcels for 4 minutes, divide them on plates and serve them with Greek yogurt on the side.
4. Enjoy!

Nutrition information:calories 182, fat 4, fiber 8, carbs 9, protein 5

35. Ham Rolls

Preparation time: 10 minutes

Cooking time: 10 minutes

Servings: 4

Ingredients:

- 1 sheet puff pastry
- 4 handful gruyere cheese, grated

- 4 teaspoons mustard
- 8 ham slices, chopped

Directions:

1. Roll out puff pastry on a working surface, divide cheese, ham and mustard, roll tight and cut into medium rounds.
2. Place all rolls in air fryer and cook for 10 minutes at 370 degrees F.
3. Divide rolls on plates and serve for breakfast.
4. Enjoy!

Nutrition information:calories 182, fat 4, fiber 7, carbs 9, protein 8

36. Shrimp Frittata

Preparation time: 10 minutes

Cooking time: 15 minutes

Servings: 4

Ingredients:

- 4 eggs
- ½ teaspoon basil, dried
- Cooking spray
- Salt and black pepper to the taste
- ½ cup rice, cooked
- ½ cup shrimp, cooked, peeled, deveined and chopped
- ½ cup baby spinach, chopped
- ½ cup Monterey jack cheese, grated

Directions:

1. In a bowl, mix eggs with salt, pepper and basil and whisk.
2. Grease your air fryer's pan with cooking spray and add rice, shrimp and spinach.
3. Add eggs mix, sprinkle cheese all over and cook in your air fryer at 350 degrees F for 10 minutes.
4. Divide among plates and serve for breakfast.
5. Enjoy!

Nutrition information:calories 162, fat 6, fiber 5, carbs 8, protein 4

37. Tuna Sandwiches

Preparation time: 10 minutes

Cooking time: 5 minutes

Servings: 4

Ingredients:

- 16 ounces canned tuna, drained
- ¼ cup mayonnaise
- 2 tablespoons mustard
- 1 tablespoons lemon juice
- 2 green onions, chopped
- 3 English muffins, halved
- 3 tablespoons butter
- 6 provolone cheese

Directions:

1. In a bowl, mix tuna with mayo, lemon juice, mustard and green onions and stir.
2. Grease muffin halves with the butter, place them in preheated air fryer and bake them at 350 degrees F for 4 minutes.
3. Spread tuna mix on muffin halves, top each with provolone cheese, return sandwiches to air fryer and cook them for 4 minutes, divide among plates and serve for breakfast

right away.

4. Enjoy!

Nutrition information:calories 182, fat 4, fiber 7, carbs 8, protein 6

38. Shrimp Sandwiches

Preparation time: 10 minutes

Cooking time: 5 minutes

Servings: 4

Ingredients:

- 1 and ¼ cups cheddar, shredded
- 6 ounces canned tiny shrimp, drained
- 3 tablespoons mayonnaise
- 2 tablespoons green onions, chopped
- 4 whole wheat bread slices
- 2 tablespoons butter, soft

Directions:

1. In a bowl, mix shrimp with cheese, green onion and mayo and stir well.
2. Spread this on half of the bread slices, top with the other bread slices, cut into halves diagonally and spread butter on top.
3. Place sandwiches in your air fryer and cook at 350 degrees F for 5 minutes.
4. Divide shrimp sandwiches on plates and serve them for breakfast.
5. Enjoy!

Nutrition information:calories 162, fat 3, fiber 7, carbs 12, protein 4

39. Breakfast Pea Tortilla

Preparation time: 10 minutes

Cooking time: 7 minutes

Servings: 8

Ingredients:

- ½ pound baby peas
- 4 tablespoons butter
- 1 and ½ cup yogurt
- 8 eggs
- ½ cup mint, chopped
- Salt and black pepper to the taste

Directions:

1. Heat up a pan that fits your air fryer with the butter over medium heat, add peas, stir and cook for a couple of minutes.
2. Meanwhile, in a bowl, mix half of the yogurt with salt, pepper, eggs and mint and whisk well.
3. Pour this over the peas, toss, introduce in your air fryer and cook at 350 degrees F for 7 minutes.
4. Spread the rest of the yogurt over your tortilla, slice and serve.
5. Enjoy!

Nutrition information:calories 192, fat 5, fiber 4, carbs 8, protein 7

40. Raspberry Rolls

Preparation time: 30 minutes

Cooking time: 20 minutes

Servings: 6

Ingredients:

- 1 cup milk
- 4 tablespoons butter
- 3 and ¼ cups flour
- 2 teaspoons yeast
- ¼ cup sugar
- 1 egg
- For the filling:
- 8 ounces cream cheese, soft
- 12 ounces raspberries
- 1 teaspoons vanilla extract
- 5 tablespoons sugar
- 1 tablespoon cornstarch
- Zest from 1 lemon, grated

Directions:

1. In a bowl, mix flour with sugar and yeast and stir.
2. Add milk and egg, stir until you obtain a dough, leave it aside to rise for 30 minutes, transfer dough to a working surface and roll well.
3. In a bowl, mix cream cheese with sugar, vanilla and lemon zest, stir well and spread over dough.
4. In another bowl, mix raspberries with cornstarch, stir and spread over cream cheese mix.
5. Roll your dough, cut into medium pieces, place them in your air fryer, spray them with cooking spray and cook them at 350 degrees F for 30 minutes.
6. Serve your rolls for breakfast.
7. Enjoy!

Nutrition information:calories 261, fat 5, fiber 8, carbs 9, protein 6

41. Potato and Leek Frittata

Preparation time: 10 minutes

Cooking time: 18 minutes

Servings: 4

Ingredients:

- 2 gold potatoes, boiled, peeled and chopped
- 2 tablespoons butter
- 2 leeks, sliced
- Salt and black pepper to the taste
- ¼ cup whole milk
- 10 eggs, whisked
- 5 ounces fromageblanc, crumbled

Directions:

1. Heat up a pan that fits your air fryer with the butter over medium heat, add leeks, stir and cook for 4 minutes.
2. Add potatoes, salt, pepper, eggs, cheese and milk, whisk well, cook for 1 minute more, introduce in your air fryer and cook at 350 degrees F for 13 minutes.
3. Slice frittata, divide among plates and serve.
4. Enjoy!

Nutrition information:calories 271, fat 6, fiber 8, carbs 12, protein 6

42. Espresso Oatmeal

Preparation time: 10 minutes

Cooking time: 17 minutes

Servings: 4

Ingredients:

- 1 cup milk

- 1 cup steel cut oats
- 2 and ½ cups water
- 2 tablespoons sugar
- 1 teaspoon espresso powder
- 2 teaspoons vanilla extract

Directions:

1. In a pan that fits your air fryer, mix oats with water, sugar, milk and espresso powder, stir, introduce in your air fryer and cook at 360 degrees F for 17 minutes.
2. Add vanilla extract, stir, leave everything aside for 5 minutes, divide into bowls and serve for breakfast.
3. Enjoy!

Nutrition information:calories 261, fat 7, fiber 6, carbs 39, protein 6

43. Mushroom Oatmeal

Preparation time: 10 minutes
Cooking time: 20 minutes
Servings: 4

Ingredients:

- 1 small yellow onion, chopped
- 1 cup steel cut oats
- 2 garlic cloves, minced
- 2 tablespoons butter
- ½ cup water
- 14 ounces canned chicken stock
- 3 thyme springs, chopped
- 2 tablespoons extra virgin olive oil
- ½ cup gouda cheese, grated
- 8 ounces mushroom, sliced
- Salt and black pepper to the taste

Directions:

1. Heat up a pan that fits your air fryer with the butter over medium heat, add onions and garlic, stir and cook for 4 minutes.
2. Add oats, water, salt, pepper, stock and thyme, stir, introduce in your air fryer and cook at 360 degrees F for 16 minutes.
3. Meanwhile, heat up a pan with the olive oil over medium heat, add mushrooms, cook them for 3 minutes, add to oatmeal and cheese, stir, divide into bowls and serve for breakfast.
4. Enjoy!

Nutrition information:calories 284, fat 8, fiber 8, carbs 20, protein 17

44. Walnuts and Pear Oatmeal

Preparation time: 5 minutes
Cooking time: 12 minutes
Servings: 4

Ingredients:

- 1 cup water
- 1 tablespoon butter, soft
- ¼ cups brown sugar
- ½ teaspoon cinnamon powder
- 1 cup rolled oats
- ½ cup walnuts, chopped
- 2 cups pear, peeled and chopped
- ½ cup raisins

Directions:

1. In a heat proof dish that fits your air fryer, mix milk with sugar, butter, oats, cinnamon, raisins, pears and walnuts, stir, introduce in your fryer and cook at 360 degrees F for 12 minutes.
2. Divide into bowls and serve.
3. Enjoy!

Nutrition information:calories 230, fat 6, fiber 11, carbs 20, protein 5

45. Cinnamon and Cream Cheese Oats

Preparation time: 10 minutes

Cooking time: 25 minutes

Servings: 4

Ingredients:

- 1 cup steel oats
- 3 cups milk
- 1 tablespoon butter
- ¾ cup raisins
- 1 teaspoon cinnamon powder
- ¼ cup brown sugar
- 2 tablespoons white sugar
- 2 ounces cream cheese, soft

Directions:

1. Heat up a pan that fits your air fryer with the butter over medium heat, add oats, stir and toast them for 3 minutes.
2. Add milk and raisins, stir, introduce in your air fryer and cook at 350 degrees F for 20 minutes.
3. Meanwhile, in a bowl, mix cinnamon with brown sugar and stir.
4. In a second bowl, mix white sugar with cream cheese and whisk.
5. Divide oats into bowls and top each with cinnamon and cream cheese.
6. Enjoy!

Nutrition information:calories 152, fat 6, fiber 6, carbs 25, protein 7

46. Cherries Risotto

Preparation time: 10 minutes

Cooking time: 12 minutes

Servings: 4

Ingredients:

- 1 and ½ cups Arborio rice
- 1 and ½ teaspoons cinnamon powder
- 1/3 cup brown sugar
- A pinch of salt
- 2 tablespoons butter
- 2 apples, cored and sliced
- 1 cup apple juice
- 3 cups milk
- ½ cup cherries, dried

1. **Directions:**
2. Heat up a pan that fist your air fryer with the butter over medium heat, add rice, stir and cook for 4-5 minutes.
3. Add sugar, apples, apple juice, milk, cinnamon and cherries, stir, introduce in your air fryer and cook at 350 degrees F for 8 minutes.
4. Divide into bowls and serve for breakfast.
5. Enjoy!

Nutrition information:calories 162, fat 12, fiber 6, carbs 23, protein 8

47. Rice, Almonds and Raisins Pudding

Preparation time: 5 minutes

Cooking time: 8 minutes

Servings: 4

Ingredients:

- 1 cup brown rice
- ½ cup coconut chips
- 1 cup milk
- 2 cups water
- ½ cup maple syrup
- ¼ cup raisins
- ¼ cup almonds
- A pinch of cinnamon powder

Directions:

- Put the rice in a pan that fits your air fryer, add the water, heat up on the stove over medium high heat, cook until rice is soft and drain.
- Add milk, coconut chips, almonds, raisins, cinnamon and maple syrup, stir well, introduce in your air fryer and cook at 360 degrees F for 8 minutes.
- Divide rice pudding in bowls and serve.
- Enjoy!

Nutrition information:calories 251, fat 6, fiber 8, carbs 39, protein 12

48. Dates and Millet Pudding

Preparation time: 10 minutes

Cooking time: 15 minutes

Servings: 4

Ingredients:

- 14 ounces milk
- 7 ounces water
- 2/3 cup millet
- 4 dates, pitted
- Honey for serving

Directions:

1. Put the millet in a pan that fits your air fryer, add dates, milk and water, stir, introduce in your air fryer and cook at 360 degrees F for 15 minutes.
2. Divide among plates, drizzle honey on top and serve for breakfast.
3. Enjoy!

Nutrition information:calories 231, fat 6, fiber 6, carbs 18, protein 6

49. Breakfast Cod Nuggets

Preparation Time:10 minutes

Servings: 4

Ingredients:

- 1 lb. of cod

For breading:

- 2 eggs, beaten
- 2 tablespoons olive oil
- 1 cup almond flour
- ¾ cup breadcrumbs
- 1 teaspoon dried parsley
- Pinch of sea salt

- ½ teaspoon black pepper

Directions:

1. Preheat the air fryer to 390°Fahrenheit. Cut the cod into strips about 1-inch by 2-inches in length. Blend breadcrumbs, olive oil, salt, parsley and pepper in a food processor. In three separate bowls add breadcrumbs, eggs, and flour. Place each piece of fish into flour, then the eggs and lastly the breadcrumbs. Add pieces of cod to air fryer basket and cook for 10-minutes. Serve warm.

Nutrition Information: Calories: 213, Total Fat: 12.6g, Carbs: 9.2g, Protein: 13.4g

50. Vegetable Egg Pancake

Preparation Time:15 minutes

Servings: 2

Ingredients:

1 cup almond flour

- ½ cup milk
- 1 tablespoon parmesan cheese, grated
- 3 eggs
- 1 potato, grated
- 1 beet, peeled and grated
- 1 carrot, grated
- 1 zucchini, grated
- 1 tablespoon olive oil
- ¼ teaspoon nutmeg
- 1 teaspoon onion powder
- 1 teaspoon garlic powder
- ½ teaspoon black pepper

Directions:

2. Preheat your air fryer to 390°Fahrenheit. Mix the zucchini, potato, beet, carrot, eggs, milk, almond flour and parmesan in bowl. Place olive oil into oven-safe dish. Form patties with vegetable mix and flatten to form patties. Place patties into oven-safe dish and cook in air fryer for 15-minutes. Serve with sliced tomatoes, sour cream, and toast.

Nutrition Information: Calories: 223, Total Fat: 11.2g, Carbs: 10.3g, Proteins: 13.4g

51. Oriental Omelet

Preparation Time:12 minutes

Servings: 1

Ingredients:

- ½ cup fresh Shimeji mushrooms, sliced
- 2 eggs, whisked
- Salt and pepper to taste
- 1 clove of garlic, minced
- A handful of sliced tofu
- 2 tablespoons onion, finely chopped
- Cooking spray

Directions:

1. Spray baking dish with cooking spray. Add onions and garlic. Air fry in preheated air fryer at 355°Fahrenheit for 4-minutes. Place the tofu and mushrooms over the onions and add salt and pepper to taste. Whisk the eggs and pour them over tofu and mushrooms. Air fry

again for 20-minutes. Serve warm.

Nutrition Information: Calories: 210, Total Fat: 11.2g, Carbs: 8.6g, Protein: 12.2g

52. Crispy Breakfast Avocado Fries

Preparation Time:8 minutes

Servings: 2

Ingredients:

- 2 eggs, beaten
- 2 large avocados, peeled, pitted, cut into 8 slices each
- ¼ teaspoon pepper
- ½ teaspoon cayenne pepper
- Salt to taste
- Juice of ½ a lemon
- ½ cup of whole wheat flour
- 1 cup whole wheat breadcrumbs
- Greek yogurt to serve

Directions:

1. Add flour, salt, pepper and cayenne pepper to bowl and mix. Add bread crumbs into another bowl. Beat eggs in a third bowl. First, dredge the avocado slices in the flour mixture. Next, dip them into the egg mixture and finally dredge them in the breadcrumbs. Place avocado fries into the air fryer basket. Preheat the air fryer to 390°Fahrenheit. Place the air fryer basket into the air fryer and cook for 6-minutes. When cook time is completed, transfer the avocado fries onto a serving platter. Sprinkle with lemon juice and serve with Greek yogurt.

Nutrition Information: Calories: 272, Total Fat: 13.4g, Carbs: 11.2g, Protein: 15.4g

53. Cheese & Egg Breakfast Sandwich

Preparation Time:6 minutes

Servings: 1

Ingredients:

- 1-2 eggs
- 1-2 slices of cheddar or Swiss cheese
- A bit of butter
- 1 roll sliced in half (your choice), Kaiser bun, English muffin, etc.

Directions:

2. Butter your sliced roll on both sides. Place the eggs in an oven-safe dish and whisk. Add seasoning if you wish such as dill, chives, oregano, and salt. Place the egg dish, roll and cheese into the air fryer. Make sure the buttered sides of roll are facing upwards. Set the air fryer to 390°Fahrenheit with a cook time of 6-minutes. Remove the ingredients when cook time is completed by air fryer. Place the egg and cheese between the pieces of roll and serve warm. You might like to try adding slices of avocado and tomatoes to this breakfast sandwich!

Nutrition Information: Calories: 212, Total Fat: 11.2g, Carbs: 9.3g, Protein: 12.4g

54. Breakfast Zucchini & Cream Muffins

Cook Time: 15 minutes

Servings: 5

Ingredients:

- 1 tablespoon cream cheese
- Half a cup zucchini, shredded
- 1 tablespoon plain yogurt
- 1 egg
- 1 cup of milk
- 2 tablespoons of warmed coconut oil
- Pinch of sea salt
- 2 teaspoons baking powder
- 1 teaspoon cinnamon
- 1 tablespoon liquid Stevia
- 4 cups whole wheat flour

Directions:

3. Mix all your dry ingredients in a mixing bowl (flour, sea salt, baking powder and cinnamon). Stir to combine. In another mixing bowl combine all of the wet ingredients (coconut oil, milk, yogurt, liquid Stevia, and egg. Whisk these until evenly combined. In a large bowl combine both the wet and dry ingredients and use a hand mixer to whisk them. Stir in the shredded zucchini and fold in the cream cheese. Place five muffin cups into your air fryer. Fill each cup ¾ full of mixture. Set air fryer to 350°Fahrenheit and cook muffins for 12-minutes. Serve warm or cold.

Nutrition Information: Calories: 217, Total Fat: 9.3g, Carbs: 8g, Protein: 10.2g

55. Peanut Butter & Banana Breakfast Sandwich

Preparation Time:6 minutes

Servings: 1

Ingredients:

- 2 slices of whole wheat bread
- 1 teaspoon of sugar-free maple syrup
- 1 sliced banana
- 2 tablespoons of peanut butter

Directions:

1. Evenly coat both sides of the slices of bread with peanut butter. Add the sliced banana and drizzle with some sugar-free maple syrup. Heat in the air fryer to 330°Fahrenheit for 6 minutes. Serve warm.

Nutrition Information: Calories: 211, Total Fat: 8.2g, Carbs: 6.3g, Protein: 11.2g

56. Eggs & Cocotte on Toast

Preparation Time:15 minutes

Servings: 2

Ingredients:

- 1/8 teaspoon of black pepper
- ¼ teaspoon salt
- ½ teaspoon Italian seasoning
- ¼ teaspoon balsamic vinegar
- ¼ teaspoon sugar-free maple syrup
- 1 cup sausages, chopped into small pieces
- 2 eggs
- 2 slices of whole wheat toast
- 3 tablespoons cheddar cheese, shredded
- 6-slices tomatoes

- Cooking spray
- A little mayonnaise to serve

Directions:

1. Spray baking dish with cooking spray. Place the bread slices at the bottom of dish. Sprinkle the sausages over bread. Lay the tomatoes over it. Sprinkle top with cheese. Beat the eggs and then pour over top of bread slices. Drizzle vinegar and maple syrup over eggs. Season with Italian seasoning, salt, and pepper, then sprinkle some more cheese on top. Place the baking dish in the air fryer basket that should be preheated at 320° Fahrenheit and cooked for 10-minutes. Remove from air fryer and add spot of mayonnaise and serve.

Nutrition Information: Calories: 232, Total Fat: 7.4g, Carbs: 6.3g, Protein: 14.2g

57. Breakfast Frittata

Preparation Time:15 minutes

Servings: 3

Ingredients:

- 6 eggs
- 8 cherry tomatoes, halved
- 2 tablespoons parmesan cheese, shredded
- 1 Italian sausage, diced
- Salt and pepper to taste

Directions:

2. Preheat your air fryer to 355°Fahrenheit. Add the tomatoes and sausage to baking dish. Place the baking dish into air fryer and cook for 5-minutes. Meanwhile, add eggs, salt, pepper, cheese, and oil into mixing bowl and whisk well. Remove the baking dish from air fryer and pour the egg mixture on top, spreading evenly. Placing the dish back into the air fryer and bake for an additional 5-minutes. Remove from air fryer and slice into wedges and serve.

Nutrition Information: Calories: 273, Total Fat: 8.2g, Carbs: 7g, Protein: 14.2g

58. Country Breakie Chicken Tenders

Preparation Time:15 minutes

Servings: 4

Ingredients:

- ¾ lb. of chicken tenders

For breading:

- 2 tablespoons olive oil
- 1 teaspoon black pepper
- ½ teaspoon salt
- ½ cup seasoned breadcrumbs
- ½ cup all-purpose flour
- 2 eggs, beaten

Directions:

1. Preheat your air fryer to 330°Fahrenheit. In three separate bowls, set aside breadcrumbs, eggs, and flour. Season the breadcrumbs with salt and pepper. Add olive oil to the breadcrumbs and mix well. Place chicken tenders into flour, then dip into eggs and finally dip into breadcrumbs. Press to ensure that

the breadcrumbs are evenly coating the chicken. Shake off excess breading in cooking basket. Cook the chicken tenders for 10-minutes in the air fryer. Serve warm.

Nutrition Information: Calories: 276, Total Fat: 8.6g, Carbs: 7g, Protein: 13.2g

59. Baked Mini Quiche

Preparation Time:15 minutes

Servings: 2

Ingredients:

- 2 eggs
- 1 large yellow onion, diced
- 1 ¾ cups whole wheat flour
- 1 ½ cups spinach, chopped
- ¾ cup cottage cheese
- Salt and black pepper to taste
- 2 tablespoons olive oil
- ¾ cup butter
- ¼ cup milk

Directions:

1. Preheat the air fryer to 355°Fahrenheit. Add the flour, butter, salt, and milk to bowl and knead dough until smooth and refrigerate for 15-minutes. Place a frying pan over medium heat and add the oil to it. When the oil is heated, add the onions into pan and sautė them. Add spinach to pan and cook until it wilts. Drain excess moisture from spinach.
2. Whisk the eggs together and add cheese to bowl and mix. Take the dough out of the fridge and divide into 8 equal parts. Roll the dough into a round that will fit into bottom of quiche mold. Place the rolled dough into molds. Place the spinach filling over dough. Place molds into air fryer basket and place basket inside of air fryer and cook for 15-minutes. Remove quiche from molds and serve warm or cold.

Nutrition Information: Calories: 262, Total Fat: 8.2g, Carbs: 7.3g, Protein: 9.5g

60. Morning Mini Cheeseburger Sliders

Preparation Time:10 minutes

Servings: 6

Ingredients:

- 1 lb. ground beef
- 6 slices of cheddar cheese
- 6 dinner rolls
- Salt and black pepper to taste

Directions:

1. Preheat your air fryer to 390°Fahrenheit. Form 6 beef patties each about 2.5 ounces and season with salt and black pepper.
2. Add the burger patties to the cooking basket and cook them for 10-minutes. Remove the burger patties from the air fryer; place the cheese on top of burgers and return to air fryer and cook for another minute. Remove and put burgers on dinner rolls and serve warm.

Nutrition Information: Calories: 262, Total Fat: 9.4g, Carbs: 8.2g, Protein: 16.2g

61. Avocado & Blueberry Muffins

Preparation Time:15 minutes

Servings: 12

Ingredients:

- 2 eggs
- 1 cup blueberries
- 2 cups almond flour
- 1 teaspoon baking soda
- 1/8 teaspoon salt
- 2 ripe avocados, peeled, pitted, mashed
- 2 tablespoons liquid Stevia
- 1 cup plain Greek yogurt
- 1 teaspoon vanilla extract

For streusel topping:

- 2 tablespoons Truvia sweetener
- 4 tablespoons butter, softened
- 4 tablespoons almond flour

Directions:

1. Make the streusel topping by mixing Truvia, flour, and butter until you form a crumbly mixture. Place this mixture in the freezer for a while. Meanwhile, make the muffins by sifting together flour, baking powder, baking soda and salt and set aside. Add avocados and liquid Stevia to a bowl and mix well. Adding in one egg at a time, continue to beat. Add the vanilla extract and yogurt and beat again. Add in flour mixture a bit at a time and mix well. Add the blueberries into mixture and gently fold them in. Pour the batter into greased muffin cups, then add mixture until they are half-full. Sprinkle the streusel topping mixture on top of muffin mixture and place muffin cups in the air fryer basket.
2. Bake in preheated air fryer at 355°Fahrenheit for 10-minutes. Remove the muffin cups from the air fryer and allow them to cool. Cool completely then serve.

Nutrition Information: Calories: 202, Total Fat: 9.2g, Carbs: 7.2g, Protein: 6.3g

62. Grilled Cheese

Preparation Time:7 minutes

Servings: 2

Ingredients:

- 4 slices of brown bread
- ½ cup sharp cheddar cheese, shredded
- ¼ cup butter, melted

Directions:

1. Preheat your air fryer to 360°Fahrenheit. Place cheese and butter into separate bowls. Melt butter and brush it onto the 4 slices of bread.
2. Place cheese on 2 sides of bread slices. Put sandwiches together and place them into cooking basket. Cook in air fryer for 5-minutes and serve warm.

Nutrition Information: Calories: 214, Total Fat: 11.2g, Carbs: 9.4g, Protein: 13.2g

63. Breakfast Muffins

Preparation Time:6 minutes

Servings: 2

Ingredients:

- 2 whole wheat English muffins
- 4 slices of bacon
- Pepper to taste
- 2 eggs

Directions:

1. Crack an egg each into ramekins. Season with pepper. Place the ramekins in your preheated air fryer at 390°Fahrenheit for 6-minutes with the bacon and muffins alongside. Remove the muffins from air fryer after a few minutes and split them. When the bacon and eggs are done cooking, add two pieces of bacon and one egg to each egg muffin and serve immediately.

Nutrition Information: Calories: 276, Total Fat: 12g, Carbs: 10.2g, Protein: 17.3g

64. Cheese Omelette

Preparation Time:15 minutes

Servings: 2

Ingredients:

- 3 eggs
- 1 large yellow onion, diced
- 2 tablespoons cheddar cheese, shredded
- ½ teaspoon soy sauce
- Salt and pepper to taste
- Olive oil cooking spray

Directions:

2. In a bowl whisk together eggs, soy sauce, pepper, and salt. Spray with olive oil cooking spray a small pan that will fit inside of your air fryer. Add onions to the pan and spread them around. Air fry onions for 7-minutes. Pour the beaten egg mixture over the cooked onions and sprinkle the top with shredded cheese. Place back into the air fryer and cook for 6-minutes more. Remove from the air fryer and serve omelet with toasted multi-grain bread.

Nutrition Information: Calories: 232, Total Fat: 8.2g, Carbs: 6.2g, Protein: 12.3g

65. Cranberry Coconut Quinoa

Preparation time: 10 minutes

Cooking time: 13 minutes

Servings: 4

Ingredients:

- 1 cup quinoa
- 3 cups coconut water
- 1 teaspoon vanilla extract
- 3 teaspoons stevia
- 1/8 cup coconut flakes
- ¼ cup cranberries, dried
- 1/8 cup almonds, chopped

Directions:

3. In your air fryer, mix quinoa with coconut water, vanilla, stevia, coconut flakes, almonds and cranberries, toss, cover and cook at 365 degrees F for 13 minutes.
4. Divide into bowls and serve for breakfast.
5. Enjoy!

Nutrition information:calories 146, fat 5, fiber 5, carbs 10, protein 7

66. Sweet Quinoa Mix

Preparation time: 10 minutes

Cooking time: 14 minutes

Servings: 6

Ingredients:

- ½ cup quinoa
- 1 and ½ cups steel cut oats
- 4 tablespoons stevia
- 4 and ½ cups almond milk
- 2 tablespoons maple syrup
- 1 and ½ teaspoons vanilla extract
- Strawberries, halved for serving
- Cooking spray

Directions:

1. Spray your air fryer with cooking spray, add oats, quinoa, stevia, almond milk, maple syrup and vanilla extract, toss, cover and cook at 365 degrees F for 14 minutes
2. Divide into bowls, add strawberries on top and serve for breakfast.
3. Enjoy!

Nutrition information:calories 207, fat 5, fiber 8, carbs 14, protein 5

67. Chia Pudding

Preparation time: 10 minutes

Cooking time: 15 minutes

Servings: 4

Ingredients:

- 1 cup chia seeds
- 2 cups coconut milk
- 2 tablespoons coconut, shredded and unsweetened
- ¼ cup maple syrup
- ½ teaspoon cinnamon powder
- 2 teaspoons cocoa powder
- ½ teaspoon vanilla extract

Directions:

1. In your air fryer, mix chia seeds, coconut milk, coconut, maple syrup, cinnamon, cocoa powder and vanilla, toss, cover and cook at 365 degrees F for 15 minutes
2. Divide chia pudding into bowls and serve for breakfast.
3. Enjoy!

Nutrition information:calories 261, fat 4, fiber 8, carbs 10, protein 4

68. Simple Creamy Breakfast Potatoes

Preparation time: 10 minutes

Cooking time: 20 minutes

Servings: 8

Ingredients:

- Cooking spray
- 2 pounds gold potatoes, halved and sliced
- 1 yellow onion, cut into medium wedges
- 10 ounces canned vegan potato cream soup
- 8 ounces coconut milk
- 1 cup tofu, crumbled
- ½ cup veggie stock
- Salt and black pepper to the taste

Directions:

1. Grease your air fryer's pan with cooking spray and arrange half of the potatoes on the bottom.
2. Layer onion wedges, half of the vegan cream soup, coconut milk, tofu, stock, salt and pepper.
3. Add the rest of the potatoes, onion wedges, cream, coconut milk, tofu and stock, cover and cook at 365 degrees F for 20 minutes.
4. Divide between plates and serve.
5. Enjoy!

Nutrition information:calories 206, fat 14, fiber 4, carbs 10, protein 12

69. Sweet Potatoes Mix

Preparation time: 10 minutes

Cooking time: 20 minutes

Servings: 10

Ingredients:

- 4 pounds sweet potatoes, thinly sliced
- 3 tablespoons stevia
- ½ cup orange juice
- Salt and black pepper to the taste
- ½ teaspoon thyme, dried
- ½ teaspoon sage, dried
- 2 tablespoons olive oil

Directions:

1. Arrange potato slices on the bottom of your air fryer's pan.
2. In a bowl, mix orange juice with salt, pepper, stevia, thyme, sage and oil and whisk well.
3. Add this over potatoes, cover and cook at 365 degrees F for 20 minutes
4. Divide between plates and serve for breakfast
5. Enjoy!

Nutrition information:calories 189, fat 4, fiber 4, carbs 16, protein 4

70. Breakfast Bowls

Preparation time: 10 minutes

Cooking time: 15 minutes

Servings: 4

Ingredients:

- 1 block firm tofu, cut into thin strips
- 1 teaspoon turmeric powder
- ¼ cup coconut aminos
- ½ teaspoon onion powder
- ½ cup nutritional yeast
- 2 tablespoons olive oil
- 1 avocado, peeled, cored and sliced
- A handful cherry tomatoes, halved
- 2 green onions, chopped
- Salt and black pepper to the taste

Directions:

1. In a bowl, mix tofu strips with turmeric, coconut aminos, onion powder, half of the oil and yeast and toss.
2. Transfer this to your preheated air fryer at 370 degrees F and cook for 15 minutes.
3. In a large bowl, mix tomatoes with green onions, salt and pepper and toss.
4. Add tofu and the rest of the oil, toss, divide between plates and serve for breakfast.

5. Enjoy!

Nutrition information:calories 200, fat 4, fiber 6, carbs 14, protein 5

71. Mediterranean Chickpeas Breakfast

Preparation time: 10 minutes

Cooking time: 12 minutes

Servings: 2

Ingredients:

- Cooking spray
- 3 shallots, chopped
- 2 garlic cloves, minced
- ½ teaspoon sweet paprika
- ½ teaspoon smoked paprika
- ½ teaspoon cinnamon powder
- Salt and black pepper to the taste
- 2 tomatoes, chopped
- 2 cup chickpeas, cooked
- 1 tablespoon parsley, chopped

Directions:

1. Spray your air fryer with cooking spray and preheat it to 365 degrees F.
2. Add shallots, garlic, sweet and smoked paprika, cinnamon, salt, pepper, tomatoes, parsley and chickpeas, toss, cover and cook for 12 minutes.
3. Divide into bowls and serve for breakfast.
4. Enjoy!

Nutrition information:calories 200, fat 4, fiber 6, carbs 12, protein 5

72. Pumpkin Breakfast Muffins

Preparation time: 10 minutes

Cooking time: 10 minutes

Servings: 2

Ingredients:

- 1 and ½ cups rolled oats
- ½ cup pumpkin, peeled and cubed
- ¼ cup maple syrup
- 1 teaspoon cinnamon powder
- ¼ teaspoon nutmeg, ground
- ¼ teaspoon ginger powder
- 1/3 cup cranberries

Directions:

1. In your blender, mix oats with pumpkin, maple syrup, cinnamon, ginger and nutmeg and pulse well.
2. Fold cranberries into the mix, spoon the whole mix into muffin cups, place them in your air fryer's basket, cover and cook at 360 degrees F for 10 minutes.
3. Serve them for breakfast.
4. Enjoy!

Nutrition information:calories 192, fat 4, fiber 5, carbs 14, protein 2

73. Delicious Porridge

Preparation time: 10 minutes

Cooking time: 16 minutes

Servings: 4

Ingredients:

- 3 cups brown rice, cooked
- 1 and ¾ cups almond milk
- 2 tablespoons coconut sugar
- 2 tablespoons flaxseed meal
- 2 tablespoons raisins

- ¼ teaspoon cinnamon powder
- ¼ teaspoon vanilla extract

Directions:

1. In your air fryer, mix rice, milk, sugar, flax meal, raisins, cinnamon and vanilla, stir, cover and cook at 360 degrees F for 16 minutes.
2. Stir porridge again, divide into bowls and serve for breakfast.
3. Enjoy!

Nutrition information:calories 221, fat 4, fiber 6, carbs 11, protein 4

74. Strawberry Quinoa

Preparation time: 10 minutes

Cooking time: 10 minutes

Servings: 1

Ingredients:

- ¾ cup water
- 1 cup strawberries, halved
- ¼ cup cashews
- 1 stevia packet
- 1 cup quinoa

Directions:

1. In your air fryer's pan, mix water with cashews, quinoa and stevia, stir, cover and cook at 400 degrees F for 10 minutes.
2. Add strawberries, stir, divide into bowls and serve for breakfast.
3. Enjoy!

Nutrition information:calories 177, fat 2, fiber 5, carbs 10, protein 4

75. Breakfast Broccoli and Tofu Bowls

Preparation time: 10 minutes

Cooking time: 15 minutes

Servings: 4

Ingredients:

- 1 block firm tofu, pressed and cubed
- 1 teaspoon rice vinegar
- 2 tablespoons coconut aminos
- 1 tablespoon olive oil
- 1 cup quinoa, cooked
- 4 cups broccoli florets
- 2 tablespoons vegan avocado pesto

Directions:

1. In a bowl, mix tofu cubes with vinegar, coconut aminos, oil and broccoli, toss and leave aside for 10 minutes.
2. Transfer tofu to your air fryer's basket and cook at 400 degrees F for 10 minutes.
3. Add broccoli, cover fryer again and cook for 5 minutes more.
4. Divide quinoa into bowls, add tofu and broccoli, top with avocado pesto and serve for breakfast.
5. Enjoy!

Nutrition information:calories 188, fat 3, fiber 5, carbs 8, protein 2

76. Cool Tofu Breakfast Mix

Preparation time: 10 minutes

Cooking time: 10 minutes

Servings: 1

Ingredients:

- 3 ounces firm tofu, pressed and crumbled
- 1 cup kale, torn
- ½ cup broccoli florets
- ½ cup mushrooms, halved
- ¼ cup cherry tomatoes, halved
- ½ cup carrot, grated
- ¼ teaspoon garlic powder
- ¼ teaspoon onion powder
- ½ teaspoon yellow curry powder
- ¼ teaspoon sweet paprika
- Salt and black pepper to the taste
- Cooking spray
- ¼ cup micro greens

Directions:

1. Heat up your air fryer at 380 degrees F, grease its pan with cooking spray, add tofu, kale, broccoli, mushrooms, tomatoes, carrot, garlic powder, onion powder, curry powder, paprika, salt and pepper, toss, cover and cook for 10 minutes.
2. Divide between plates, add micro greens, toss and serve.
3. Enjoy!

Nutrition information:calories 199, fat 2, fiber 5, carbs 12, protein 3

77. Cinnamon Oatmeal

Preparation time: 10 minutes

Cooking time: 15 minutes

Servings: 3

Ingredients:

- 3 cups water
- 1 cup steel cut oats
- 1 apple, cored and chopped
- 1 tablespoon cinnamon powder

Directions:

1. In your air fryer, mix water with oats, cinnamon and apple, stir, cover and cook at 365 degrees F for 15 minutes.
2. Stir again, divide into bowls and serve for breakfast.
3. Enjoy!

Nutrition information:calories 200, fat 1, fiber 7, carbs 12, protein 10

78. Coconut Rice

Preparation time: 10 minutes

Cooking time: 15 minutes

Servings: 4

Ingredients:

- 1 cup Arborio rice
- 2 cups almond milk
- 1 cup coconut milk
- 1/3 cup agave nectar
- 2 teaspoons vanilla extract
- ¼ cup coconut flakes, toasted

Directions:

1. In your air fryer, mix rice with almond milk, coconut milk, agave nectar, vanilla extract and coconut flakes, cover and cook at 360 degrees F for 15 minutes.
2. Divide into bowls and serve warm.
3. Enjoy!

Nutrition information:calories 192, fat 1, fiber 1, carbs 20, protein 4

LUNCH

79. Asian Chicken

Preparation Time:40 Minutes

Servings: 4

Ingredients:

- 2 chicken breasts; skinless, boneless and sliced
- 1 tsp. olive oil
- 1 yellow onion; sliced
- 1 tbsp. Worcestershire sauce
- 14 oz. pizza dough
- 1 ½ cups cheddar cheese; grated
- 1/2 cup jarred cheese sauce
- Salt and black pepper to the taste

Directions:

1. Preheat your air fryer at 400 degrees F; add half of the oil and onions and fry them for 8 minutes, stirring once.
2. Add chicken pieces, Worcestershire sauce, salt and pepper; toss, air fry for 8 minutes more, stirring once and transfer everything to a bowl.
3. Roll pizza dough on a working surface and shape a rectangle.
4. Spread half of the cheese all over, add chicken and onion mix and top with cheese sauce.
5. Roll your dough and shape into a U.
6. Place your roll in your air fryer's basket, brush with the rest of the oil and cook at 370 degrees for 12 minutes, flipping the roll halfway. Slice your roll when it's warm and serve for lunch.

Nutrition information:Calories: 300; Fat: 8; Fiber: 17; Carbs: 20; Protein: 6

80. Japanese Style Chicken

Preparation Time:18 Minutes

Servings: 2

Ingredients:

- 2 chicken thighs; skinless and boneless
- 1/8 cup sake
- 1/2 tsp. sesame oil
- 1/8 cup water
- 2 ginger slices; chopped
- 3 garlic cloves; minced
- 1/4 cup soy sauce
- 1/4 cup mirin
- 2 tbsp. sugar
- 1 tbsp. cornstarch mixed with 2 tbsp. water
- Sesame seeds for serving

Directions:

In a bowl; mix chicken thighs with ginger, garlic, soy sauce, mirin, sake, oil, water, sugar and cornstarch; toss well, transfer to preheated air fryer and cook at 360 °F, for 8 minutes. Divide among plates; sprinkle sesame seeds on top and serve with a side salad for lunch.

Nutrition information:Calories: 300; Fat: 7; Fiber: 9; Carbs: 17; Protein: 10

81. Beef Cubes

Preparation Time:22 Minutes

Servings: 4

Ingredients:

- 1 lb. sirloin; cubed
- 16 oz. jarred pasta sauce
- 1 ½ cups bread crumbs
- 1/2 tsp. marjoram; dried
- 2 tbsp. olive oil
- White rice; already cooked for serving

Directions:

1. In a bowl; mix beef cubes with pasta sauce and toss well.
2. In another bowl; mix bread crumbs with marjoram and oil and stir well.
3. Dip beef cubes in this mix, place them in your air fryer and cook at 360 °F, for 12 minutes. Divide among plates and serve with white rice on the side.

Nutrition information:Calories: 271; Fat: 6; Fiber: 9; Carbs: 18; Protein: 12

82. Chicken Salad

Preparation Time:30 Minutes

Servings: 4

Ingredients:

- 2 ears of corn; hulled
- 1 lb. chicken tenders; boneless
- 12 cherry tomatoes; sliced
- Olive oil as needed
- 1/4 cup ranch dressing
- 3 tbsp. BBQ sauce
- 1 tsp. sweet paprika
- 1 tbsp. brown sugar
- 1/2 tsp. garlic powder
- 1/2 iceberg lettuce head; cut into medium strips
- 1/2 romaine lettuce head; cut into medium strips
- 1 cup canned black beans; drained
- 1 cup cheddar cheese; shredded
- 3 tbsp. cilantro; chopped.
- 4 green onions; chopped.
- Salt and black pepper to the taste

Directions:

1. Put corn in your air fryer; drizzle some oil, toss, cook at 400 °F, for 10 minutes; transfer to a plate and leave aside for now.
2. Put chicken in your air fryer's basket, add salt, pepper, brown sugar, paprika and garlic powder; toss, drizzle some more oil, cook at 400 °F, for 10 minutes; flipping them halfway, transfer tenders to a cutting board and chop them.
3. Cur kernels off the cob, transfer corn to a bowl; add chicken, iceberg lettuce, romaine lettuce, black beans, cheese, cilantro, tomatoes, onions, BBQ sauce and ranch dressing; toss well and serve for lunch.

Nutrition information:Calories: 372; Fat: 6; Fiber: 9; Carbs: 17; Protein: 6

83. Different Pasta Salad

Preparation Time:22 Minutes

Servings: 6

Ingredients:

- 1 zucchini; sliced in half and roughly chopped.

- 1 orange bell pepper; roughly chopped.
- 1 green bell pepper; roughly chopped.
- 1 lb. penne rigate; already cooked
- 1 cup cherry tomatoes; halved
- 1/2 cup kalamata olive; pitted and halved
- 1 red onion; roughly chopped.
- 4 oz. brown mushrooms; halved
- 1 tsp. Italian seasoning
- 1/4 cup olive oil
- 3 tbsp. balsamic vinegar
- 2 tbsp. basil; chopped.
- Salt and black pepper to the taste

Directions:

1. In a bowl; mix zucchini with mushrooms, orange bell pepper, green bell pepper, red onion, salt, pepper, Italian seasoning and oil; toss well, transfer to preheated air fryer at 380 °F and cook them for 12 minutes.
2. In a large salad bowl; mix pasta with cooked veggies, cherry tomatoes, olives, vinegar and basil; toss and serve for lunch.

Nutrition information:Calories: 200; Fat: 5; Fiber: 8; Carbs: 10; Protein: 6

84. Tasty Turkey Burgers

Preparation Time:18 Minutes

Servings: 4

Ingredients:

- 1 lb. turkey meat; ground
- 1 shallot; minced
- A drizzle of olive oil
- 1 small jalapeno pepper; minced
- 2 tsp. lime juice
- Zest from 1 lime; grated
- 1 tsp. cumin; ground
- 1 tsp. sweet paprika
- Salt and black pepper to the taste
- Guacamole for serving

Directions:

1. In a bowl; mix turkey meat with salt, pepper, cumin, paprika, shallot, jalapeno, lime juice and zest; stir well, shape burgers from this mix, drizzle the oil over them; introduce in preheated air fryer and cook them at 370 °F, for 8 minutes on each side. Divide among plates and serve with guacamole on top.

Nutrition information:Calories: 200; Fat: 12; Fiber: 0; Carbs: 0; Protein: 12

85. Shrimp Croquettes

Preparation Time:18 Minutes

Servings: 4

Ingredients:

- 2/3 lb. shrimp; cooked; peeled; deveined and chopped.
- 1 ½ cups bread crumbs
- 1 egg; whisked
- 2 tbsp. olive oil
- 2 tbsp. lemon juice
- 3 green onions; chopped.
- 1/2 tsp. basil; dried
- Salt and black pepper to the taste

Directions:

2. In a bowl; mix half of the bread crumbs with egg and lemon juice and stir well.
3. Add green onions, basil, salt, pepper and shrimp and stir really well.
4. In a separate bowl; mix the rest of the bread crumbs with the oil and toss well.
5. Shape round balls out of shrimp mix, dredge them in bread crumbs; place them in preheated air fryer and cook the for 8 minutes at 400 degrees F. Serve them with a dip for lunch.

Nutrition information:Calories: 142; Fat: 4; Fiber: 6; Carbs: 9; Protein: 4

86. Tasty Hot Dogs

Preparation Time:17 Minutes

Servings: 2

Ingredients:

- 2 hot dog buns
- 1 tbsp. Dijon mustard
- 2 hot dogs
- 2 tbsp. cheddar cheese; grated

Directions:

1. Put hot dogs in preheated air fryer and cook them at 390 °F, for 5 minutes.
2. Divide hot dogs into hot dog buns, spread mustard and cheese; return everything to your air fryer and cook for 2 minutes more at 390 degrees F. Serve for lunch.

Nutrition information:Calories: 211; Fat: 3; Fiber: 8; Carbs: 12; Protein: 4

87. Delicious Lentils Fritters

Preparation Time:20 Minutes

Servings: 2

Ingredients:

- 1 cup yellow lentils; soaked in water for 1 hour and drained
- 1 hot chili pepper; chopped.
- 1-inch ginger piece; grated
- 1/2 tsp. turmeric powder
- 1 tsp. garam masala
- 1 tsp. baking powder
- 2 tsp. olive oil
- 1/3 cup water
- 1/2 cup cilantro; chopped
- 1 ½ cup spinach; chopped
- 4 garlic cloves; minced
- 3/4 cup red onion; chopped
- Salt and black pepper to the taste
- Mint chutney for serving

Directions:

1. In your blender; mix lentils with chili pepper, ginger, turmeric, garam masala, baking powder, salt, pepper, olive oil, water, cilantro, spinach, onion and garlic, blend well and shape medium balls out of this mix.
2. Place them all in your preheated air fryer at 400 °F and cook for 10 minutes. Serve your veggie fritters with a side salad for lunch.

Nutrition information:Calories: 142; Fat: 2; Fiber: 8; Carbs: 12; Protein: 4

88. Stuffed Portobello Mushrooms

Preparation Time:30 Minutes

Servings: 4

Ingredients:

- 4 big Portobello mushroom caps
- 1/3 cup bread crumbs
- 1/4 tsp. rosemary; chopped.
- 1 tbsp. olive oil
- 1/4 cup ricotta cheese
- 5 tbsp. parmesan; grated
- 1 cup spinach; torn

Directions:

1. Rub mushrooms caps with the oil; place them in your air fryer's basket and cook them at 350 °F, for 2 minutes.
2. Meanwhile; in a bowl, mix half of the parmesan with ricotta, spinach, rosemary and bread crumbs and stir well.
3. Stuff mushrooms with this mix; sprinkle the rest of the parmesan on top; place them in your air fryer's basket again and cook at 350 °F, for 10 minutes. Divide them on plates and serve with a side salad for lunch.

Nutrition information:Calories: 152; Fat: 4; Fiber: 7; Carbs: 9; Protein: 5

89. Mouthwatering Chicken Kabobs

Preparation Time:30 Minutes

Servings: 2

Ingredients:

- 2 chicken breasts; skinless, boneless and roughly cubed
- 3 orange bell peppers; cut into squares
- 1/4 cup honey
- 1/3 cup soy sauce
- Cooking spray
- 6 mushrooms; halved
- Salt and black pepper to the taste

Directions:

1. In a bowl; mix chicken with salt, pepper, honey, say sauce and some cooking spray and toss well.
2. Thread chicken, bell peppers and mushrooms on skewers; place them in your air fryer and cook at 338 °F, for 20 minutes. Divide among plates and serve for lunch.

Nutrition information:Calories: 261; Fat: 7; Fiber: 9; Carbs: 12; Protein: 6

90. Delicious Fajitas

Preparation Time:20 Minutes

Servings: 4

Ingredients:

- 1 lb. chicken breasts; cut into strips
- 1 tsp. garlic powder
- 1/4 tsp. cumin; ground
- 1/2 tsp. chili powder
- 1 green bell pepper; sliced
- 1 yellow onion; chopped.
- 1 tbsp. lime juice
- 1/4 tsp. coriander; ground
- 1 red bell pepper; sliced

- Salt and black pepper to the taste
- Cooking spray
- 4 tortillas; warmed up
- Salsa for serving
- 1 cup lettuce leaves; torn for serving
- Sour cream for serving

Directions:

1. In a bowl; mix chicken with garlic powder, cumin, chili, salt, pepper, coriander, lime juice, red bell pepper, green bell pepper and onion; toss, leave aside for 10 minutes, transfer to your air fryer and drizzle some cooking spray all over.
2. Toss and cook at 400 °F, for 10 minutes. Arrange tortillas on a working surface, divide chicken mix, also add salsa, sour cream and lettuce; wrap and serve for lunch.

Nutrition information:Calories: 317; Fat: 6; Fiber: 8; Carbs: 14; Protein: 4

91. Fried Thai Salad

Preparation Time:15 Minutes

Servings: 4

Ingredients:

- 12 big shrimp; cooked, peeled and deveined
- 1 cup carrots; grated
- 1 cup red cabbage; shredded
- A handful cilantro; chopped.
- 1 small cucumber; chopped.
- Juice from 1 lime
- 2 tsp. red curry paste
- A pinch of salt and black pepper

Directions:

1. In a pan, mix cabbage with carrots, cucumber and shrimp; toss, introduce in your air fryer and cook at 360 °F, for 5 minutes. Add salt, pepper, cilantro, lime juice and red curry paste; toss again, divide among plates and serve right away.

Nutrition information:Calories: 172; Fat: 5; Fiber: 7; Carbs: 8; Protein: 5

92. Awesome Buttermilk Chicken

Preparation Time:28 Minutes

Servings: 4

Ingredients:

- 1 ½ lbs. chicken thighs
- 2 cups buttermilk
- 1 tbsp. baking powder
- 1 tbsp. sweet paprika
- A pinch of cayenne pepper
- 2 cups white flour
- 1 tbsp. garlic powder
- Salt and black pepper to the taste

Directions:

2. In a bowl; mix chicken thighs with buttermilk, salt, pepper and cayenne; toss and leave aside for 6 hours.
3. In a separate bowl; mix flour with paprika, baking powder and garlic powder and stir.
4. Drain chicken thighs, dredge them in flour mix; arrange them in your air fryer and cook at 360 °F, for 8 minutes. Flip chicken pieces, cook them for 10 minutes more; arrange

on a platter and serve for lunch.

Nutrition information:Calories: 200; Fat: 3; Fiber: 9; Carbs: 14; Protein: 4

93. Succulent Turkey Breast

Preparation Time:57 Minutes
Servings: 4

- **Ingredients:**

- 1 big turkey breast
- 2 tsp. olive oil
- 1/2 tsp. smoked paprika
- 1 tsp. thyme; dried
- 1/2 tsp. sage; dried
- 2 tbsp. mustard
- 1/4 cup maple syrup
- 1 tbsp. butter; soft
- Salt and black pepper to the taste

Directions:

1. Brush turkey breast with the olive oil; season with salt, pepper, thyme, paprika and sage, rub, place in your air fryer's basket and fry at 350 °F, for 25 minutes.
2. Flip turkey; cook for 10 minutes more; flip one more time and cook for another 10 minutes.
3. Meanwhile; heat up a pan with the butter over medium heat, add mustard and maple syrup; stir well, cook for a couple of minutes and take off heat. Slice turkey breast, divide among plates and serve with the maple glaze drizzled on top.

Nutrition information:Calories: 280; Fat: 2; Fiber: 7; Carbs: 16; Protein: 14

94. Special Gnocchi

Preparation Time:27 Minutes
Servings: 4

Ingredients:

- 1/4 cup parmesan; grated
- 1 yellow onion; chopped
- 16 oz. gnocchi
- 1 tbsp. olive oil
- 3 garlic cloves; minced
- 8 oz. spinach pesto

Directions:

1. Grease your air fryer's pan with olive oil, add gnocchi, onion and garlic, toss; put pan in your air fryer and cook at 400 °F, for 10 minutes.
2. Add pesto, toss and cook for 7 minutes more at 350 degrees F. Divide among plates and serve for lunch.

Nutrition information:Calories: 200; Fat: 4; Fiber: 4; Carbs: 12; Protein: 4

95. Tasty Hash Brown Toasts

Preparation Time:17 Minutes
Servings: 4

Ingredients:

- 4 hash brown patties; frozen
- 1 tbsp. olive oil
- 1 tbsp. balsamic vinegar
- 1 tbsp. basil; chopped.
- 1/4 cup cherry tomatoes; chopped.
- 3 tbsp. mozzarella; shredded
- 2 tbsp. parmesan; grated

Directions:

1. Put hash brown patties in your air fryer; drizzle the oil over them and cook them at 400 °F, for 7 minutes.
2. In a bowl; mix tomatoes with mozzarella, parmesan, vinegar and basil and stir well. Divide hash brown patties on plates; top each with tomatoes mix and serve for lunch.

Nutrition information:Calories: 199; Fat: 3; Fiber: 8; Carbs: 12; Protein: 4

96. Italian Eggplant Sandwich

Preparation time: 10 minutes

Cooking time: 16 minutes

Servings: 2

Ingredients:

- 1 eggplant, sliced
- 2 teaspoons parsley, dried
- Salt and black pepper to the taste
- ½ cup breadcrumbs
- ½ teaspoon Italian seasoning
- ½ teaspoon garlic powder
- ½ teaspoon onion powder
- 2 tablespoons milk
- 4 bread slices
- Cooking spray
- ½ cup mayonnaise
- ¾ cup tomato sauce
- 2 cups mozzarella cheese, grated

Directions:

1. Season eggplant slices with salt and pepper, leave aside for 10 minutes and then pat dry them well.
2. In a bowl, mix parsley with breadcrumbs, Italian seasoning, onion and garlic powder, salt and black pepper and stir.
3. In another bowl, mix milk with mayo and whisk well.
4. Brush eggplant slices with mayo mix, dip them in breadcrumbs, place them in your air fryer's basket, spray with cooking oil and cook them at 400 degrees F for 15 minutes, flipping them after 8 minutes.
5. Brush each bread slice with olive oil and arrange 2 on a working surface.
6. Add mozzarella and parmesan on each, add baked eggplant slices, spread tomato sauce and basil and top with the other bread slices, greased side down.
7. Divide sandwiches on plates, cut them in halves and serve for lunch.
8. Enjoy!

Nutrition information:calories 324, fat 16, fiber 4, carbs 39, protein 12

97. Creamy Chicken Stew

Preparation time: 10 minutes

Cooking time: 25 minutes

Servings: 4

Ingredients:

- 1 and ½ cups canned cream of celery soup
- 6 chicken tenders
- Salt and black pepper to the taste
- 2 potatoes, chopped
- 1 bay leaf
- 1 thyme spring, chopped
- 1 tablespoon milk

- 1 egg yolk
- ½ cup heavy cream

Directions:

1. In a bowl, mix chicken with cream of celery, potatoes, heavy cream, bay leaf, thyme, salt and pepper, toss, pour into your air fryer's pan and cook at 320 degrees F for 25 minutes.
2. Leave your stew to cool down a bit, discard bay leaf, divide among plates and serve right away.
3. Enjoy!

Nutrition information:calories 300, fat 11, fiber 2, carbs 23, protein 14

98. Lunch Pork and Potatoes

Preparation time: 10 minutes

Cooking time: 25 minutes

Servings: 2

Ingredients:

- 2 pounds pork loin
- Salt and black pepper to the taste
- 2 red potatoes, cut into medium wedges
- ½ teaspoon garlic powder
- ½ teaspoon red pepper flakes
- 1 teaspoon parsley, dried
- A drizzle of balsamic vinegar

Directions:

1. In your air fryer's pan, mix pork with potatoes, salt, pepper, garlic powder, pepper flakes, parsley and vinegar, toss and cook at 390 degrees F for 25 minutes.
2. Slice pork, divide it and potatoes on plates and serve for lunch.
3. Enjoy!

Nutrition information:calories 400, fat 15, fiber 7, carbs 27, protein 20

99. Turkey Cakes

Preparation time: 10 minutes

Cooking time: 10 minutes

Servings: 4

Ingredients:

- 6 mushrooms, chopped
- 1 teaspoon garlic powder
- 1 teaspoon onion powder
- Salt and black pepper to the taste
- 1 and ¼ pounds turkey meat, ground
- Cooking spray
- Tomato sauce for serving

Directions:

1. In your blender, mix mushrooms with salt and pepper, pulse well and transfer to a bowl.
2. Add turkey, onion powder, garlic powder, salt and pepper, stir and shape cakes out of this mix.
3. Spray them with cooking spray, transfer them to your air fryer and cook at 320 degrees F for 10 minutes.
4. Serve them with tomato sauce on the side and a tasty side salad.
5. Enjoy!

Nutrition information:calories 202, fat 6, fiber 3, carbs 17, protein 10

100. Cheese Ravioli and Marinara Sauce

Preparation time: 10 minutes
Cooking time: 8 minutes
Servings: 6

Ingredients:

- 20 ounces cheese ravioli
- 10 ounces marinara sauce
- 1 tablespoon olive oil
- 1 cup buttermilk
- 2 cups bread crumbs
- ¼ cup parmesan, grated

Directions:

1. Put buttermilk in a bowl and breadcrumbs in another bowl.
2. Dip ravioli in buttermilk, then in breadcrumbs and place them in your air fryer on a baking sheet.
3. Drizzle olive oil over them, cook at 400 degrees F for 5 minutes, divide them on plates, sprinkle parmesan on top and serve for lunch
4. Enjoy!

Nutrition information:calories 270, fat 12, fiber 6, carbs 30, protein 15

101. Beef Stew

Preparation time: 10 minutes
Cooking time: 20 minutes
Servings: 4

Ingredients:

- 2 pounds beef meat, cut into medium chunks
- 2 carrots, chopped
- 4 potatoes, chopped
- Salt and black pepper to the taste
- 1 quart veggie stock
- ½ teaspoon smoked paprika
- A handful thyme, chopped

Directions:

1. In a dish that fits your air fryer, mix beef with carrots, potatoes, stock, salt, pepper, paprika and thyme, stir, place in air fryer's basket and cook at 375 degrees F for 20 minutes.
2. Divide into bowls and serve right away for lunch.
3. Enjoy!

Nutrition information:calories 260, fat 5, fiber 8, carbs 20, protein 22

102. Meatballs Sandwich

Preparation time: 10 minutes
Cooking time: 22 minutes
Servings: 4

Ingredients:

- 3 baguettes, sliced more than halfway through
- 14 ounces beef, ground
- 7 ounces tomato sauce
- 1 small onion, chopped
- 1 egg, whisked
- 1 tablespoon bread crumbs
- 2 tablespoons cheddar cheese, grated
- 1 tablespoon oregano, chopped
- 1 tablespoon olive oil
- Salt and black pepper to the taste

- 1 teaspoon thyme, dried
- 1 teaspoon basil, dried

Directions:

1. In a bowl, combine meat with salt, pepper, onion, breadcrumbs, egg, cheese, oregano, thyme and basil, stir, shape medium meatballs and add them to your air fryer after you've greased it with the oil.
2. Cook them at 375 degrees F for 12 minutes, flipping them halfway.
3. Add tomato sauce, cook meatballs for 10 minutes more and arrange them on sliced baguettes.
4. Serve them right away.
5. Enjoy!

Nutrition information:calories 380, fat 5, fiber 6, carbs 34, protein 20

103. Bacon Pudding

Preparation time: 10 minutes

Cooking time: 30 minutes

Servings: 6

Ingredients:

- 4 bacon strips, cooked and chopped
- 1 tablespoon butter, soft
- 2 cups corn
- 1 yellow onion, chopped
- ¼ cup celery, chopped
- ½ cup red bell pepper, chopped
- 1 teaspoon thyme, chopped
- 2 teaspoons garlic, minced
- Salt and black pepper to the taste
- ½ cup heavy cream
- 1 and ½ cups milk
- 3 eggs, whisked
- 3 cups bread, cubed
- 4 tablespoons parmesan, grated
- Cooking spray

Directions:

1. Grease your air fryer's pan with coking spray.
2. In a bowl, mix bacon with butter, corn, onion, bell pepper, celery, thyme, garlic, salt, pepper, milk, heavy cream, eggs and bread cubes, toss, pour into greased pan and sprinkle cheese all over
3. Add this to your preheated air fryer at 320 degrees and cook for 30 minutes.
4. Divide among plates and serve warm for a quick lunch.
5. Enjoy!

Nutrition information:calories 276, fat 10, fiber 2, carbs 20, protein 10

104. Special Lunch Seafood Stew

Preparation time: 10 minutes

Cooking time: 20 minutes

Servings: 4

Ingredients:

- 5 ounces white rice
- 2 ounces peas
- 1 red bell pepper, chopped
- 14 ounces white wine
- 3 ounces water
- 2 ounces squid pieces
- 7 ounces mussels

- 3 ounces sea bass fillet, skinless, boneless and chopped
- 6 scallops
- ounces clams
- 4 shrimp
- 4 crayfish
- Salt and black pepper to the taste
- 1 tablespoon olive oil

Directions:

1. In your air fryer's pan, mix sea bass with shrimp, mussels, scallops, crayfish, clams and squid.
2. Add the oil, salt and pepper and toss to coat.
3. In a bowl, mix peas salt, pepper, bell pepper and rice and stir.
4. Add this over seafood, also add whine and water, place pan in your air fryer and cook at 400 degrees F for 20 minutes, stirring halfway.
5. Divide into bowls and serve for lunch.
6. Enjoy!

Nutrition information:calories 300, fat 12, fiber 2, carbs 23, protein 25

105. Air Fried Thai Salad

Preparation time: 10 minutes

Cooking time: 5 minutes

Servings: 4

Ingredients:

- 1 cup carrots, grated
- 1 cup red cabbage, shredded
- A pinch of salt and black pepper
- A handful cilantro, chopped
- 1 small cucumber, chopped
- Juice from 1 lime
- 2 teaspoons red curry paste
- 12 big shrimp, cooked, peeled and deveined

Directions:

1. In a pan that fits your, mix cabbage with carrots, cucumber and shrimp, toss, introduce in your air fryer and cook at 360 degrees F for 5 minutes.
2. Add salt, pepper, cilantro, lime juice and red curry paste, toss again, divide among plates and serve right away.
3. Enjoy!

Nutrition information:calories 172, fat 5, fiber 7, carbs 8, protein 5

106. Sweet Potato Lunch Casserole

Preparation time: 10 minutes

Cooking time: 50 minutes

Servings: 6

Ingredients:

- 3 big sweet potatoes, pricked with a fork
- 1 cup chicken stock
- Salt and black pepper to the taste
- A pinch of cayenne pepper
- ¼ teaspoon nutmeg, ground
- 1/3 cup coconut cream

Directions:

1. Place sweet potatoes in your air fryer, cook them at 350 degrees F for

40 minutes, cool them down, peel, roughly chop and transfer to a pan that fits your air fryer.

2. Add stock, salt, pepper, cayenne and coconut cream, toss, introduce in your air fryer and cook at 360 degrees F for 10 minutes more.
3. Divide casserole into bowls and serve.
4. Enjoy!

Nutrition information:calories 245, fat 4, fiber 5, carbs 10, protein 6

107. Zucchini Casserole

Preparation time: 10 minutes

Cooking time: 16 minutes

Servings: 8

Ingredients:

- 1 cup veggie stock
- 2 tablespoons olive oil
- 2 sweet potatoes, peeled and cut into medium wedges
- 8 zucchinis, cut into medium wedges
- 2 yellow onions, chopped
- 1 cup coconut milk
- Salt and black pepper to the taste
- 1 tablespoon soy sauce
- ¼ teaspoon thyme, dried
- ¼ teaspoon rosemary, dried
- 4 tablespoons dill, chopped
- ½ teaspoon basil, chopped

Directions:

1. Heat up a pan that fits your air fryer with the oil over medium heat, add onion, stir and cook for 2 minutes.
2. Add zucchinis, thyme, rosemary, basil, potato, salt, pepper, stock, milk, soy sauce and dill, stir, introduce in your air fryer, cook at 360 degrees F for 14 minutes, divide among plates and serve right away.
3. Enjoy!

Nutrition information:calories 133, fat 3, fiber 4, carbs 10, protein 5

108. Coconut and Chicken Casserole

Preparation time: 10 minutes

Cooking time: 25 minutes

Servings: 4

Ingredients:

- 4 lime leaves, torn
- 1 cup veggie stock
- 1 lemongrass stalk, chopped
- 1 inch piece, grated
- 1 pound chicken breast, skinless, boneless and cut into thin strips
- 8 ounces mushrooms, chopped
- 4 Thai chilies, chopped
- 4 tablespoons fish sauce
- 6 ounces coconut milk
- ¼ cup lime juice
- ¼ cup cilantro, chopped
- Salt and black pepper to the taste

Directions:

1. Put stock into a pan that fits your air fryer, bring to a simmer over medium heat, add lemongrass, ginger and lime leaves, stir and cook for 10 minutes.

2. Strain soup, return to pan, add chicken, mushrooms, milk, chilies, fish sauce, lime juice, cilantro, salt and pepper, stir, introduce in your air fryer and cook at 360 degrees F for 15 minutes.
3. Divide into bowls and serve.
4. Enjoy!

Nutrition information:calories 150, fat 4, fiber 4, carbs 6, protein 7

109. Turkey Burgers

Preparation time: 10 minutes

Cooking time: 8 minutes

Servings: 4

Ingredients:

- 1 pound turkey meat, ground
- 1 shallot, minced
- A drizzle of olive oil
- 1 small jalapeno pepper, minced
- 2 teaspoons lime juice
- Zest from 1 lime, grated
- Salt and black pepper to the taste
- 1 teaspoon cumin, ground
- 1 teaspoon sweet paprika
- Guacamole for serving

Directions:

1. In a bowl, mix turkey meat with salt, pepper, cumin, paprika, shallot, jalapeno, lime juice and zest, stir well, shape burgers from this mix, drizzle the oil over them, introduce in preheated air fryer and cook them at 370 degrees F for 8 minutes on each side.
2. Divide among plates and serve with guacamole on top.
3. Enjoy!

Nutrition information:calories 200, fat 12, fiber 0, carbs 0, protein 12

110. Salmon and Asparagus

Preparation time: 10 minutes

Cooking time: 23 minutes

Servings: 4

Ingredients:

- 1 pound asparagus, trimmed
- 1 tablespoon olive oil
- A pinch of sweet paprika
- Salt and black pepper to the taste
- A pinch of garlic powder
- A pinch of cayenne pepper
- 1 red bell pepper, cut into halves
- 4 ounces smoked salmon

Directions:

1. Put asparagus spears and bell pepper on a lined baking sheet that fits your air fryer, add salt, pepper, garlic powder, paprika, olive oil, cayenne pepper, toss to coat, introduce in the fryer, cook at 390 degrees F for 8 minutes, flip and cook for 8 minutes more.
2. Add salmon, cook for 5 minutes, more, divide everything on plates and serve.
3. Enjoy!

Nutrition information:calories 90, fat 1, fiber 1, carbs 1.2, protein 4

111. Easy Chicken Lunch

Preparation time: 10 minutes

Cooking time: 20 minutes

Servings: 6

Ingredients:

- 1 bunch kale, chopped
- Salt and black pepper to the taste
- ¼ cup chicken stock
- 1 cup chicken, shredded
- 3 carrots, chopped
- 1 cup shiitake mushrooms, roughly sliced

Directions:

1. In a blender, mix stock with kale, pulse a few times and pour into a pan that fits your air fryer.
2. Add chicken, mushrooms, carrots, salt and pepper to the taste, toss, introduce in your air fryer and cook at 350 degrees F for 18 minutes.
3. Enjoy!

Nutrition information:calories 180, fat 7, fiber 2, carbs 10, protein 5

112. Chicken and Corn Casserole

Preparation time: 10 minutes

Cooking time: 30 minutes

Servings: 6

Ingredients:

- 1 cup clean chicken stock
- 2 teaspoons garlic powder
- Salt and black pepper to the taste
- 6 ounces canned coconut milk
- 1 and ½ cups green lentils
- 2 pounds chicken breasts, skinless, boneless and cubed
- 1/3 cup cilantro, chopped
- 3 cups corn
- 3 handfuls spinach
- 3 green onions, chopped

Directions:

1. In a pan that fits your air fryer, mix stock with coconut milk, salt, pepper, garlic powder, chicken and lentils.
2. Add corn, green onions, cilantro and spinach, stir well, introduce in your air fryer and cook at 350 degrees F for 30 minutes.
3. Enjoy!

Nutrition information:calories 345, fat 12, fiber 10, carbs 20, protein 44

113. Chicken and Zucchini Lunch Mix

Preparation time: 10 minutes

Cooking time: 20 minutes

Servings: 4

Ingredients:

- 4 zucchinis, cut with a spiralizer
- 1 pound chicken breasts, skinless, boneless and cubed
- 2 garlic cloves, minced
- 1 teaspoon olive oil
- Salt and black pepper to the taste
- 2 cups cherry tomatoes, halved
- ½ cup almonds, chopped

- For the pesto:
- 2 cups basil
- 2 cups kale, chopped
- 1 tablespoon lemon juice
- 1 garlic clove
- ¾ cup pine nuts
- ½ cup olive oil
- A pinch of salt

Directions:

1. In your food processor, mix basil with kale, lemon juice, garlic, pine nuts, oil and a pinch of salt, pulse really well and leave aside.
2. Heat up a pan that fits your air fryer with the oil over medium heat, add garlic, stir and cook for 1 minute.
3. Add chicken, salt, pepper, stir, almonds, zucchini noodles, garlic, cherry tomatoes and the pesto you've made at the beginning, stir gently, introduce in preheated air fryer and cook at 360 degrees F for 17 minutes.
4. Divide among plates and serve for lunch.
5. Enjoy!

Nutrition information:calories 344, fat 8, fiber 7, carbs 12, protein 16

114. Chicken, Beans, Corn and Quinoa Casserole

Preparation time: 10 minutes

Cooking time: 30 minutes

Servings: 8

Ingredients:

- 1 cup quinoa, already cooked
- 3 cups chicken breast, cooked and shredded
- 14 ounces canned black beans
- 12 ounces corn
- ½ cup cilantro, chopped
- 6 kale leaves, chopped
- ½ cup green onions, chopped
- 1 cup clean tomato sauce
- 1 cup clean salsa
- 2 teaspoons chili powder
- 2 teaspoons cumin, ground
- 3 cups mozzarella cheese, shredded
- 1 tablespoon garlic powder
- Cooking spray
- 2 jalapeno peppers, chopped

Directions:

1. Spray a baking dish that fits your air fryer with cooking spray, add quinoa, chicken, black beans, corn, cilantro, kale, green onions, tomato sauce, salsa, chili powder, cumin, garlic powder, jalapenos and mozzarella, toss, introduce in your fryer and cook at 350 degrees F for 17 minutes.
2. Slice and serve warm for lunch.
3. Enjoy!

Nutrition information:calories 365, fat 12, fiber 6, carbs 22, protein 26

115. Roly Poly Air Fried White Fish

Preparation Time:10 minutes

Servings: 4

Ingredients:

- 4 lbs. of white fish fillets

- 2 ½ teaspoons of sea salt
- 4 mushrooms, sliced
- 1 teaspoon liquid stevia
- 2 tablespoons of Chinese winter pickle
- 2 tablespoons of vinegar
- 2 teaspoons chili powder
- 2 onions, thinly sliced
- 1 cup vegetable stock
- 2 tablespoons soy sauce

Directions:

1. Fill the fish fillets with mushrooms and pickle. Cut the onions into thinly sliced pieces. Spread the onions over the fish fillets. Combine the stock, soy sauce, vinegar, sea salt, and stevia. Sprinkle the mixture over the fish fillets. Place the fish fillets into your air fryer and cook at 350°Fahrenheit for 10-minutes. Serve warm.

Nutrition Information: Calories: 278, Total Fat: 9.2g, Carbs: 7.4g, Protein: 33.2g

116. Air Fried Dragon Shrimp

Preparation Time:15 minutes

Servings: 2

Ingredients:

- ½ lb. shrimp
- ¼ cup almond flour
- Pinch of ginger
- 1 cup chopped green onions
- 2 tablespoons olive oil
- 2 eggs, beaten
- ½ cup soy sauce

Directions:

1. Boil the shrimps for 5-minutes. Prepare a paste made of ginger and onion. Now, beat the eggs, add the ginger paste, soya sauce and almond flour and combine well. Add the shrimps to the mixture then place them in a baking dish and spray with oil. Cook shrimps at 390°Fahrenheit for 10-minutes.

Nutrition Information: Calories: 278, Total Fat: 8.6g, Carbs: 6.2g, Protein: 28.6g

117. Lasagna Zucchini Cups

Preparation Time:25 minutes

Servings: 6

Ingredients:

- Chopped parsley, for garnish
- ¼ cup parmesan, freshly grated
- ½ cup mozzarella, shredded
- ½ cup ricotta
- 1-14.5-ounce can of crushed tomatoes
- Black pepper and salt to taste
- ½ teaspoon oregano, dried
- ½ lb. ground beef
- 2 garlic cloves, minced
- ½ onion, chopped
- 1 tablespoon olive oil
- 3 zucchinis

Directions:

1. In a large pan over medium heat, add the oil. Add onion and garlic and cook for 5-minutes. Add in the ground beef and cook for 10-minutes stirring

often. Season with oregano, salt, pepper, cook until meat is no longer pink. Add crushed tomatoes and simmer mixture for 5-minutes. Stir in the ricotta and remove from heat. Cut zucchini in half crosswise in two. Using a spoon scoop out zucchini flesh to create wells. Fill wells with meat mixture. Top with mozzarella and parmesan cheese. Place directly in air fryer and cook at 350°Fahrenheit for 15-minutes. Garnish with parsley and parmesan.

118. Spinach Artichoke Stuffed Peppers

Preparation Time:15 minutes

Servings: 4

Ingredients:

- 4 assorted bell peppers,
- halved and seeded
- Salt and black pepper to taste
- Olive oil for drizzling
- 2 cups shredded rotisserie chicken
- Fresh parsley, chopped for garnish
- 2 cloves garlic, minced
- ¼ cup mayonnaise
- ¼ cup sour cream
- ½ cup mozzarella, shredded, divided
- 6-ounces cream cheese, softened
- 1 (10-ounce) package frozen spinach, thawed, well-drained, and chopped
- 1 (14-ounce) can artichoke hearts, drained and chopped

Directions:

1. On a large, rimmed baking sheet, place bell peppers cut side-up and drizzle with olive oil, then season with salt and pepper. In a large bowl, combine chicken, artichoke hearts, spinach, cream cheese, ½ cup mozzarella, parmesan, sour cream, mayo and garlic. Season with more salt and pepper and mix until well blended. Divide the chicken mixture between pepper halves, top with remaining mozzarella, and bake in air fryer at 400°Fahrenheit for 15-minutes. Garnish with parsley and serve.

Nutrition Information: Calories: 284, Total Fat: 13.4g, Carbs: 9.2g, Protein: 34.3g

119. Cauliflower Shepherd's Pie

Preparation Time:43 minutes

Servings: 4

Ingredients:

- 1 medium head of cauliflower, cut into florets
- ¼ cup whole milk
- 3-ounces cream cheese, softened
- 1 tablespoon parsley, chopped for garnish
- 2/3 cup chicken broth
- 2 tablespoons almond flour
- 1 cup frozen peas
- 1 lb. ground beef
- 2 cloves garlic, minced
- 2 carrots, peeled, and chopped
- 1 large onion, chopped
- 1 tablespoon olive oil
- Salt and black pepper to taste

Directions:

2. Make mashed cauliflower. Bring a pot of water to boil, add the florets and cook for 10-minutes. Drain pot and then use paper towel to absorb excess water. Return florets to pot and mash with potato masher until smooth. Stir in cream cheese, milk and season with salt and pepper. Set aside. Make the beef mixture: in large pan over medium heat, heat oil. Add onion, garlic and cook for 5-minutes.
3. Add ground beef for 5-minutes or until meat is no longer pink. Stir in frozen peas and corn and cook another 3-minutes. Sprinkle meat mixture with almond flour and stir to even distribute. Cook for another minute then add chicken broth. Bring to a simmer and let mixture thicken slightly, for 5-minutes. Place beef mixture in air fryer baking dish. Top beef mixture with an even layer of cauliflower and bake in air fryer at 400°Fahrenheit for 15-minutes. Garnish with parsley and serve.

Nutrition Information: Calories: 279, Total Fat: 13.2g, Carbs: 10.2g, Protein: 34.2g

120. Coconut Lime Skirt Steak

Preparation Time:5 minutes

Servings: 2

Ingredients:

1. ½ cup coconut oil, melted
2. Zest of one lime
3. 2-1lb. grass fed skirt steaks
4. ¾ teaspoon sea salt
5. 1 teaspoon red pepper flakes
6. 1 teaspoon ginger, fresh, grated
7. 1 tablespoon garlic, minced
8. 2 tablespoons freshly squeezed lime juice

Directions:

1. In a mixing bowl, combine lime juice, coconut oil, garlic, ginger, red pepper, salt, and zest. Add the steaks and toss and rub with marinade. Allow the meat to marinate for about 20-minutes at room temperature. Transfer steaks to your air fryer directly on the rack. Cook steaks in air fryer at 400°Fahrenhet for 5-minutes.

Nutrition Information: Calories: 312, Total Fat: 12.3g, Carbs: 6.4g, Protein: 42.1g

121. Spicy Chicken Enchilada Casserole

Preparation Time:40 minutes

Servings: 2

Ingredients:

- 1 lb. of chicken breasts, skinless and boneless
- Salt and pepper to taste
- ½ cup cilantro, fresh, minced
- Olive oil spray
- 2 cups cheddar cheese, shredded
- Lime wedges (optional)
- Sour cream (optional)
- 1 (4-ounce) can of green chilies, chopped
- 1 cup feta cheese, finely crumbled
- 1 ½ cup enchilada sauce

Directions:

1. Pat the chicken breasts dry and season with salt and pepper. Combine the chicken and enchilada sauce in a pan and simmer for 15-minutes over medium-low heat. Flip chicken over and cover and cook for an additional 15-minutes. Remove the chicken from pan and shred into bite-size pieces. Combine shredded chicken, feta cheese, enchilada sauce, chiles, and cilantro in a bowl. Add salt and pepper. Spray the air fryer basking dish with olive oil. Coat the entire bottom and sides. Evenly spread a cup of shredded cheese on the bottom of baking dish. Add the chicken mixture, then add another cup of cheese on top. Bake in your air fryer at 350°Fahrenheit for 10-minutes. Serve with optional lime wedges and sour cream.

Nutrition Information: Calories: 338, Total Fat: 12.3g, Carbs: 8.3g, Protein: 32.2g

122. Kale & Ground Beef Casserole

Preparation Time:16 minutes

Servings: 4

Ingredients:

- 4-ounces mozzarella, shredded
- 2 cups marinara sauce
- 10-ounces kale, fresh
- 1 teaspoon oregano
- 1 teaspoon onion powder
- ½ teaspoon sea salt
- 1 lb. lean ground beef
- 2 tablespoons olive oil

Directions:

2. In a deep skillet, heat the olive oil for 2-minutes, add in the ground beef and cook for an additional 8-minutes or until meat is browned. Stir in salt, pepper, garlic powder, onion powder and oregano. In batches, stir the kale into beef mixture, cooking for another 2-minutes. Stir in the marinara sauce and cook for 2-minutes more. Mix in half the cheese into mixture. Transfer mixture into the air fryer baking dish. Sprinkle the remaining cheese on top. Broil in air fryer at 400°Fahrenheit for 2-minutes. Allow to rest for 5-minutes before serving.

Nutrition Information: Calories: 312, Total Fat: 13.2, Carbs: 9.2g, Protein: 43.2g

123. Cauliflower-Cottage Pie

Preparation Time:40 minutes

Servings: 4

Ingredients:

Half a cup of bacon bits

- 2 cups cauliflower rice
- ¼ cup tomato puree
- 1 tablespoon coconut oil
- ½ white onion, chopped
- 2lbs. lean ground beef
- 1 tablespoon mixed spice blend

Directions:

3. In the frying pan add coconut oil and onions cook for 2-minutes. Add the ground beef into pan and cook for an

additional 5-minutes or until meat is browned. Add spices and stir to combine. Add the tomato puree and mix well and cook for another 10-minutes. Transfer to air fryer baking dish. Top with cauliflower rice and bacon bits. Bake in air fryer at 350°Fahrenheit for 20-minutes. Serve warm.

Nutrition Information: Calories: 367, Total Fat: 13.4g, Carbs: 11.2g, Protein: 43.1g

124. Roasted Asian Shrimp & Brussels Sprouts

Preparation Time:19 minutes

Servings: 4

Ingredients:

- 1 lb. jumbo frozen shrimp, thawed and drained
- 1 lb. brussels sprouts
- 2 tablespoons olive oil
- Salt and pepper to taste

Asian Marinade Sauce:

- 2 tablespoons rice vinegar
- 2 tablespoons Splenda
- 2 teaspoons liquid stevia
- 1 tablespoon Asian sesame oil
- ½ teaspoon garlic powder
- 1/3 cup soy sauce

Directions:

1. About 20-minutes before you start cooking, place the shrimp into a colander and place it in the sink and let shrimp drain. Mix the soy sauce, stevia, rice vinegar, sesame oil, and garlic powder to make marinade mixture. After the shrimp have drained well, layer them on a paper towel an blot dry, so they are as dry as you can get them. Place dried shrimp into Ziploc bag with half of the marinade and allow the shrimp to marinate while you cook the brussels sprouts. Trim the stem ends off each brussels sprout and cut in half. Place brussels sprouts into a bowl and toss with desired amount of olive oil, salt and pepper.
2. Spread brussels sprouts out in a single layer in your air fryer and roast at 400°Fahrenheit for 15-minutes. Keep brussels sprouts in air fryer and move to one side. Add shrimp beside them in air fryer. Roast for an additional 4-minutes. Remove from air fryer and place into serving bowl, add remaining marinade into bowl and give dish a stir. Serve immediately.

Nutrition Information: Calories: 267, Total Fat: 11.2g, Carbs: 8.3g, Protein: 9.2g

125. Grilled Chicken with Garlic Sauce

Preparation Time:15-minutes

Servings: 4

Ingredients:

- 1lb. chicken breast, cut into large cubes
- 2 bell peppers, chopped
- 1 zucchini
- 1 onion, chopped

For Garlic Sauce:

- 1 head garlic, peeled
- ¼ cup lemon juice
- 1 cup olive oil
- 1 teaspoon salt

Additional ingredients for the marinade:

- 1 teaspoon salt
- ½ cup olive oil

Directions:

1. Soak 4 wooden skewers in water. For your garlic sauce, place garlic cloves and salt into blender. Then, add in about 1/8 of a cup of lemon juice and ½ a cup of olive oil. Blend for about 10-seconds. Keep half of the garlic sauce to serve with. Take the other half of garlic sauce and add an additional ½ cup of olive oil and a teaspoon of salt and mix well—this will make your marinade. Chop up the chicken, onion, bell peppers, and zucchini into 1-inch cubes or squares. Mix them in a bowl with the marinade. Place the cubes onto the skewers and cook them directly on the air fryer rack at 400°Fahrenheit for 15-minutes. Serve warm.

Nutrition Information: Calories: 321, Total Fat: 12.5g, Carbs: 9.2g, Protein: 32.1g

126. Bacon-Wrapped Stuffed Zucchini Boats

Preparation Time:15 minutes

Servings: 4

Ingredients:

- ½ a teaspoon of fresh ground black pepper
- 1 teaspoon sea salt
- 5-ounces cream cheese
- 8-mushrooms, finely chopped
- 1 tablespoon Italian parsley, chopped
- 1 tablespoon finely chopped dill
- 3 garlic cloves, peeled, pressed
- 1 sweet red pepper, finely chopped
- 2 large zucchinis
- 12 bacon strips
- 1 medium onion, chopped

Directions:

1. Preheat your air fryer to 350°Fahrenheit. Trim the ends off zucchini. Cut zucchini in half length-wise. Scoop out pulp, leaving ¼-inch thick shells. Stir pulp in mixing bowl. Add onion, garlic, herbs, pepper, cream cheese, salt, and pepper. Mix well to combine. Fill individual shells with the same amount of stuffing. Wrap three bacon strips around each zucchini boat such that the ends end up underneath. Place them directly on the air fryer rack and bake turning the temperature up to 375°Fahrenheit for 15-minutes. Remove and serve immediately.

Nutrition Information: Calories: 282, Total Fat: 9.1g, Carbs: 6.3g, Protein: 24.2g

127. Parmesan Chicken Wings

Preparation Time:22 minutes

Servings: 4

Ingredients:

- 2 lbs. chicken wings

- 2 tablespoons olive oil
- 1 teaspoon sea salt
- 1 teaspoon black pepper
- 3 tablespoons butter
- 3 tablespoons olive oil
- 3 garlic cloves, minced
- 4 tablespoons parmesan cheese
- 1/8 teaspoon smoked paprika
- ¼ teaspoon red pepper flakes
- Salt and pepper to taste

Directions:

1. Add chicken to a bowl and pat the chicken dry. Drizzle with 2 tablespoons of olive oil, 1 teaspoon of sea salt, and 1 teaspoon black pepper. Gently toss to coat chicken. Place chicken wings into air fryer directly on the rack. Bake at 400°Fahrenheit for 20-minutes, flipping wings half-way through cook time. In a pan over medium heat add butter and 3 tablespoons olive oil and melt the butter down, for about 3-minutes. Add 2 tablespoons of parmesan cheese, smoked paprika, red pepper flakes, salt and pepper to taste. Cook sauce for about 2-minutes. Remove the wings from air fryer and place in large bowl. Pour the garlic parmesan sauce over the wings toss to coat. Serve wings topped with additional a2 tablespoons of parmesan cheese.

Nutrition Information: Calories: 324, Total Fat: 12.3g, Carbs: 9.3g, Protein: 39.3g

128. Beef Burgers

Preparation Time:10 minutes

Servings: 4

Ingredients:

- 1 lb. ground beef
- 1 teaspoon parsley, dried
- ½ teaspoon oregano, dried
- ½ teaspoon ground black pepper
- ½ teaspoon salt
- ½ teaspoon onion powder
- ½ teaspoon garlic powder
- 1 tablespoon Worcestershire sauce
- Olive oil cooking spray

Directions:

1. In a mixing bowl, mix the seasonings. Add the seasoning to beef in a bowl. Mix well to combine. Divide the beef into four patties, put an indent in the middle of patties with your thumb to prevent patties from bunching up in the middle. Place burgers into air fryer and spray the tops of them with olive oil. Cook for 10-minutes at 400°Fahrenheit, no need to flip patties. Serve on a bun with a side dish of your choice.

Nutrition Information: Calories: 312, Total Fat: 11.3g, Carbs: 7.2g, Protein: 39.2g

129. Bacon Wrapped Avocado

Preparation Time:10 minutes

Servings: 2

Ingredients:

- 2 avocados, fresh and firm
- Chili powder
- Ground cumin

- 4 thick slices of hickory smoked bacon

Directions:

1. Slice the avocados into wedges and peel off the skin. Stretch the bacon strips this will help to elongate them. Slice avocados in half. Next, take half a bacon strip and wrap one around each avocado wedge and tuck the ends under the bottom. Sprinkle wedges with chili powder and cumin. Bake the bacon wrapped avocado wedges in air fryer at 400°Fahrenheit for 10-minutes. Serve with your favorite salad!

Nutrition Information: Calories: 276, Total Fat: 7.3g, Carbs: 6.3g, Protein: 21g

130. Buffalo Chicken Meatballs

Preparation Time:20 minutes

Servings: 4

Ingredients:

- 1 lb. ground chicken
- 1 egg, beaten
- 1 celery stalk, trimmed and finely diced
- 1 cup buffalo wing sauce
- 1 teaspoon black pepper
- 1 teaspoon pink sea salt
- 1 teaspoon garlic powder
- 1 teaspoon onion powder
- 1 tablespoon mayonnaise
- 1 tablespoon almond flour
- 2 sprigs of green onion, finely chopped

Directions:

1. Place the baking pan in air fryer and spray with olive oil. In a bowl, combine all ingredients, except buffalo sauce. Mix well. Use your hands to form 2-inch balls. Place the meatballs in air fryer and bake at 350°Fahrenheit for 15-minutes. Remove the meatballs from the air fryer. Add them to a pan over medium-low heat. Coat meatballs with buffalo sauce and stir cooking in pan for 5-minutes. Serve.

Nutrition Information: Calories: 302, Total Fat: 12.4g, Carbs: 7.6g, Protein: 32.1g

131. Caprese Grilled Chicken with Balsamic Vinegar

Preparation Time:20 minutes

Servings: 6

Ingredients:

- 6 grilled chicken breasts, boneless, skinless
- 6 large basil leaves
- 6 slices of tomato
- 6 slices of mozzarella cheese
- 1 tablespoon butter
- ¼ cup balsamic vinegar

Directions:

1. Prepare chicken in air fryer at 400°Fahrenheit for 15-minutes or until chicken is cooked. As chicken is cooking, pour balsamic vinegar into the pan and cook until reduced by half, for about 5-minutes. Add in the butter and stir with a flat whisk until

well combined. Set aside. Top chicken with mozzarella cheese slices, basil leaves, and tomato slice each. Drizzle with balsamic reduction and serve warm.

Nutrition Information: Calories: 289, Total Fat: 11.3g, Carbs: 7.2g, Protein: 28g

132. Philly Cheese Steak Stuffed Peppers

Preparation Time:40 minutes

Servings: 2

Ingredients:

- 8-ounces of roast beef, thinly sliced
- 8-slices of provolone cheese
- 2 large green bell peppers
- 1 medium sweet onion, diced
- 1 (6-ounce) package of baby Bella mushrooms
- 1 tablespoon garlic, minced
- 2 tablespoons olive oil
- 2 tablespoons butter

Directions:

1. Cut your peppers in half lengthwise, removing ribs and seeds. Slice onions and mushrooms. Sautė over medium heat with butter, olive oil, a dash of salt, pepper, and minced garlic. Cook for 20-minutes or until the mushrooms and onions are sweet and caramelized. Slice the roast beef into thin strips and add to the onion/mushroom mixture. Allow cooking for 10-minutes. In the inside of each pepper line it with a slice of provolone cheese. Fill each pepper with meat mixture. Garnish top of each pepper with another slice of provolone cheese. Bake in the air fryer at 375°Fahrenhiet for 10-minutes.

Nutrition Information: Calories: 298, Total Fat: 11.5g, Carbs: 8.2g, Protein: 39.2g

133. Parmesan, Garlic, Lemon Roasted Zucchini

Preparation Time:10 minutes

Servings: 4

Ingredients:

- 1 ½ lbs. zucchini (about 4 small zucchini)
- Salt and pepper to taste
- ¾ cup parmesan cheese, finely shredded
- 2 cloves garlic, minced
- Zest of 1 lemon
- 2 tablespoons olive oil

Directions:

1. Cut zucchini into thick wedges or halves (cut each zucchini in half then that half in half, so you have 4 wedges from each zucchini. In a bowl, stir olive oil, garlic, and lemon zest. Align zucchini in air fryer space them evenly apart. Brush olive oil mixture over tops of zucchini. Sprinkle tops with parmesan cheese and season lightly with salt and pepper. Bake in air fryer at 375°Fahrenheit for 10-minutes. Serve warm.

134. Chicken Filet Stuffed with Sausage

Preparation Time:15 minutes

Servings: 4

Ingredients:

- 4 chicken fillets
- 4 sausages, casings removed

Directions:

1. Place the sausage inside the chicken filets and roll the fillets. Seal with 2 toothpicks each. Air fry the chicken filets at 375°Fahrenheit for 15-minutes. Serve warm.

Nutrition Information: Calories: 276, Total Fat: 12.2g, Carbs: 8.2g, Protein: 28g

135. Bourbon Chicken

Preparation Time:22 minutes

Servings: 4

Ingredients:

- 3lbs. of chicken wings
- ¾ cups ketchup
- ¼ teaspoon cayenne
- ¼ cup Bourbon
- 2 teaspoons smoked paprika
- ½ cup water
- 2 garlic cloves, crushed
- ¼ cup onion, minced
- 2 teaspoons stevia
- 1 tablespoon liquid smoke
- 1 teaspoon salt
- ½ teaspoon black pepper

Directions:

1. In a bowl, mix liquid smoke, onion, garlic, ketchup, stevia and cook for 5-minutes in an electric pressure cooker on Sautė function. Combine the rest of your ingredients and cook on high pressure for 5-minutes. Do a quick release of pressure and then transfer the chicken wings into the air fryer basket. Cook wings in air fryer for 6-minutes at 400°Fahrenheit. Dip wings into sauce and air fry for another 6-minutes. Serve hot!

Nutrition Information: Calories: 302, Total Fat: 12.5g, Carbs: 8.4g, Protein: 32.4g

136. Roasted Chicken Legs

Preparation Time:35 minutes

Servings: 2

Ingredients:

- 2 chicken legs
- 2 teaspoons sweet smoked paprika
- 1 teaspoon honey
- Salt and pepper to taste
- ½ teaspoon garlic powder
- Fresh parsley, chopped for garnish
- 1 lime sliced for garnish

Directions:

1. Combine all the ingredients except the chicken in a bowl. Rub the mixture over the chicken and preheat your air fryer for 3-minutes. Cook the chicken in air fryer at 390°Fahrenheit for 35-minutes. Serve with a favorite salad of your choice.

Nutrition Information: Calories: 232, Total Fat: 9.3g, Carbs: 7.5g, Protein: 22.1g

137. Mongolian Chicken

Preparation Time:17 minutes

Servings: 4

Ingredients:

- 4 chicken breasts, boneless, skinless, chopped small pieces
- 1 yellow onion, thinly sliced
- Olive oil for frying
- 1 Chili Padi, chopped
- 3 garlic cloves, minced
- 5 curry leaves
- 1 teaspoon ginger, grated
- ¾ cup evaporated milk

Marinade:

1. 1 egg
2. 1 tablespoon light soy sauce
3. Self-raising flour to coat
4. ½ tablespoon cornstarch

Seasonings:

- 1 teaspoon liquid stevia
- 1 tablespoon chili sauce
- ½ teaspoon sea salt
- Dash of black pepper

Directions:

1. Combine all of you marinade ingredients in a bowl and marinate the chicken with it for an hour. Dredge the chicken in the self-raising flour and spray some oil over. Cook in air fryer for 10-minutes at 390°Fahrenheit. Heat a wok and sautė the ginger, garlic, chili padi, curry leaves and onions for 2-minutes. Add the chicken and seasonings, stirring to combine well. Add your milk and cook until thickened. Serve hot!

Nutrition Information: Calories: 286, Total Fat: 11.3g, Carbs: 6.4g, Protein: 28g

138. Corn and Cabbage Salad

Preparation time: 10 minutes

Cooking time: 15 minutes

Servings: 4

Ingredients:

- 1 small yellow onion, chopped
- 1 tablespoon olive oil
- 2 garlic cloves, minced
- 1 and ½ cups mushrooms, sliced
- 3 teaspoons ginger, grated
- A pinch of salt and black pepper
- 2 cups corn
- 4 cups red cabbage, chopped
- 1 tablespoon nutritional yeast
- 2 teaspoons tomato paste
- 1 teaspoon coconut aminos
- 1 teaspoon sriracha sauce

Directions:

1. In your air fryer's pan, mix the oil with onion, garlic, mushrooms, ginger, salt, pepper, corn, cabbage, yeast and tomato paste, stir, cover and cook at 365 degrees F for 15 minutes
2. Add sriracha sauce and aminos, stir, divide between plates and serve.

3. Enjoy!

Nutrition information:calories 360, fat 4, fiber 4, carbs 10, protein 4

139. Okra and Corn Mix

Preparation time: 10 minutes

Cooking time: 15 minutes

Servings: 6

Ingredients:

- 1 green bell pepper, chopped
- 1 small yellow onion, chopped
- 3 garlic cloves, minced
- 16 ounces okra, sliced
- 2 cup corn
- 12 ounces canned tomatoes, crushed
- 1 and ½ teaspoon smoked paprika
- 1 teaspoon marjoram, dried
- 1 teaspoon thyme, dried
- 1 teaspoon oregano, dried
- Salt and black pepper to the taste

Directions:

1. In your air fryer, mix bell pepper with onion, garlic, okra, corn, tomatoes, smoked paprika, marjoram, thyme, oregano, salt and pepper, stir, cover and cook at 360 degrees F for 15 minutes.
2. Stir, divide between plates and serve.
3. Enjoy!

Nutrition information:calories 243, fat 4, fiber 6, carbs 10, protein 3

140. Potato and Carrot Mix

Preparation time: 10 minutes

Cooking time: 16 minutes

Servings: 6

Ingredients:

- 2 potatoes, cubed
- 3 pounds carrots, cubed
- 1 yellow onion, chopped
- Salt and black pepper to the taste
- 1 teaspoon thyme, dried
- 3 tablespoons coconut milk
- 2 teaspoons curry powder
- 3 tablespoons vegan cheese, crumbled
- 1 tablespoon parsley, chopped

Directions:

1. In your air fryer's pan, mix onion with potatoes, carrots, salt, pepper, thyme and curry powder, stir, cover and cook at 365 degrees F for 16 minutes.
2. Add coconut milk, sprinkle vegan cheese, divide between plates and serve.
3. Enjoy!

Nutrition information:calories 241, fat 4, fiber 7, carbs 8, protein 4

141. Winter Green Beans

Preparation time: 10 minutes

Cooking time: 16 minutes

Servings: 4

Ingredients:

- 1 and ½ cups yellow onion, chopped

- 1 pound green beans, halved
- 4 ounces canned tomatoes, chopped
- 4 garlic cloves, chopped
- 2 teaspoons oregano, dried
- 1 jalapeno, chopped
- Salt and black pepper to the taste
- 1 and ½ teaspoons cumin, ground
- 1 tablespoons olive oil

Directions:

1. Preheat your air fryer to 365 degrees F, add oil to the pan, also add onion, green beans, tomatoes, garlic, oregano, jalapeno, salt, pepper and cumin, cover and cook for 16 minutes.
2. Divide between plates and serve.
3. Enjoy!

Nutrition information:calories 261, fat 5, fiber 8, carbs 10, protein 12

142. Green Beans Casserole

Preparation time: 10 minutes

Cooking time: 20 minutes

Servings: 4

Ingredients:

- 1 teaspoon olive oil
- 2 red chilies, dried
- ¼ teaspoon fenugreek seeds
- ½ teaspoon black mustard seeds
- 10 curry leaves, chopped
- ½ cup red onion, chopped
- 3 garlic cloves, minced
- 2 teaspoons coriander powder
- 2 tomatoes, chopped
- 2 cups eggplant, chopped
- ½ teaspoon turmeric powder
- ½ cup green bell pepper, chopped
- A pinch of salt and black pepper
- 1 cup green beans, trimmed and halved
- 2 teaspoons tamarind paste
- 1 tablespoons cilantro, chopped

Directions:

1. In a baking dish that fits your air fryer, combine oil with chilies, fenugreek seeds, black mustard seeds, curry leaves, onion, coriander, tomatoes, eggplant, turmeric, green bell pepper, salt, pepper, green beans, tamarind paste and cilantro, toss, put in your air fryer and cook at 365 degrees F for 20 minutes.
2. Divide between plates and serve.

Nutrition information:calories 251, fat 5, fiber 4, carbs 8, protein 12

143. Chipotle Green Beans

Preparation time: 10 minutes

Cooking time: 16 minutes

Servings: 6

Ingredients:

- 1 yellow onion, chopped
- 1 pound green beans, halved
- 2 teaspoons cumin, ground
- A drizzle of olive oil
- 12 ounces corn
- ¼ teaspoon chipotle powder
- 1 cup salsa

Directions:

1. In a pan that fits your air fryer, combine oil with onion, green beans, cumin, corn, chipotle powder and salsa, toss, introduce in your air fryer and cook at 365 degrees F for 16 minutes.
2. Divide between plates and serve.
3. Enjoy!

Nutrition information:calories 224, fat 2, fiber 12, carbs 14, protein 10

144. Cranberry Beans Pasta

Preparation time: 10 minutes

Cooking time: 15 minutes

Servings: 8

Ingredients:

- 2 cups canned cranberry beans, drained
- 2 celery ribs, chopped
- 1 yellow onion, chopped
- 7 garlic cloves, minced
- 1 teaspoon rosemary, chopped
- 26 ounces canned tomatoes, chopped
- ¼ teaspoon red pepper flakes
- 2 teaspoons oregano, dried
- 3 teaspoons basil, dried
- ½ teaspoon smoked paprika
- A pinch of salt and black pepper
- 10 ounces kale, roughly chopped
- 2 cups whole wheat vegan pasta, cooked

Directions:

1. In a pan that fits your air fryer, combine beans with celery, onion, garlic, rosemary, tomatoes, pepper flakes, oregano, basil, paprika, salt, pepper and kale, introduce in your air fryer and cook at 365 degrees F for 15 minutes.
2. Divide vegan pasta between plates, add cranberry mix on top and serve.
3. Enjoy!

Nutrition information:calories 251, fat 2, fiber 12, carbs 12, protein 6

145. Mexican Casserole

Preparation time: 10 minutes

Cooking time: 15 minutes

Servings: 4

Ingredients:

- 1 tablespoon olive oil
- 4 garlic cloves, minced
- 1 yellow onion, chopped
- 2 tablespoons cilantro, chopped
- 1 small red chili, chopped
- 2 teaspoons cumin, ground
- Salt and black pepper to the taste
- 1 teaspoon sweet paprika
- 1 teaspoon coriander seeds
- 1 pound sweet potatoes, cubed
- Juice of ½ lime
- 10 ounces green beans
- 2 cups tomatoes, chopped
- 1 tablespoon parsley, chopped

Directions:

1. Grease a pan that fits your air fryer with the oil, add garlic, onion, cilantro, red chili, cumin, salt, pepper,

paprika, coriander, potatoes, lime juice, green beans and tomatoes, toss, place in your air fryer and cook at 365 degrees F for 15 minutes.
2. Add parsley, divide between plates and serve.
3. Enjoy!

Nutrition information:calories 223, fat 5, fiber 4, carbs 7, protein 8

146. Endives and Rice Casserole

Preparation time: 10 minutes

Cooking time: 20 minutes

Servings: 4

Ingredients:

- 1 tablespoon olive oil
- 2 scallions, chopped
- 3 garlic cloves chopped
- 1 tablespoon ginger, grated
- 1 teaspoon chili sauce
- A pinch of salt and black pepper
- ½ cup white rice
- 1 cup veggie stock
- 3 endives, trimmed and chopped

Directions:

1. Grease a pan that fits your air fryer with the oil, add scallions, garlic, ginger, chili sauce, salt, pepper, rice, stock and endives, place in your air fryer, cover and cook at 365 degrees F for 20 minutes.
2. Divide casserole between plates and serve.
3. Enjoy!

Nutrition information:calories 220, fat 5, fiber 8, carbs 12, protein 6

147. Cabbage and Tomatoes

Preparation time: 10 minutes

Cooking time: 12 minutes

Servings: 4

Ingredients:

- 1 tablespoon olive oil
- 1 green cabbage head, chopped
- Salt and black pepper to the taste
- 15 ounces canned tomatoes, chopped
- ½ cup yellow onion, chopped
- 2 teaspoons turmeric powder

Directions:

1. In a pan that fits your air fryer, combine oil with green cabbage, salt, pepper, tomatoes, onion and turmeric, place in your air fryer and cook at 365 degrees F for 12 minutes.
2. Divide between plates and serve.
3. Enjoy!

Nutrition information:calories 202, fat 5, fiber 8, carbs 9, protein 10

148. Simple Endive Mix

Preparation time: 10 minutes

Cooking time: 10 minutes

Servings: 4

Ingredients:

- 8 endives, trimmed
- Salt and black pepper to the taste
- 3 tablespoons olive oil
- Juice of ½ lemon
- 1 tablespoon tomato paste
- 2 tablespoons parsley, chopped

- 1 teaspoon stevia

Directions:

1. In a bowl, combine endives with salt, pepper, oil, lemon juice, tomato paste, parsley and stevia, toss, place endives in your air fryer's basket and cook at 365 degrees F for 10 minutes.
2. Divide between plates and serve.
3. Enjoy!

Nutrition information:calories 160, fat 4, fiber 7, carbs 9, protein 4

149. Eggplant and Tomato Sauce

Preparation time: 10 minutes

Cooking time: 12 minutes

Servings: 2

Ingredients:

- 4 cups eggplant, cubed
- 1 tablespoon olive oil
- 1 tablespoon garlic powder
- A pinch of salt and black pepper
- 3 garlic cloves, minced
- 1 cup tomato sauce

Directions:

1. In a pan that fits your air fryer, combine eggplant cubes with oil, garlic, salt, pepper, garlic powder and tomato sauce, toss, place in your air fryer and cook at 370 degrees F for 12 minutes.
2. Divide between plates and serve.
3. Enjoy!

Nutrition information:calories 250, fat 7, fiber 5, carbs 10, protein 4

150. Brown Rice and Mung Beans Mix

Preparation time: 10 minutes

Cooking time: 16 minutes

Servings: 2

Ingredients:

- ½ teaspoon olive oil
- ½ cup brown rice, cooked
- ½ cup mung beans
- ½ teaspoon cumin seeds
- ½ cup red onion, chopped
- 2 tomatoes, chopped
- 1 small ginger piece, grated
- 4 garlic cloves, minced
- 1 teaspoon coriander, ground
- ½ teaspoon turmeric powder
- A pinch of cayenne pepper
- ½ teaspoon garam masala
- 1 cup veggie stock
- Salt and black pepper to the taste
- 1 teaspoon lemon juice

Directions:

1. In your blender, mix tomato with garlic, onions, ginger, salt, pepper, garam masala, cayenne, coriander and turmeric and pulse really well.
2. In a pan that fits your air fryer, combine oil with blended tomato mix, mung beans, rice, stock, cumin and lemon juice, place in your air fryer and cook at 365 degrees F for 16 minutes.
3. Divide everything between plates and serve.
4. Enjoy!

Nutrition information:calories 200, fat 6,

fiber 7, carbs 10, protein 8

151. Lentils and Spinach Casserole

Preparation time: 10 minutes

Cooking time: 16 minutes

Servings: 3

Ingredients:

- 1 teaspoon olive oil
- 1/3 cup canned brown lentils, drained
- 1 small ginger piece, grated
- 4 garlic cloves, minced
- 1 green chili pepper, chopped
- 2 tomatoes, chopped
- ½ teaspoon garam masala
- ½ teaspoon turmeric powder
- 2 potatoes, cubed
- Salt and black pepper to the taste
- ¼ teaspoon cardamom, ground
- ¼ teaspoon cinnamon powder
- 6 ounces spinach leaves

Directions:

1. In a pan that fits your air fryer combine oil with canned lentils, ginger, garlic, chili pepper, tomatoes, garam masala, turmeric, potatoes, salt, pepper, cardamom, cinnamon and spinach, toss, place in your air fryer and cook at 356 degrees F for 16 minutes.
2. Divide casserole between plates and serve.
3. Enjoy!

Nutrition information:calories 250, fat 3, fiber 11, carbs 16, protein 10

152. Red Potatoes and Tasty Chutney

Preparation time: 10 minutes

Cooking time: 14 minutes

Servings: 4

Ingredients:

- 2 pounds red potatoes, cubed
- 1 cup green beans
- 1 cup carrots, shredded
- 16 ounces canned chickpeas, drained
- 2 tablespoons olive oil
- 1 teaspoon coriander seeds
- 1 and ½ teaspoons cumin seeds
- 1 and ½ teaspoons garam masala
- ½ teaspoon mustard seeds
- 1 teaspoon garlic, minced
- For the chutney:
- ¼ cup water
- ½ cup mint
- ½ cup cilantro
- 1 small ginger piece, grated
- 2 teaspoons lime juice
- A pinch of salt

Directions:

1. In a baking dish that fits your air fryer, combine oil with potatoes, green beans, carrots, chickpeas, coriander, cumin, garam masala, mustard seeds and garlic, place in your air fryer and cook at 365 degrees F for 20 minutes.
2. In your blender, mix water with mint, cilantro, ginger, lime juice and salt and pulse really well.
3. Divide potato mix between plates, add mint chutney on top and serve.
4. Enjoy!

Nutrition information:calories 241, fat 4, fiber 7, carbs 11, protein 6

153. Simple Veggie Salad

Preparation time: 10 minutes

Cooking time: 10 minutes

Servings: 8

Ingredients:

- 1 and ½ cups tomatoes, chopped
- 3 cups eggplant, chopped
- 2 teaspoons capers
- Cooking spray
- 3 garlic cloves, minced
- 2 teaspoons balsamic vinegar
- 1 tablespoon basil, chopped
- A pinch of salt and black pepper

Directions:

1. Grease a pan that fits your air fryer with cooking spray, add tomatoes, eggplant, capers, garlic, salt and pepper, place in your air fryer and cook at 365 degrees F for 10 minutes.
2. Divide between plates, drizzle balsamic vinegar all over, sprinkle basil and serve cold.
3. Enjoy!

Nutrition information:calories 171, fat 3, fiber 1, carbs 8, protein 12

SEAFOOD

154. Salmon & Blackberry Glaze

Preparation Time:43 Minutes

Servings: 4

Ingredients:

- 4 medium salmon fillets; skinless
- 1 cup water
- 1-inch ginger piece; grated
- Juice from 1/2 lemon
- 12 oz. blackberries
- 1 tbsp. olive oil
- 1/4 cup sugar
- Salt and black pepper to the taste

Directions:

1. Heat up a pot with the water over medium high heat, add ginger, lemon juice and blackberries; stir, bring to a boil, cook for 4-5 minutes; take off heat, strain into a bowl, return to pan and combine with sugar.
2. Stir this mix, bring to a simmer over medium low heat and cook for 20 minutes.
3. Leave blackberry sauce to cool down, brush salmon with it, season with salt and pepper, drizzle olive oil all over and rub fish well.
4. Place fish in your preheated air fryer at 350 °F and cook for 10 minutes; flipping fish fillets once. Divide among plates, drizzle some of the remaining blackberry sauce all over and serve.

Nutrition information:Calories: 312; Fat: 4; Fiber: 9; Carbs: 19; Protein: 14

155. Special Salmon Recipe

Preparation Time:35 Minutes

Servings: 4

Ingredients:

- 1 lb. medium beets; sliced
- 1 ½ lbs. salmon fillets; skinless and boneless
- 6 tbsp. olive oil
- 1 tbsp. chives; chopped
- 1 tbsp. parsley; chopped.
- 1 tbsp. fresh tarragon; chopped
- 3 tbsp. shallots; chopped
- 1 tbsp. grated lemon zest
- 1/4 cup lemon juice
- 4 cups mixed baby greens
- Salt and pepper to the taste

Directions:

1. In a bowl; mix beets with 1/2 tbsp. oil and toss to coat.
2. Season them with salt and pepper, arrange them on a baking sheet; introduce in the oven at 450 °F and bake for 20 minutes.
3. Take beets out of the oven, add salmon on top, brush it with the rest if the oil and season with salt and pepper.
4. In a bowl; mix chives with parsley and tarragon and sprinkle 1 tbsp. of this mix over salmon.
5. Introduce in the oven again and bake for 15 minutes.

6. Meanwhile; in a boil with shallots with lemon peel, salt, pepper and lemon juice and the rest of the herbs mixture and stir gently.
7. Combine 2 tbsp. of shallots dressing with mixed greens and toss gently. Take salmon out of the oven, arrange on plates, add beets and greens on the side, drizzle the rest of the shallot dressing on top and serve right away.

Nutrition information:Calories: 312; Fat: 2; Fiber: 2; Carbs: 2; Protein: 4

156. Chinese Style Cod

Preparation Time:20 Minutes

Servings: 2

Ingredients:

- 2 medium cod fillets; boneless
- 1 tbsp. light soy sauce
- 1/2 tsp. ginger; grated
- 1 tsp. peanuts; crushed
- 2 tsp. garlic powder

Directions:

1. Put fish fillets in a heat proof dish that fits your air fryer, add garlic powder, soy sauce and ginger; toss well, put in your air fryer and cook at 350 °F, for 10 minutes. Divide fish on plates, sprinkle peanuts on top and serve.

Nutrition information:Calories: 254; Fat: 10; Fiber: 11; Carbs: 14; Protein: 23

157. Coconut Tilapia Recipe

Preparation Time:20 Minutes

Servings: 4

Ingredients:

- 4 medium tilapia fillets
- 1/2 cup coconut milk
- 1 tsp. ginger; grated
- 1/2 cup cilantro; chopped
- 2 garlic cloves; chopped
- 1/2 tsp. garam masala
- Salt and black pepper to the taste
- Cooking spray
- 1/2 jalapeno; chopped.

Directions:

2. In your food processor, mix coconut milk with salt, pepper, cilantro, ginger, garlic, jalapeno and garam masala and pulse really well.
3. Spray fish with cooking spray, spread coconut mix all over, rub well, transfer to your air fryer's basket and cook at 400 °F, for 10 minutes. Divide among plates and serve hot.

Nutrition information:Calories: 200; Fat: 5; Fiber: 6; Carbs: 25; Protein: 26

158. Roasted Cod & Prosciutto

Preparation Time:20 Minutes

Servings: 4

Ingredients:

- 4 medium cod filets
- 1 tbsp. parsley; chopped
- 1/4 cup butter; melted
- 2 garlic cloves; minced
- 2 tbsp. lemon juice

- 3 tbsp. prosciutto; chopped.
- 1 tsp. Dijon mustard
- 1 shallot; chopped
- Salt and black pepper to the taste

Directions:

1. In a bowl; mix mustard with butter, garlic, parsley, shallot, lemon juice, prosciutto, salt and pepper and whisk well.
2. Season fish with salt and pepper; spread prosciutto mix all over, put in your air fryer and cook at 390 °F, for 10 minutes. Divide among plates and serve.

Nutrition information:Calories: 200; Fat: 4; Fiber: 7; Carbs: 12; Protein: 6

159. Lemon Sole & Swiss Chard

Preparation Time:24 Minutes

Servings: 4

Ingredients:

- 2 bunches Swiss chard; chopped
- 4 tbsp. butter
- 1/4 cup lemon juice
- 3 tbsp. capers
- 2 garlic cloves; minced
- 1 tsp. lemon zest; grated
- 4 white bread slices; quartered
- 1/4 cup walnuts; chopped.
- 1/4 cup parmesan; grated
- 4 tbsp. olive oil
- 4 sole fillets; boneless
- Salt and black pepper to the taste

Directions:

1. In your food processor, mix bread with walnuts, cheese and lemon zest and pulse well.
2. Add half of the olive oil, pulse really well again and leave aside for now.
3. Heat up a pan with the butter over medium heat, add lemon juice, salt, pepper and capers; stir well, add fish and toss it.
4. Transfer fish to your preheated air fryer's basket, top with bread mix you've made at the beginning and cook at 350 °F, for 14 minutes.
5. Meanwhile; heat up another pan with the rest of the oil, add garlic, Swiss chard, salt and pepper; stir gently, cook for 2 minutes and take off heat. Divide fish on plates and serve with sautéed chard on the side.

Nutrition information:Calories: 321; Fat: 7; Fiber: 18; Carbs: 27; Protein: 12

160. Mustard Salmon Recipe

Preparation Time:20 Minutes

Servings: 1

Ingredients:

- 1 big salmon fillet; boneless
- 2 tbsp. mustard
- 1 tbsp. coconut oil
- 1 tbsp. maple extract
- Salt and black pepper to the taste

Directions:

1. In a bowl; mix maple extract with mustard, whisk well, season salmon with salt and pepper and brush

salmon with this mix.

2. Spray some cooking spray over fish; place in your air fryer and cook at 370 °F, for 10 minutes; flipping halfway. Serve with a tasty side salad.

Nutrition information:Calories: 300; Fat: 7; Fiber: 14; Carbs: 16; Protein: 20

161. Salmon and Orange Marmalade Recipe

Preparation Time:25 Minutes

Servings: 4

Ingredients:

- 1 lb. wild salmon; skinless, boneless and cubed
- 2 lemons; sliced
- 1/4 cup orange juice
- 1/3 cup orange marmalade
- 1/4 cup balsamic vinegar
- A pinch of salt and black pepper

Directions:

1. Heat up a pot with the vinegar over medium heat; add marmalade and orange juice; stir, bring to a simmer, cook for 1 minute and take off heat.
2. Thread salmon cubes and lemon slices on skewers, season with salt and black pepper, brush them with half of the orange marmalade mix, arrange in your air fryer's basket and cook at 360 °F, for 3 minutes on each side. Brush skewers with the rest of the vinegar mix; divide among plates and serve right away with a side salad.

Nutrition information:Calories: 240; Fat: 9; Fiber: 12; Carbs: 14; Protein: 10

162. Salmon and Avocado Sauce Recipe

Preparation Time:20 Minutes

Servings: 4

Ingredients:

- 1 avocado; pitted, peeled and chopped
- 4 salmon fillets; boneless
- 1/4 cup cilantro; chopped
- 1/3 cup coconut milk
- 1 tbsp. lime juice
- 1 tbsp. lime zest; grated
- 1 tsp. onion powder
- 1 tsp. garlic powder
- Salt and black pepper to the taste

Directions:

1. Season salmon fillets with salt, black pepper and lime zest, rub well, put in your air fryer, cook at 350 °F, for 9 minutes; flipping once and divide among plates.
2. In your food processor, mix avocado with cilantro, garlic powder, onion powder, lime juice, salt, pepper and coconut milk; blend well, drizzle over salmon and serve right away.

Nutrition information:Calories: 260; Fat: 7; Fiber: 20; Carbs: 28; Protein: 18

163. Tilapia & Chives Sauce

Preparation Time:18 Minutes

Servings: 4

Ingredients:

- 4 medium tilapia fillets
- 2 tsp. honey
- 1/4 cup Greek yogurt
- Juice from 1 lemon
- 2 tbsp. chives; chopped
- Cooking spray
- Salt and black pepper to the taste

Directions:

1. Season fish with salt and pepper, spray with cooking spray, place in preheated air fryer 350 °F and cook for 8 minutes; flipping halfway.
2. Meanwhile; in a bowl, mix yogurt with honey, salt, pepper, chives and lemon juice and whisk really well. Divide air fryer fish on plates, drizzle yogurt sauce all over and serve right away.

Nutrition information:Calories: 261; Fat: 8; Fiber: 18; Carbs: 24; Protein: 21

164. Buttery Shrimp Skewers

Preparation Time:16 Minutes

Servings: 2

Ingredients:

- 8 shrimps; peeled and deveined
- 8 green bell pepper slices
- 1 tbsp. rosemary; chopped.
- 1 tbsp. butter; melted
- 4 garlic cloves; minced
- Salt and black pepper to the taste

1. **Directions:**

2. In a bowl; mix shrimp with garlic, butter, salt, pepper, rosemary and bell pepper slices; toss to coat and leave aside for 10 minutes.
3. Arrange 2 shrimp and 2 bell pepper slices on a skewer and repeat with the rest of the shrimp and bell pepper pieces.
4. Place them all in your air fryer's basket and cook at 360 °F, for 6 minutes. Divide among plates and serve right away.

Nutrition information:Calories: 140; Fat: 1; Fiber: 12; Carbs: 15; Protein: 7

165. Special Swordfish and Mango Salsa

Preparation Time:16 Minutes

Servings: 2

Ingredients:

- 2 medium swordfish steaks
- 2 tsp. avocado oil
- 1 tbsp. cilantro; chopped.
- 1 mango; chopped
- 1 avocado; pitted, peeled and chopped
- A pinch of cumin
- A pinch of onion powder
- A pinch of garlic powder
- 1 orange; peeled and sliced
- 1/2 tbsp. balsamic vinegar
- Salt and black pepper to the taste

Directions:

1. Season fish steaks with salt, pepper, garlic powder, onion powder and cumin and rub with half of the oil;

place in your air fryer and cook at 360 °F, for 6 minutes; flipping halfway.
2. Meanwhile; in a bowl, mix avocado with mango, cilantro, balsamic vinegar, salt, pepper and the rest of the oil and stir well. Divide fish on plates; top with mango salsa and serve with orange slices on the side.

Nutrition information:Calories: 200; Fat: 7; Fiber: 2; Carbs: 14; Protein: 14

166. Crusted Salmon Recipe

Preparation Time:20 Minutes

Servings: 4

Ingredients:

- 1 cup pistachios; chopped.
- 4 salmon fillets
- 1/4 cup lemon juice
- 2 tbsp. honey
- 1 tbsp. mustard
- 1 tsp. dill; chopped
- Salt and black pepper to the taste

Directions:

1. In a bowl; mix pistachios with mustard, honey, lemon juice, salt, black pepper and dill; whisk and spread over salmon.
2. Put in your air fryer and cook at 350 °F, for 10 minutes. Divide among plates and serve with a side salad.

Nutrition information:Calories: 300; Fat: 17; Fiber: 12; Carbs: 20; Protein: 22

167. Stuffed Salmon Delight

Preparation Time:30 Minutes

Servings: 2

Ingredients:

- 2 salmon fillets; skinless and boneless
- 5 oz. tiger shrimp; peeled, deveined and chopped
- 1 tbsp. olive oil
- 6 mushrooms; chopped.
- 3 green onions; chopped
- 2 cups spinach; torn
- 1/4 cup macadamia nuts; toasted and chopped
- Salt and black pepper to the taste

Directions:

1. Heat up a pan with half of the oil over medium high heat, add mushrooms, onions, salt and pepper; stir and cook for 4 minutes.
2. Add macadamia nuts, spinach and shrimp; stir, cook for 3 minutes and take off heat.
3. Make an incision lengthwise in each salmon fillet, season with salt and pepper, divide spinach and shrimp mix into incisions and rub with the rest of the olive oil.
4. Place in your air fryer's basket and cook at 360 °F and cook for 10 minutes; flipping halfway. Divide stuffed salmon on plates and serve.

Nutrition information:Calories: 290; Fat: 15; Fiber: 3; Carbs: 12; Protein: 31

168. Delightful French Cod

Preparation Time:32 Minutes

Servings: 4

Ingredients:

- 2 tbsp. olive oil
- 1 yellow onion; chopped
- 1/2 cup white wine
- 2 garlic cloves; minced
- 3 tbsp. parsley; chopped.
- 2 lbs. cod; boneless
- 14 oz. canned tomatoes; stewed
- Salt and black pepper to the taste
- 2 tbsp. butter

Directions:

1. Heat up a pan with the oil over medium heat, add garlic and onion; stir and cook for 5 minutes.
2. Add wine; stir and cook for 1 minute more.
3. Add tomatoes; stir, bring to a boil, cook for 2 minutes; add parsley; stir again and take off heat.
4. Pour this mix into a heat proof dish that fits your air fryer, add fish, season it with salt and pepper and cook in your fryer at 350 °F, for 14 minutes. Divide fish and tomatoes mix on plates and serve.

Nutrition information:Calories: 231; Fat: 8; Fiber: 12; Carbs: 26; Protein: 14

169. Fish and Couscous Recipe

Preparation Time:25 Minutes

Servings: 4

Ingredients:

- 2½ lbs. sea bass; gutted
- 5 tsp. fennel seeds
- 3/4 cup whole wheat couscous; cooked
- 2 red onions; chopped
- Cooking spray
- 2 small fennel bulbs; cored and sliced
- 1/4 cup almonds; toasted and sliced

Salt and black pepper to the taste

Directions:

1. Season fish with salt and pepper, spray with cooking spray; place in your air fryer and cook at 350 °F, for 10 minutes.
2. Meanwhile; spray a pan with some cooking oil and heat it up over medium heat.
3. Add fennel seeds to this pan; stir and toast them for 1 minute.
4. Add onion, salt, pepper, fennel bulbs, almonds and couscous; stir, cook for 2-3 minutes and divide among plates. Add fish next to couscous mix and serve right away.

Nutrition information:Calories: 354; Fat: 7; Fiber: 10; Carbs: 20; Protein: 30

170. Marinated Salmon Recipe

Preparation Time:1 hour 20 Minutes

Servings: 6

Ingredients:

- 1 whole salmon
- 1 tbsp. dill; chopped.
- 1 tbsp. tarragon; chopped
- 1 tbsp. garlic; minced

- Juice from 2 lemons
- 1 lemon; sliced
- A pinch of salt and black pepper

Directions:

1. In a large fish, mix fish with salt, pepper and lemon juice; toss well and keep in the fridge for 1 hour.
2. Stuff salmon with garlic and lemon slices, place in your air fryer's basket and cook at 320 °F, for 25 minutes. Divide among plates and serve with a tasty coleslaw on the side.

Nutrition information:Calories: 300; Fat: 8; Fiber: 9; Carbs: 19; Protein: 27

171. Clam with Lemons on the Grill

Servings: 6

Preparation Time: 6 minutes

Ingredients:

- 4 pounds littleneck clams
- Salt and pepper to taste
- 1 clove of garlic, minced
- ½ cup parsley, chopped
- 1 teaspoon crushed red pepper flakes
- 5 tablespoons olive oil
- 1 loaf crusty bread, halved
- ½ cup parmesan cheese, grated

Directions:

1. Preheat the air fryer at 3900F.
2. Place the grill pan accessory in the air fryer.
3. Place the clams on the grill pan and cook for 6 minutes.
4. Once the clams have opened, take them out and extract the meat.
5. Transfer the meat into a bowl and season with salt and pepper.
6. Stir in the garlic, parsley, red pepper flakes, and olive oil.
7. Serve on top of bread and sprinkle with parmesan cheese.

Nutrition information:

Calories: 341; Carbs: 26g; Protein:48.3g; Fat: 17.2g

172. Salmon Steak with Garlic Sauce

Servings: 2

Preparation Time: 15 minutes

Ingredients:

- 2 salmon steaks
- Salt and pepper to taste
- 2 tablespoons vegetable oil
- 2 cloves of garlic, minced
- 1 cup cilantro leaves
- ½ cup Greek yogurt
- 1 teaspoon honey

Directions:

1. Preheat the air fryer at 3900F.
2. Place the grill pan accessory in the air fryer.
3. Season the salmon steaks with salt and pepper. Brush with oil.
4. Grill for 15 minutes and make sure to flip halfway through the cooking time.
5. In a food processor, mix the garlic, cilantro leaves, yogurt and honey. Season with salt and pepper to taste.Pulse until smooth.
6. Serve the salmon steaks with the cilantro sauce.

Nutrition information:

Calories: 485; Carbs: 6.3g; Protein: 47.6g; Fat: 29.9g

173. Tasty Grilled Red Mullet

Servings: 8

Preparation Time: 15 minutes

Ingredients:

- 8 whole red mullets, gutted and scales removed
- Salt and pepper to taste
- Juice from 1 lemon
- 1 tablespoon olive oil

Directions:

1. Preheat the air fryer at 3900F.
2. Place the grill pan accessory in the air fryer.
3. Season the red mullet with salt, pepper, and lemon juice.
4. Brush with olive oil.
5. Grill for 15 minutes.

Nutrition information:

Calories: 152; Carbs: 0.9g; Protein: 23.1g; Fat: 6.2g

174. Chargrilled Halibut With Vegetables

Servings: 6

Preparation Time: 15 minutes

Ingredients:

- 1 ½ pounds halibut fillets
- Salt and pepper to taste
- 2 tablespoons olive oil
- 2 pounds mixed vegetables
- 4 cups torn lettuce leaves
- 1 cup cherry tomatoes, halved
- 4 large hard-boiled eggs, peeled and sliced

Directions:

1. Preheat the air fryer at 3900F.
2. Place the grill pan accessory in the air fryer.
3. Rub the halibut with salt and pepper. Brush the fish with oil.
4. Place on the grill.
5. Surround the fish fillet with the mixed vegetables and cook for 15 minutes.
6. Assemble the salad by serving the fish fillet with grilled mixed vegetables, lettuce, cherry tomatoes, and hard-boiled eggs.

Nutrition information:

Calories: 312; Carbs:16.8 g; Protein: 19.8g; Fat: 18.3g

175. Spiced Salmon Kebabs

Servings: 3

Preparation Time: 15 minutes

Ingredients:

- 2 tablespoons chopped fresh oregano
- 2 teaspoons sesame seeds
- 1 teaspoon ground cumin
- Salt and pepper to taste
- 1 ½ pounds salmon fillets

- 2 tablespoons olive oil
- 2 lemons, sliced into rounds

Directions:

1. Preheat the air fryer at 3900F.
2. Place the grill pan accessory in the air fryer.
3. Create the dry rub by combining the oregano, sesame seeds, cumin, salt and pepper.
4. Rub the salmon fillets with the dry rub and brush with oil.
5. Grill the salmon for 15 minutes.
6. Serve with lemon slices once cooked.

Nutrition information:

Calories per serving 447 ; Carbs: 4.1g; Protein:47.6 g; Fat:26.6 g

176. Roasted Tuna on Linguine

Servings: 2

Preparation Time: 20 minutes

Ingredients:

- 1-pound fresh tuna fillets
- Salt and pepper to taste
- 1 tablespoon olive oil
- 12 ounces linguine, cooked according to package Directions:
- 2 cups parsley leaves, chopped
- 1 tablespoon capers, chopped
- Juice from 1 lemon

Directions:

1. 1.Preheat the air fryer at 3900F.
2. 2.Place the grill pan accessory in the air fryer.
3. 3.Season the tuna with salt and pepper. Brush with oil.
4. 4.Grill for 20 minutes.
5. 5.Once the tuna is cooked, shred using forks and place on top of cooked linguine. Add parsley and capers. Season with salt and pepper and add lemon juice.

Nutrition information:

Calories: 520; Carbs: 60.6g; Protein: 47.7g; Fat: 9.6g

177. Chili Lime Clams with Tomatoes

Servings: 3

Preparation Time: 15 minutes

Ingredients:

- 25 littleneck clams
- 1 tablespoon fresh lime juice
- Salt and pepper to taste
- 6 tablespoons unsalted butter
- 4 cloves of garlic, minced
- ½ cup tomatoes, chopped
- ½ cup basil leaves

Directions:

1. Preheat the air fryer at 3900F.
2. Place the grill pan accessory in the air fryer.
3. On a large foil, place all ingredients. Fold over the foil and close by crimping the edges.
4. Place on the grill pan and cook for 15 minutes.
5. Serve with bread.

Nutrition information:

Calories: 163; Carbs: 4.1g; Protein: 1.7g; Fat: 15.5g

178. Garlicky-Grilled Turbot

Servings: 2

Preparation Time: 20 minutes

Ingredients:

- 2 whole turbot, scaled and head removed
- Salt and pepper to taste
- 1 clove of garlic, minced
- ½ cup chopped celery leaves
- 2 tablespoons olive oil

Directions:

1. Preheat the air fryer at 3900F.
2. Place the grill pan accessory in the air fryer.
3. Season the turbot with salt, pepper, garlic, and celery leaves.
4. Brush with oil.
5. Place on the grill pan and cook for 20 minutes until the fish becomes flaky.

Nutrition information:

Calories: 269; Carbs: 3.3g; Protein: 66.2g; Fat: 25.6g

179. Broiled Spiced-Lemon Squid

Servings: 4

Preparation Time: 15 minutes

Ingredients:

- 2 pounds squid, gutted and cleaned
- Salt and pepper to taste
- 1 tablespoon fresh lemon juice
- 5 cloves of garlic
- ½ cup tomatoes, chopped
- ½ cup green onions, chopped
- 2 tablespoons olive oil

Directions:

1. Preheat the air fryer at 3900F.
2. Place the grill pan accessory in the air fryer.
3. Season the squid with salt, pepper, and lemon juice.
4. Stuff the cavity with garlic, tomatoes, and onions.
5. Brush the squid with olive oil.
6. Place on the grill pan and cook for 15 minutes.
7. Halfway through the cooking time, flip the squid.

Nutrition information:

Calories: 277; Carbs: 10.7g; Protein: 36g; Fat: 10g

180. Tuna Grill with Ginger Sauce

Servings: 3

Preparation Time: 20 minutes

Ingredients:

- 1 ½ pounds tuna, thick slices
- 2 tablespoons rice vinegar
- 2 tablespoons grated fresh ginger
- 2 tablespoons peanut oil
- 2 tablespoons soy sauce

- 2 tablespoons honey
- 1 serrano chili, seeded and minced

Directions:

1. Place all ingredients in a Ziploc bag.
2. Allow to marinate in the fridge for at least 2 hours.
3. Preheat the air fryer at 3900F.
4. Place the grill pan accessory in the air fryer.
5. Grill the fish for 15 to 20 minutes.
6. Flip the fish halfway through the cooking time.
7. Meanwhile, pour the marinade in a saucepan and allow to simmer for 10 minutes until the sauce thickens.
8. 8.Brush the tuna with the sauce before serving.

Nutrition information:

Calories: 357; Carbs:14.8 g; Protein: 44.9g; Fat: 13.1g

181. Char-Grilled Spicy Halibut

Servings: 6

Preparation Time: 20 minutes

Ingredients:

- 3 pounds halibut fillet, skin removed
- Salt and pepper to taste
- 4 tablespoons dry white wine
- 4 tablespoons olive oil
- 2 cloves of garlic, minced
- 1 tablespoon chili powder

Directions:

1. Place all ingredients in a Ziploc bag.
2. Allow to marinate in the fridge for at least 2 hours.
3. Preheat the air fryer at 3900F.
4. Place the grill pan accessory in the air fryer.
5. Grill the fish for 20 minutes making sure to flip every 5 minutes.

Nutrition information:

Calories: 385; Carbs: 1.7g; Protein: 33g; Fat: 40.6g

182. Swordfish with Charred Leeks

Servings: 4

Preparation Time: 20 minutes

Ingredients:

- 4 swordfish steaks
- Salt and pepper to taste
- 3 tablespoons lime juice
- 2 tablespoons olive oil
- 4 medium leeks, cut into an inch long

Directions:

1. Preheat the air fryer at 3900F.
2. Place the grill pan accessory in the air fryer.
3. Season the swordfish with salt, pepper and lime juice.
4. Brush the fish with olive oil
5. Place fish fillets on grill pan and top with leeks.
6. Grill for 20 minutes.

Nutrition information:

Calories: 611; Carbs: 14.6g; Protein: 48g;

Fat: 40g

183. Citrusy Branzini on the Grill

Servings: 2

Preparation Time: 15 minutes

Ingredients:

- 2 branzini fillets
- Salt and pepper to taste
- 3 lemons, juice freshly squeezed
- 2 oranges, juice freshly squeezed

Directions:

1. Place all ingredients in a Ziploc bag. Allow to marinate in the fridge for 2 hours.
2. Preheat the air fryer at 3900F.
3. Place the grill pan accessory in the air fryer.
4. Place the fish on the grill pan and cook for 15 minutes until the fish is flaky.

Nutrition information:

Calories: 318; Carbs: 20.8g; Protein: 23.5g; Fat: 15.6g

184. Grilled Squid Rings with Kale

Servings: 3

Preparation Time: 15 minutes

Ingredients:

- 1 2-pound squid, cleaned and sliced into rings
- Salt and pepper to taste
- 3 cloves of garlic, minced
- 1 sprig rosemary, chopped
- ¼ cup red wine vinegar
- 3 pounds kale, torn
- 3 tomatoes, chopped

Directions:

1. Preheat the air fryer at 3900F.
2. Place the grill pan accessory in the air fryer.
3. Season the squid rings with salt, pepper, garlic, rosemary, and wine vinegar.
4. Grill for 15 minutes.
5. Serve octopus on a bed of kale leaves and garnish with tomatoes on top.

Nutrition information:

Calories: 575; Carbs: 56.2g; Protein: 68.1g; Fat: 8.6g

185. Butterflied Sriracha Prawns

Servings: 2

Preparation Time: 15 minutes

Ingredients:

- 1-pound large prawns, shells removed and cut lengthwise or butterflied
- 1 tablespoon sriracha
- 2 tablespoons melted butter
- 2 tablespoons minced garlic
- 1teaspoon fish sauce
- 1 tablespoon lime juice
- Salt and pepper to taste

Directions:

1. Preheat the air fryer at 3900F.
2. Place the grill pan accessory in the air fryer.
3. Season the prawns with the rest of the ingredients.
4. Place on the grill pan and cook for 15 minutes. Make sure to flip the prawns halfway through the cooking time.

Nutrition information:

Calories: 443; Carbs:9.7 g; Protein: 62.8g; Fat: 16.9g

186. Grilled Shrimp with Butter

Servings: 4

Preparation Time: 15 minutes

Ingredients:

- 6 tablespoons unsalted butter
- ½ cup red onion, chopped
- 1 ½ teaspoon red pepper
- 1 teaspoon shrimp paste or fish sauce
- 1 ½ teaspoon lime juice
- Salt and pepper to taste
- 24 large shrimps, shelled and deveined

Directions:

1. Preheat the air fryer at 3900F.
2. Place the grill pan accessory in the air fryer.
3. Place all ingredients in a Ziploc bag and give a good shake.
4. Skewer the shrimps through a bamboo skewer and place on the grill pan.
5. Cook for 15 minutes.
6. Flip the shrimps halfway through the cooking time.

Nutrition information:

Calories: 153; Carbs: 2.3g; Protein: 6.9g; Fat: 12.9g

187. Cajun-Seasoned Lemon Salmon

Preparation Time:7 minutes

Servings: 1

Ingredients:

- 1 salmon fillet
- 1 teaspoon Cajun seasoning
- 2 lemon wedges, for serving
- 1 teaspoon liquid stevia
- ½ lemon, juiced

Directions:

1. Preheat your air fryer to 350°Fahrenheit. Combine lemon juice and liquid stevia and coat salmon with this mixture. Sprinkle Cajun seasoning all over salmon. Place salmon on parchment paper in air fryer and cook for 7-minutes. Serve with lemon wedges.

Nutrition Information: Calories: 287, Total Fat: 9.3g, Carbs: 8.4g, Protein: 15.3g

188. Grilled Salmon Fillets

Preparation Time:8 minutes

Servings: 2

Ingredients:

- 2 salmon fillets
- 2 tablespoons olive oil
- 1 teaspoon liquid stevia
- 1/3 cup of light soy sauce
- 1/3 cup of water
- Salt and black pepper to taste

Directions:

1. Season salmon fillets with salt and pepper. Whisk the rest of the ingredients in a bowl. Allow the salmon fillets to marinate in mixture for 2-hours. Preheat your air fryer to 355°Fahrenheit for 5-minutes. Drain salmon fillets and air fry for 8-minutes.

Nutrition Information: Calories: 302, Total Fat: 8.6g, Carbs: 7.3g, Protein: 15.3g

189. Salmon Patties

Preparation Time:10 minutes

Servings: 2

Ingredients:

- 3 large russet potatoes, boiled, mashed
- 1 salmon fillet
- 1 egg
- Breadcrumbs
- 2 tablespoons olive oil
- Parsley, fresh, chopped
- Handful of parboiled vegetables
- ½ teaspoon dill
- Salt and pepper to taste

Directions:

1. Peel, chop, and mash cooked potatoes. Set aside. Preheat your air fryer for 5-minutes at 355°Fahrenheit. Air fry salmon for five minutes. Use a fork to flake salmon then set aside. Add vegetables, parsley, flaked salmon, dill, salt, and pepper to mashed potatoes. Add egg and combine. Shape the mixture into six patties. Cover with breadcrumbs. Cook in air fryer for 10-minutes.

Nutrition Information: Calories: 297, Total Fat: 8.5g, Carbs: 7.2g, Protein: 14.7g

190. Cheesy Breaded Salmon

Preparation Time:20 minutes

Servings: 4

Ingredients:

- 2 cups breadcrumbs
- 4 salmon fillets
- 2 eggs, beaten
- 1 cup Swiss cheese, shredded

Directions:

1. Preheat your air fryer to 390°Fahrenheit. Dip each salmon filet into eggs. Top with Swiss cheese. Dip into breadcrumbs, coating entire fish. Put into an oven-safe dish and cook for 20-minutes.

Nutrition Information: Calories: 296, Total Fat: 9.2g, Carbs: 8.7g, Protein: 15.2g

200. Cajun Salmon

Preparation Time:7 minutes

Servings: 1

Ingredients:

- 1 salmon fillet
- Cajun seasoning
- Juice of half a lemon, to serve

Directions:

1. Preheat your air fryer to 355°Fahrenheit. Sprinkle Cajun seasoning all over fish. Cook fish for 7-minutes, skin side up on grill pan. Squeeze lemon juice over fish and serve.

Nutrition Information: Calories: 298, Total Fat: 8.9g, Carbs: 7.6g, Protein: 15.4g

201. Coconut Shrimp

Preparation Time:10 minutes

Servings: 4

Ingredients:

- 1 cup breadcrumbs
- 1 cup dried coconut, unsweetened
- 1 cup almond flour
- Sea salt to taste
- 2 lbs. shrimp
- 1 cup egg whites

Directions:

1. In a mixing bowl, combine coconut and breadcrumbs. Season lightly with sea salt. In another bowl, add flour, and in a third bowl, add egg whites. Preheat your air fryer to 340°Fahrenheit. Dip each shrimp into flour, egg whites, then the breadcrumbs. Cook the shrimps for 10-minutes and serve with preferred dipping sauce.

Nutritional Value Nutrition Information: Calories: 296, Total Fat: 9.2g, Carbs: 7.9g, Protein: 14.9g

202. Air-Fried Cajun Shrimp

Preparation Time:5 minutes

Servings: 4

Ingredients:

- 1 ¼ lbs. shrimp, peeled and deveined
- ¼ teaspoon salt
- ½ teaspoon paprika
- 1 tablespoon olive oil
- ¼ cayenne pepper
- ½ teaspoon Old Bay seasoning

Directions:

1. Preheat air fryer to 400°Fahrenheit. Mix all the ingredients in a bowl. Place the seasoned shrimp into air fryer basket and cook for 5-minutes.

Nutrition Information: Calories: 300, Total Fat: 9.3g, Carbs: 8.2g, Protein: 14.6g

203. Air-Fried Crab Herb Croquettes

Preparation Time:18 minutes

Servings: 6

Ingredients:

- 1 lb. crab meat

- 1 cup breadcrumbs
- 2 egg whites
- Salt and black pepper to taste
- ½ teaspoon parsley, chopped
- ¼ teaspoon chives
- ¼ teaspoon tarragon
- 2 tablespoon celeries, chopped
- 4 tablespoon mayonnaise
- 4 tablespoons light sour cream
- 1 teaspoon olive oil
- ½ teaspoon lime juice
- ½ cup red pepper, chopped
- ¼ cup onion, chopped

Directions:

2. Preheat your air fryer to 355°Fahrenheit. Add breadcrumbs with salt and pepper in a bowl. In another small bowl add the egg whites. Add all the remaining ingredients into another bowl and mix well. Make croquettes from crab mixture and dip into egg whites, and then into breadcrumbs. Place into air fryer and cook for 18-minutes.

Nutrition Information: Calories: 295, Total Fat: 9.3g, Carbs: 8.6g, Protein: 15.3g

204. Creamy Air Fryer Salmon

Preparation Time:10 minutes

Servings: 2

Ingredients:

- ¾ lb. salmon, cut into 6 pieces
- Salt to taste
- ¼ cup plain yogurt
- 1 tablespoon dill, chopped
- 3 tablespoons light sour cream
- 1 tablespoon olive oil

Directions:

1. Season the salmon with salt and place it in air fryer. Drizzle the salmon with olive oil. Air-fry salmon at 285°Fahrenheit and cook for 10-minutes. Mix the dill, yogurt, sour cream and some salt. Place salmon on serving dish and drizzle with creamy sauce.

Nutrition Information: Calories: 289, Total Fat: 9.8g, Carbs: 8.6g, Protein: 14.7g

205. Air-Fried Cod Sticks

Preparation Time:12 minutes

Servings: 5

Ingredients:

- 2 large eggs, beaten
- 3 tablespoon milk
- 2 cups breadcrumbs
- 1 lb. cod fillets
- 1 cup almond meal
- Salt and pepper to taste

Directions:

1. In a bowl, mix egg and milk. In a shallow dish, combine breadcrumbs, pepper, and salt. In another dish, add the almond meal. Roll the cod sticks into almond meal, dip in egg, and coat in breadcrumbs. Place the coated cod sticks in air fryer basket. Air fry at 350°Fahrenheit for 12-minutes and shake basket halfway through cook time. Serve hot.

Nutrition Information: Calories: 298, Total Fat: 10.2g, Carbs: 9.5g, Protein: 14.8g

206. Barbecued Lime Shrimp

Preparation Time:15 minutes

Servings: 4

Ingredients:

- 4 cups of shrimp
- 1 ½ cups barbeque sauce
- 1 fresh lime, cut into quarters

Directions:

1. Preheat your air fryer to 360°Fahrenheit. Place the shrimp in a bowl with barbeque sauce. Stir gently. Allow shrimps to marinade for at least 5-minutes. Place the shrimp in air fryer and cook for 15-minutes. Remove from air fryer and squeeze lime over shrimps.

Nutrition Information: Calories: 289, Total Fat: 9.8g, Carbs: 8.7g, Protein: 14.9g

207. Crispy Shrimp

Preparation Time:8 minutes

Servings: 8

Ingredients:

- 4 egg whites
- 1 cup almond flour
- 2 lbs. shrimp, peeled and deveined
- ½ teaspoon cayenne pepper
- 2 tablespoon olive oil
- 1 cup breadcrumbs
- Salt and black pepper to taste

Directions:

1. In a dish mix flour, pepper, and salt. In a small bowl, whisk egg whites. In another bowl, mix breadcrumbs, cayenne pepper, and salt. Preheat your air fryer to 400°Fahrenheit. Coat the shrimp with flour mixture, dip in egg white, then finally coat with breadcrumbs. Place shrimp in air fryer basket and drizzle with olive oil and cook in batches for 8-minutes each.

Nutrition Information: Calories: 295, Total Fat: 9.2g, Carbs: 8.3g, Protein: 15.3g

208. Spicy Air-Fried Cheese Tilapia

Preparation Time:10 minutes

Servings: 4

Ingredients:

- 1 lb. tilapia fillets
- 1 tablespoon olive oil
- Salt and pepper to taste
- 2 teaspoons paprika
- 1 tablespoon parsley, chopped
- ¾ cup parmesan cheese, grated

Directions:

1. Preheat your air fryer to 400°Fahrenheit. Mix the parmesan cheese, parsley, paprika, salt, and pepper. Drizzle olive oil over the tilapia fillets and coat with paprika and cheese mixture. Place the coated tilapia fillets on aluminum foil. Place into the air fryer and cook for 10-

minutes.

Nutrition Information: Calories: 289, Total Fat: 8.9g, Carbs: 7.8g, Protein: 14.9g

209. Cheese Salmon

Preparation Time:11 minutes

Servings: 5

Ingredients:

- 2 lbs. salmon fillet
- Salt and pepper to taste
- ½ cup parmesan cheese, grated
- ¼ cup parsley, fresh, chopped
- 2 garlic cloves, minced

Directions:

1. Preheat your air fryer to 350°Fahrenheit. Put the salmon skin side facing down on aluminum foil and cover with another piece of foil. Cook salmon for 10-minutes. Remove the salmon from foil and top it with minced garlic, parsley, parmesan cheese, and pepper. Return salmon to air fryer for 1-minute cook time.

Nutrition Information: Calories: 297, Total Fat: 9.5g, Carbs: 8.3g, Protein: 14.9g

210. Herb Salmon Fillet

Preparation Time:8 minutes

Servings: 2

Ingredients:

- ½ lb. salmon fillet
- ¼ teaspoon thyme
- 1 teaspoon garlic powder
- ½ teaspoon cayenne pepper
- ½ teaspoon paprika
- ¼ teaspoon sage
- ¼ teaspoon oregano
- Salt and pepper to taste

Directions:

1. Rub the seasoning all over the salmon. Preheat your air fryer to 350°Fahrenheit. Place the seasoned salmon fillet into air fryer basket and cook for 8-minutes.

Nutrition Information: Calories: 298, Total Fat: 9.3g, Carbs: 8.6g, Protein: 10.2g

211. Crunchy Fish Taco

Preparation Time:13 minutes

Servings: 4

Ingredients:

- 12-ounce cod fillet
- Salt and black pepper to taste
- 1 cup tempura butter
- 1 cup breadcrumbs
- ½ cup guacamole
- 6-flour tortillas
- 2 tablespoons cilantro, freshly chopped
- ½ cup salsa
- 1 lemon, juiced

Directions:

1. Cut the cod fillets lengthwise into 2-inch pieces and season with salt and pepper. Dip each cod strip into tempura butter then into

breadcrumbs. Preheat your air fryer to 340°Fahrenheit and cook cod for 13-minutes. Spread guacamole on each tortilla. Place cod stick on tortilla and top with chopped cilantro and salsa. Squeeze lemon juice on top, then fold and serve.

Nutrition Information: Calories: 300, Total Fat: 10.3g, Carbs: 8.9g, Protein: 14.8g

212. Air-Fryer Baked Salmon & Asparagus

Preparation Time:15 minutes

Servings: 4

Ingredients:

- 4 salmon fillets
- 4 asparagus
- 2 tablespoons butter
- 3 lemons, sliced
- Salt and pepper to taste

Directions:

1. Preheat the air fryer to 300°Fahrenheit. Take four pieces of aluminum foil. Add asparagus, half lemon juice, pepper and salt in a bowl and toss. Divide seasoned asparagus evenly on four aluminum foil pieces. Place 1 salmon fillet on top of each asparagus. Place lemon slices on top of salmon fillets. Fold foil tightly to seal parcel. Place in air fryer basket and cook for 15-minutes. Serve warm.

Nutrition Information: Calories: 291, Total Fat: 16g, Carbs: 1g, Protein: 35g

213. Potato Fish Cake

Preparation Time:15 minutes

Servings: 2

Ingredients:

- 1 ½ cups white fish, cooked
- Pepper and salt to taste
- 1 ½ tablespoons of milk
- ½ cup of mashed potatoes
- 1 tablespoon butter
- 2 teaspoons gluten-free flour
- 1 teaspoon parsley
- ½ teaspoon sage

Directions:

1. Add ingredients to a mixing bowl and combine well. Make round patties and place them in the fridge for 1 hour. Place the patties into the air fryer at 375°Fahrenheit for 15-minutes.

Nutrition Information: Calories: 167, Total Fat: 9g, Carbs: 14g, Protein: 5g

214. Parmesan Baked Salmon

Preparation Time:11 minutes

Servings: 5

Ingredients:

- 2 lbs. fresh salmon fillet
- Salt and pepper to taste
- ½ cup parmesan cheese, grated
- ¼ cup fresh parsley, chopped
- 2 garlic cloves, minced

Directions:

1. Preheat the air fryer to 300°Fahrenheit. Place the salmon with the skin side down on foil and cover with more foil. Bake the salmon in the air fryer basket for 10-minutes. Open the foil and top salmon with cheese, garlic, pepper, salt, and parsley. Return for an additional minute in the air fryer.

Nutrition Information: Calories: 267, Total Fat: 12g, Carbs: 6g, Protein: 37g

215. Garlic Salmon Patties

Preparation Time:15 minutes

Servings: 4

Ingredients:

- 1 egg
- 14-ounce can of salmon, drained
- Salt and pepper to taste
- 2 tablespoons mayonnaise
- ½ teaspoon garlic powder
- 4 tablespoons onion, minced
- 4 tablespoons gluten-free flour
- 4 tablespoons cornmeal

Directions:

1. Add drained salmon into a bowl, and with a fork flake the salmon. Add garlic powder, mayonnaise, flour, cornmeal, onion, egg, pepper, and salt. Mix well. Make round patties with mix and place them in the air fryer. Air fry at 300°Fahrenheit for 15-minutes.

Nutrition Information: Calories: 244, Total Fat: 11g, Carbs: 14g, Protein: 22g

216. Grilled Prawns

Preparation Time:15 minutes

Servings: 4

Ingredients:

- 8 medium prawns
- Salt and pepper to taste
- 3 garlic cloves, minced
- 1 tablespoons butter, melted
- 1 rosemary sprig

Directions:

1. Add ingredients to a bowl and toss well. Add the marinated prawns to air fryer basket and cook at 300°Fahrenheit for 7-minutes. Serve hot!

Nutrition Information: Calories: 137, Total Fat: 4g, Carbs: 3g, Protein: 20g

POULTRY

217. Marinated Duck Breasts Recipe

Preparation Time:1 day 15 Minutes

Servings: 2

Ingredients:

- 2 duck breasts
- 2 garlic cloves; minced
- 6 tarragon springs
- 1 tbsp. butter
- 1/4 cup sherry wine
- 1 cup white wine
- 1/4 cup soy sauce
- Salt and black pepper to the taste

Directions:

1. In a bowl, mix duck breasts with white wine, soy sauce, garlic, tarragon, salt and pepper; toss well and keep in the fridge for 1 day.
2. Transfer duck breasts to your preheated air fryer at 350 °F and cook for 10 minutes; flipping halfway.
3. Meanwhile; pour the marinade in a pan, heat up over medium heat, add butter and sherry; stir, bring to a simmer, cook for 5 minutes and take off heat. Divide duck breasts on plates, drizzle sauce all over and serve.

Nutrition information:Calories: 475; Fat: 12; Fiber: 3; Carbs: 10; Protein: 48

218. Chicken Breasts with Passion Fruit Sauce

Preparation Time:20 Minutes

Servings: 4

Ingredients:

- 4 chicken breasts
- 4 passion fruits; halved, deseeded and pulp reserved
- 1 tbsp. whiskey
- 2-star anise
- 2 oz. maple syrup
- 1 bunch chives; chopped
- Salt and black pepper to the taste

Directions:

1. Heat up a pan with the passion fruit pulp over medium heat, add whiskey, star anise, maple syrup and chives; stir well, simmer for 5-6 minutes and take off heat.
2. Season chicken with salt and pepper, put in preheated air fryer and cook at 360 °F, for 10 minutes; flipping halfway. Divide chicken on plates, heat up the sauce a bit, drizzle it over chicken and serve.

Nutrition information:Calories: 374; Fat: 8; Fiber: 22; Carbs: 34; Protein: 37

219. Turkey, Mushrooms and Peas Casserole

Preparation Time:30 Minutes

Servings: 4

Ingredients:

- 2 lbs. turkey breasts; skinless, boneless
- 1 yellow onion; chopped
- 1 celery stalk; chopped.
- 1/2 cup peas
- 1 cup chicken stock
- 1 cup cream of mushrooms soup
- 1 cup bread cubes
- Salt and black pepper to the taste

Directions:

1. In a pan that fits your air fryer, mix turkey with salt, pepper, onion, celery, peas and stock, introduce in your air fryer and cook at 360 °F, for 15 minutes.
2. Add bread cubes and cream of mushroom soup; stir toss and cook at 360 °F, for 5 minutes more. Divide among plates and serve hot.

Nutrition information:Calories: 271; Fat: 9; Fiber: 9; Carbs: 16; Protein: 7

220. Chicken and Creamy Veggie Mix Recipe

Preparation Time:40 Minutes

Servings: 6

Ingredients:

- 29 oz. chicken stock
- 2 cups whipping cream
- 40 oz. chicken pieces; boneless and skinless
- 3 tbsp. butter; melted
- 1/2 cup yellow onion; chopped.
- 3/4 cup red peppers; chopped
- 1 bay leaf
- 8 oz. mushrooms; chopped
- 17 oz. asparagus; trimmed
- 3 tsp. thyme; chopped.
- Salt and black pepper to the taste

Directions:

1. Heat up a pan with the butter over medium heat, add onion and peppers; stir and cook for 3 minutes.
2. Add stock, bay leaf, salt and pepper, bring to a boil and simmer for 10 minutes.
3. Add asparagus, mushrooms, chicken, cream, thyme, salt and pepper to the taste; stir, introduce in your air fryer and cook at 360 °F, for 15 minutes. Divide chicken and veggie mix on plates and serve.

Nutrition information:Calories: 360; Fat: 27; Fiber: 13; Carbs: 24; Protein: 47

221. Cider Glazed Chicken Recipe

Preparation Time:24 Minutes

Servings: 4

Ingredients:

- 6 chicken thighs; bone in and skin on
- 1 sweet potato; cubed
- 2 apples; cored and sliced
- 1 tbsp. olive oil
- 1 tbsp. rosemary; chopped.
- 2/3 cup apple cider
- 1 tbsp. mustard
- 2 tbsp. honey
- 1 tbsp. butter

- Salt and black pepper to the taste

Directions:

1. Heat up a pan that fits your air fryer with half of the oil over medium high heat, add cider, honey, butter and mustard, whisk well, bring to a simmer, take off heat, add chicken and toss really well.
2. In a bowl, mix potato cubes with rosemary, apples, salt, pepper and the rest of the oil; toss well and add to chicken mix.
3. Place pan in your air fryer and cook at 390 °F, for 14 minutes. Divide everything on plates and serve.

Nutrition information:Calories: 241; Fat: 7; Fiber: 12; Carbs: 28; Protein: 22

222. Duck Breasts with Red Wine and Orange Sauce Recipe

Preparation Time:45 Minutes

Servings: 4

Ingredients:

- 2 duck breasts; skin on and halved
- 2 cups chicken stock
- 2 cups orange juice
- 2 tsp. pumpkin pie spice
- 2 tbsp. olive oil
- 2 tbsp. butter
- 1/2 cup honey
- 2 tbsp. sherry vinegar
- 4 cups red wine
- Salt and black pepper to the taste

Directions:

1. Heat up a pan with the orange juice over medium heat, add honey; stir well and cook for 10 minutes.
2. Add wine, vinegar, stock, pie spice and butter; stir well, cook for 10 minutes more and take off heat.
3. Season duck breasts with salt and pepper, rub with olive oil, place in preheated air fryer at 370 °F and cook for 7 minutes on each side.
4. Divide duck breasts on plates, drizzle wine and orange juice all over and serve right away.

Nutrition information:Calories: 300; Fat: 8; Fiber: 12; Carbs: 24; Protein: 11

223. Coconut Creamy Chicken

Preparation Time:2 hours 25 Minutes

Servings: 4

Ingredients:

- 4 big chicken legs
- 5 tsp. turmeric powder
- 2 tbsp. ginger; grated
- 4 tbsp. coconut cream
- Salt and black pepper to the taste

Directions:

1. In a bowl, mix cream with turmeric, ginger, salt and pepper, whisk, add chicken pieces, toss them well and leave aside for 2 hours.
2. Transfer chicken to your preheated air fryer, cook at 370 °F, for 25 minutes; divide among plates and serve with a side salad.

Nutrition information:Calories: 300; Fat: 4; Fiber: 12; Carbs: 22; Protein: 20

224. Duck and Cherries Recipe

Preparation Time:30 Minutes

Servings: 4

- **Ingredients:**

- 4 duck breasts; boneless, skin on and scored
- 1 tbsp. ginger; grated
- 1 tsp. cumin; ground
- 1/2 tsp. clove; ground
- 2 cups cherries; pitted
- 1/2 cup sugar
- 1/4 cup honey
- 1/3 cup balsamic vinegar
- 1/2 cup yellow onion; chopped
- 1/2 tsp. cinnamon powder
- 4 sage leaves; chopped
- 1 tsp. garlic; minced
- 1 jalapeno; chopped
- 2 cups rhubarb; sliced
- Salt and black pepper to the taste

Directions:

1. Season duck breast with salt and pepper, put in your air fryer and cook at 350 °F, for 5 minutes on each side.
2. Meanwhile; heat up a pan over medium heat, add sugar, honey, vinegar, garlic, ginger, cumin, clove, cinnamon, sage, jalapeno, rhubarb, onion and cherries; stir, bring to a simmer and cook for 10 minutes.
3. Add duck breasts; toss well, divide everything on plates and serve.

Nutrition information:Calories: 456; Fat: 13; Fiber: 4; Carbs: 64; Protein: 31

225. Easy Duck Breasts Recipe

Preparation Time:25 Minutes

Servings: 4

Ingredients:

- 4 duck breasts; skinless and boneless
- 4 garlic heads; peeled, tops cut off and quartered
- 2 tbsp. lemon juice
- 1/2 tsp. lemon pepper
- 1 ½ tbsp. olive oil
- Salt and black pepper to the taste

Directions:

1. In a bowl, mix duck breasts with garlic, lemon juice, salt, pepper, lemon pepper and olive oil and toss everything.
2. Transfer duck and garlic to your air fryer and cook at 350 °F, for 15 minutes. Divide duck breasts and garlic on plates and serve.

Nutrition information:Calories: 200; Fat: 7; Fiber: 1; Carbs: 11; Protein: 17

226. Duck and Tea Sauce Recipe

Preparation Time:30 Minutes

Servings: 4

Ingredients:

- 2 duck breast halves; boneless
- 3/4 cup shallot; chopped
- 2 ¼ cup chicken stock
- 1 ½ cup orange juice
- 3 tsp. earl gray tea leaves

- 3 tbsp. butter; melted
- 1 tbsp. honey
- Salt and black pepper to the taste

Directions:

1. Season duck breast halves with salt and pepper, put in preheated air fryer and cook at 360 °F, for 10 minutes.
2. Meanwhile; heat up a pan with the butter over medium heat, add shallot; stir and cook for 2-3 minutes.
3. Add stock; stir and cook for another minute.
4. Add orange juice, tea leaves and honey; stir, cook for 2-3 minutes more and strain into a bowl.
5. Divide duck on plates, drizzle tea sauce all over and serve.

Nutrition information:Calories: 228; Fat: 11; Fiber: 2; Carbs: 20; Protein: 12

227. Chicken and Radish Mix Recipe

Preparation Time:40 Minutes

Servings: 4

Ingredients:

- 4 chicken things; bone-in
- 1 tbsp. olive oil
- 3 carrots; cut into thin sticks
- 6 radishes; halved
- 2 tbsp. chives; chopped
- 1 cup chicken stock
- 1 tsp. sugar
- Salt and black pepper to the taste

Directions:

1. Heat up a pan that fits your air fryer over medium heat, add stock, carrots, sugar and radishes; stir gently, reduce heat to medium, cover pot partly and simmer for 20 minutes.
2. Rub chicken with olive oil, season with salt and pepper, put in your air fryer and cook at 350 °F, for 4 minutes. Add chicken to radish mix; toss, introduce everything in your air fryer, cook for 4 minutes more, divide among plates and serve.

Nutrition information:Calories: 237; Fat: 10; Fiber: 4; Carbs: 19; Protein: 29

228. Quick Creamy Chicken Casserole Recipe

Preparation Time:22 Minutes

Servings: 4

Ingredients:

1. 10 oz. spinach; chopped
2. 1/2 cup parmesan; grated
3. 1/2 cup heavy cream
4. 4 tbsp. butter
5. 3 tbsp. flour
6. 1 ½ cups milk
7. 2 cup chicken breasts; skinless, boneless and cubed
8. 1 cup bread crumbs
9. Salt and black pepper to the taste

Directions:

1. Heat up a pan with the butter over medium heat, add flour and stir well.
2. Add milk, heavy cream and parmesan; stir well, cook for 1-2

minutes more and take off heat.

3. In a pan that fits your air fryer, spread chicken and spinach.
4. Add salt and pepper and toss.
5. Add cream mix and spread, sprinkle bread crumbs on top, introduce in your air fryer and cook at 350 for 12 minutes. Divide chicken and spinach mix on plates and serve.

Nutrition information:Calories: 321; Fat: 9; Fiber: 12; Carbs: 22; Protein: 17

229. Duck Breasts with Endives Recipe

Preparation Time:35 Minutes

Servings: 4

Ingredients:

- 2 duck breasts
- 1 tbsp. sugar
- 1 tbsp. olive oil
- 6 endives; julienned
- 2 tbsp. cranberries
- 8 oz. white wine
- 1 tbsp. garlic; minced
- 2 tbsp. heavy cream
- Salt and black pepper to the taste

Directions:

1. Score duck breasts and season them with salt and pepper, put in preheated air fryer and cook at 350 °F, for 20 minutes; flipping them halfway.
2. Meanwhile; heat up a pan with the oil over medium heat, add sugar and endives; stir and cook for 2 minutes.
3. Add salt, pepper, wine, garlic, cream and cranberries; stir and cook for 3 minutes. Divide duck breasts on plates, drizzle the endives sauce all over and serve.

Nutrition information:Calories: 400; Fat: 12; Fiber: 32; Carbs: 29; Protein: 28

230. Chicken and Garlic Sauce Recipe

Preparation Time:30 Minutes

Servings: 4

Ingredients:

- 4 chicken breasts; skin on and bone-in
- 1 tbsp. butter; melted
- 1 tbsp. olive oil
- Salt and black pepper to the taste
- 40 garlic cloves; peeled and chopped.
- 2 thyme springs
- 1/4 cup chicken stock
- 2 tbsp. parsley; chopped
- 1/4 cup dry white wine

Directions:

1. Season chicken breasts with salt and pepper, rub with the oil, place in your air fryer, cook at 360 °F, for 4 minutes on each side and transfer to a heat proof dish that fits your air fryer.
2. Add melted butter, garlic, thyme, stock, wine and parsley; toss, introduce in your air fryer and cook at 350 °F, for 15 minutes more. Divide everything on plates and serve.

Nutrition information:Calories: 227; Fat:

9; Fiber: 13; Carbs: 22; Protein: 12**

231. Lemony Chicken

Preparation Time:40 Minutes

Servings: 6

Ingredients:

- 1 whole chicken; cut into medium pieces
- 1 tbsp. olive oil
- Juice from 2 lemons
- Zest from 2 lemons; grated
- Salt and black pepper to the taste

Directions:

1. Season chicken with salt, pepper, rub with oil and lemon zest, drizzle lemon juice, put in your air fryer and cook at 350 °F, for 30 minutes; flipping chicken pieces halfway. Divide among plates and serve with a side salad.

Nutrition information:Calories: 334; Fat: 24; Fiber: 12; Carbs: 26; Protein: 20

232. Pepperoni Chicken Recipe

Preparation Time:32 Minutes

Servings: 6

Ingredients:

- 4 medium chicken breasts; skinless and boneless
- 14 oz. tomato paste
- 1 tbsp. olive oil
- 1 tsp. oregano; dried
- 6 oz. mozzarella; sliced
- 1 tsp. garlic powder
- 2 oz. pepperoni; sliced
- Salt and black pepper to the taste

Directions:

1. In a bowl, mix chicken with salt, pepper, garlic powder and oregano and toss.
2. Put chicken in your air fryer, cook at 350 °F, for 6 minutes and transfer to a pan that fits your air fryer.
3. Add mozzarella slices on top, spread tomato paste, top with pepperoni slices, introduce in your air fryer and cook at 350 °F, for 15 minutes more. Divide among plates and serve.

Nutrition information:Calories: 320; Fat: 10; Fiber: 16; Carbs: 23; Protein: 27

233. Chicken and Chestnuts Mix Recipe

Preparation Time:22 Minutes

Servings: 2

Ingredients:

- 1/2 lb. chicken pieces
- 1 small yellow onion; chopped
- 2 tsp. garlic; minced
- 2 tbsp. soy sauce
- 4 tbsp. water chestnuts
- 2 tbsp. chicken stock
- 2 tbsp. balsamic vinegar
- 2 tortillas for serving
- A pinch of ginger; grated
- A pinch of allspice; ground

Directions:

1. In a pan that fits your air fryer, mix chicken meat with onion, garlic, ginger, allspice, chestnuts, soy sauce, stock and vinegar; stir, transfer to your air fryer and cook at 360 °F, for 12 minutes. Divide everything on plates and serve.

Nutrition information:Calories: 301; Fat: 12; Fiber: 7; Carbs: 24; Protein: 12

234. Chicken Tenders and Flavored Sauce Recipe

Preparation Time:20 Minutes

Servings: 6

Ingredients:

- 2 lbs. chicken tenders
- 2 tbsp. cornstarch
- 1 tsp. chili powder
- 2 tsp. garlic powder
- 1 tsp. onion powder
- 1 tsp. sweet paprika
- 2 tbsp. butter
- 2 tbsp. olive oil
- 1/2 cup chicken stock
- 2 cups heavy cream
- 2 tbsp. water
- 2 tbsp. parsley; chopped
- Salt and black pepper to the taste

Directions:

1. In a bowl, mix garlic powder with onion powder, chili, salt, pepper and paprika; stir, add chicken and toss.
2. Rub chicken tenders with oil, place in your air fryer and cook at 360 °F, for 10 minutes.
3. Meanwhile; heat up a pan with the butter over medium high heat, add cornstarch, stock, cream, water and parsley; stir, cover and cook for 10 minutes. Divide chicken on plates, drizzle sauce all over and serve.

Nutrition information:Calories: 351; Fat: 12; Fiber: 9; Carbs: 20; Protein: 17

235. Turmeric Chicken Legs

Preparation time: 5 minutes

Cooking time: 20 minutes

Servings: 4

Ingredients:

- 4 chicken legs
- 5 teaspoons turmeric powder
- 2 tablespoons ginger, grated
- Salt and black pepper to taste
- 4 tablespoons heavy cream

Directions:

1. Place all ingredients in a bowl and mix well.
2. Transfer the chicken to your air fryer and cook at 380 degrees F for 20 minutes.
3. Divide between plates and serve.

Nutrition information:calories 300, fat 4, fiber 12, carbs 22, protein 20

236.Flavored Turkey Breast

Preparation time: 10 minutes

Cooking time: 50 minutes

Servings: 4

Ingredients:

- 2 turkey breasts, skinless, boneless and halved
- Salt and black pepper to taste
- 1 teaspoon garlic powder
- 1 teaspoon onion powder
- ½ teaspoon thyme, dried
- 1 teaspoon rosemary, dried
- 1 tablespoon lemon juice
- 2 tablespoons olive oil

Directions:

1. In a bowl, mix all the ingredients and rub the turkey well.
2. Transfer to your air fryer's basket and cook at 370 degrees F for 25 minutes on each side.
3. Serve hot with a side salad.

Nutrition information:calories 271, fat 10, fiber 5, carbs 18, protein 15

237. Salsa Verde Chicken Breast

Preparation time: 10 minutes

Cooking time: 20 minutes

Servings: 4

Ingredients:

- 16 ounces salsa Verde
- 1 tablespoon avocado oil
- Salt and black pepper to taste
- 1 pound chicken breast, boneless and skinless
- 1½ cups cheddar cheese, grated
- ¼ cup parsley, chopped
- 1 teaspoon sweet paprika

Directions:

1. In a baking dish that fits your air fryer, place all ingredients except the cheese; toss well.
2. Put the pan into the fryer and cook at 380 degrees F for 17 minutes.
3. Sprinkle with the cheese and cook for 3-4 minutes more.
4. Divide between plates and serve.

Nutrition information:calories 280, fat 18, fiber 9, carbs 17, protein 14

238. Creamy Chicken Thighs

Preparation time: 10 minutes

Cooking time: 20 minutes

Servings: 4

Ingredients:

- 5 chicken thighs
- 1 tablespoon olive oil
- 2 garlic cloves, minced
- 1 tablespoon rosemary
- ½ cup heavy cream
- ¾ cup chicken stock
- 1 teaspoon chili powder
- ¼ cup cheddar cheese, grated
- ½ cup tomatoes, chopped
- 2 tablespoons basil, chopped
- Salt and black pepper to taste

Directions:

1. Season the chicken with salt and pepper and rub it with ½ tablespoon of the oil.
2. Put the chicken in your air fryer's basket and cook at 350 degrees F for

4 minutes.

3. Heat up a pan that fits your air fryer with the remaining ½ tablespoon of oil over medium heat.
4. Add rosemary, garlic, chili powder, tomatoes, cream, stock, cheese, salt, and pepper; stir / combine.
5. Bring the mixture to a simmer, take off the heat, and then add the chicken thighs and toss everything.
6. Place the pan in the air fryer and cook at 340 degrees F for 12 minutes.
7. Divide between plates, sprinkle the basil on top, serve, and enjoy.

Nutrition information:calories 232, fat 9, fiber 12, carbs 27, protein 16

239. Chinese Chicken Thighs

Preparation time: 10 minutes

Cooking time: 30 minutes

Servings: 4

Ingredients:

- 4 chicken thighs
- 2 green chilies, chopped
- 1 tablespoon olive oil
- 1 bunch spring onions, chopped
- 1 tablespoon ginger, grated
- 1 tablespoon fish sauce
- 1 tablespoon soy sauce
- 1 teaspoon sesame oil
- 14 ounces water
- 1 tablespoon rice wine

Directions:

1. Heat up a pan that fits your air fryer with the olive and sesame oil over medium heat.
2. Add the chilies, onions, ginger, fish sauce, soy sauce, rice wine, and the water; whisk, bring to a simmer, cook for 3-4 minutes, and then take off the heat.
3. Add the chicken thighs and toss everything.
4. Place the pan into the air fryer and cook at 370 degrees F for 25 minutes.
5. Divide between plates and serve.

Nutrition information:calories 280, fat 12, fiber 12, carbs 20, protein 13

240. Oregano Chicken Thighs

Preparation time: 5 minutes

Cooking time: 30 minutes

Servings: 4

Ingredients:

- 8 chicken thighs
- 2 tablespoons olive oil
- 4 teaspoons oregano, chopped
- ½ teaspoon sweet paprika
- Salt and black pepper to taste
- 2 garlic cloves, minced
- 1 red onion, chopped

Directions:

1. In a baking dish that fits your air fryer, place all of the ingredients and mix well.
2. Transfer the dish to your air fryer and cook at 400 degrees F for 30 minutes, shaking halfway.
3. Divide between plates and serve.

Nutrition information:calories 264, fat

14, fiber 13, carbs 21, protein 15

241. Herbed Chicken

Preparation time: 5 minutes

Cooking time: 30 minutes

Servings: 8

Ingredients:

- 8 chicken thighs
- Salt and black pepper to taste
- 3 garlic cloves, minced
- 3 tablespoons butter, melted
- 1 cup chicken stock
- ¼ cup heavy cream
- ½ teaspoon basil, dried
- ½ teaspoon thyme, dried
- ½ teaspoon oregano, dried
- 1 tablespoon mustard
- ¼ cup cheddar cheese, grated

Directions:

1. In a baking dish that fits your air fryer, place all ingredients except the cheddar cheese; mix well.
2. Transfer the dish to your air fryer and cook at 370 degrees F for 25 minutes.
3. Sprinkle the cheese on top and cook for 5 more minutes.
4. Divide everything between plates and serve.

Nutrition information:calories 280, fat 11, fiber 13, carbs 22, protein 14

242. Honey Duck Breasts

Preparation time: 10 minutes

Cooking time: 20 minutes

Servings: 6

Ingredients:

- 6 duck breasts, boneless
- 4 tablespoons soy sauce
- 1 teaspoon olive oil
- 2 tablespoons honey
- Salt and black pepper to taste
- 20 ounces chicken stock
- 1 tablespoon ginger, grated
- 4 tablespoons hoisin sauce

Directions:

1. Place all of the ingredients in a bowl and toss well.
2. Put the bowl in the fridge for 10 minutes.
3. Transfer the duck breasts to your air fryer's basket and cook at 400 degrees F for 10 minutes on each side.
4. Divide between plates and serve with a side salad.

Nutrition information:calories 286, fat 9, fiber 1, carbs 20, protein 17

243. Duck and Sauce

Preparation time: 5 minutes

Cooking time: 25 minutes

Servings: 4

Ingredients:

- 2 duck breasts, skin scored

- Salt and black pepper to taste
- 1 tablespoon sugar
- 1 tablespoon olive oil
- 2 tablespoons cranberries
- 8 ounces white wine
- 1 tablespoons garlic, minced
- 2 tablespoons heavy cream

Directions:

1. Season the duck breasts with salt and pepper and put them in preheated air fryer.
2. Cook at 350 degrees F for 10 minutes on each side and divide between plates.
3. Heat up a pan with the oil over medium heat, and add the cranberries, sugar, wine, garlic, and the cream; whisk well.
4. Cook for 3-4 minutes, drizzle over the duck, and serve.

Nutrition information:calories 280, fat 11, fiber 32, carbs 19, protein 20

244. Chicken Wings and Endives

Preparation time: 10 minutes

Cooking time: 30 minutes

Servings: 4

Ingredients:

- 8 chicken wings, halved
- 6 endives, shaved
- 1 tablespoon olive oil
- 2 garlic cloves, minced
- ¼ cup white wine
- Salt and black pepper to taste
- 1 tablespoon rosemary, chopped
- 1 teaspoon cumin, ground

Directions:

1. Season the chicken wings with the salt, pepper, cumin, and rosemary.
2. Place the wings in your air fryer's basket and cook at 360 degrees F for 10 minutes on each side; divide between plates.
3. Heat up a pan with the oil over medium heat, and then add the garlic, endives, salt, pepper, and the wine; bring to a simmer.
4. Cook for 8 minutes, spread over the chicken, and serve.

Nutrition information:calories 270, fat 8, fiber 12, carbs 20, protein 22

245. Indian Spiced Chicken Eggplant

Servings: 4

Preparation Time: 25 minutes

Ingredients:

- 4 cloves of garlic, minced
- 1-inch ginger, grated
- 1 can coconut milk
- 3 teaspoons lime zest
- 2 tablespoons fresh lime juice
- 2 tablespoons tomato paste
- Salt and pepper to taste
- 1 ½ teaspoon ground turmeric
- ¼ teaspoon cayenne pepper
- ¼ teaspoon ground cardamom
- 2 pounds boneless chicken breasts, cut into cubes

- 1 medium eggplant, cut into cubes
- 1 onion, cut into wedges
- 1 cup cherry tomatoes

Directions:

1. Place in a bowl the garlic, ginger, coconut milk, lime zest, lime juice, tomato paste, salt, pepper, turmeric, cayenne pepper, cardamom, and chicken breasts. Allow to marinate in the fridge for at least for 2 hours.
2. Preheat the air fryer at 3900F.
3. Place the grill pan accessory in the air fryer.
4. Skewer the chicken cubes with eggplant, onion, and cherry tomatoes on bamboo skewers.
5. Place on the grill pan and cook for 25 minutes making sure to flip the chicken every 5 minutes for even cooking.

Nutrition information:

Calories: 479; Carbs:19.7 g; Protein: 55.2g; Fat: 20.6g

246. Hot Spicy Turkey Meatloaf

Preparation time: 55 minutes

Servings 6

Nutrition Information:373 Calories; 20.9g Fat; 10.6g Carbs; 35.7g Protein; 4.8g Sugars

Ingredients

- 1½ pounds turkey breasts, ground
- 1/2 pound Cheddar cheese, cubed
- 1/2 cup hot spicy ketchup
- 1/2 cup turkey or chicken stock
- 1/3 teaspoon hot paprika
- 3 eggs, lightly beaten
- 1 ½ tablespoon olive oil
- 2 cloves garlic, pressed
- 1 ½ teaspoons dried rosemary
- 1/2 cup yellow onion,chopped
- 1/3 cup ground quick oats
- 1/2 teaspoon pepper
- A few dashes of Tabasco sauce
- 1 teaspoon seasoned salt

Directions

1. Heat the olive oil in a medium-sized saucepan that is placed over a moderate flame; now, sauté the onions, garlic, and dried rosemary until just tender, or about 3 to 4 minutes.
2. In the meantime, set the air fryer to cook at 385 degrees F.
3. Place all the ingredients, minus the hot spicy ketchup, in a mixing dish together with the sautéed mixture; thoroughly mix to combine.
4. Shape into meatloaf and top with the hot spicy ketchup. Air-fry for 47 minutes. Bon appétit!

247. Mustard and Sage Turkey Breasts

Preparation time: 30 minutes

Servings 4

Nutrition Information:373 Calories; 19.9g Fat; 5g Carbs; 41.9g Protein; 1.8g Sugars

Ingredients

- 1/2 teaspoon smoked paprika
- 1 1/2 tablespoons mustard

- 1 ½ tablespoons soy sauce
- 1/3 cup chopped fresh sage
- 1 ½ tablespoons sesame oil
- 1/3 cup lemon juice
- 1/3 turkey breast, quartered lengthwise
- 1/2 teaspoon marjoram
- Sea salt flakes, to taste
- 1 teaspoon freshly ground pepper, or to savor

Directions

1. Firstly, pat the turkey breast dry; brush it with the sesame oil. Now, add the soy sauce, lemon juice, fresh sage, and the mustard; let it marinate for at least 2 hours.
2. After that, discard the marinade; season the turkey breasts with the paprika, salt, black pepper, and marjoram.
3. Now, bake in the air fryer cooking basket for about 22 minutes at 365 degrees F.

248. Wine and Coriander Turkey Wings

Preparation time: 2 hours 30 minutes

Servings 4

Nutrition Information:126 Calories; 7g Fat; 2.8g Carbs; 12.2g Protein; 1.2g Sugars

Ingredients

- 1 teaspoon freshly cracked pink peppercorns
- 1 ½ teaspoons all-purpose flour
- ½ pound turkey wings, cut into smaller pieces
- 2 teaspoon garlic powder
- 1/3 cup white wine
- 1/2 teaspoon garlic salt
- 1/2 tablespoon coriander,ground

Directions

1. Toss all of the above ingredients in a mixing dish. Let it marinate at least 3 hours.
2. Air-fry turkey wings for 28 minutes at 355 degrees F. Bon appétit!

249. Baked Eggs with Ground Turkey

Preparation time: 30 minutes

Servings 6

Nutrition Information:234 Calories; 15.6g Fat; 6.2g Carbs; 16g Protein; 1.9g Sugars

Ingredients

- 1½ pounds ground turkey
- 6 whole eggs, well beaten
- 1/3 teaspoon smoked paprika
- 2 egg whites, beaten
- Tabasco sauce, for drizzling
- 2 tablespoons sesame oil
- 2 leeks, chopped
- 3 cloves garlic, finely minced
- 1 teaspoon ground black pepper
- 1/2 teaspoon sea salt

Directions

1. Warm the oil in a pan over moderate heat; then, sweat the leeks and garlic

until tender; stir periodically.
2. Next, grease 6 oven safe ramekins with pan spray. Divide the sautéed mixture among six ramekins.
3. In a bowl, beat the eggs and egg whites using a wire whisk. Stir in the smoked paprika, salt and black pepper; whisk until everything is thoroughly combined. Divide the egg mixture among the ramekins.
4. Air-fry approximately 22 minutes at 345 degrees F. Drizzle Tabasco sauce over each portion and serve.

250. Winter Turkey Breasts with Leeks

Preparation time: 35 minutes

Servings 4

Nutrition Information:176 Calories; 8.6g Fat; 9.1g Carbs; 9g Protein; 3.1g Sugars

Ingredients

- 4 turkey breasts, boneless and skinless
- 1/2 palmful chopped fresh sage leaves
- 1 ½ tablespoons freshly squeezed lemon juice
- 1/3 teaspoon dry mustard
- 1/3 cup dry white wine
- 3 cloves garlic, minced
- 2 leeks, cut into thick slices
- 1/2 teaspoon smoked paprika
- 2 tablespoons olive oil

Directions

1. Combine the first six ingredients in a small-sized mixing bowl; mix thoroughly until everything is well combined
2. Then, smear this mixture on the turkey breast. Add white wine and let it marinate about 2 hours.
3. Transfer to the cooking basket along with the leeks.

Bake at 375 degrees F for 48 minutes, turning once or twice. Bon appétit!

251. Easy Honey Mustard Turkey Breast

Preparation time: 40 minutes

Servings 4

Nutrition Information:201 Calories; 9.6g Fat; 4.7g Carbs; 20.6g Protein; 1.5g Sugars

Ingredients

- 1/2 teaspoon dried thyme
- 4 medium-sized turkey breasts
- 1/2 teaspoon dried sage
- 3 whole star anise
- 1 ½ tablespoons olive oil
- 1 ½ tablespoons honey mustard
- 1 teaspoon smoked cayenne pepper
- 1 teaspoon fine sea salt

Directions

1. Set your air fryer to cook at 365 degrees F.
2. Brush the turkey breast with olive oil and sprinkle with seasonings.
3. Cook at 365 degrees F for 45 minutes, turning twice. Now, pause the machine and spread the cooked breast with honey mustard.

4. Air-fry for 6 to 8 more minutes. Let it rest before slicing and serving.

252. Asiago Turkey Wrapped in Bacon

Preparation time: 10 minutes

Servings 12

Nutrition Information:306 Calories; 30.6g Fat; 1g Carbs; 43.9g Protein; 0.6g Sugars

Ingredients

- 1 ½ small-sized turkey breast, chop into 12 pieces
- 12 thin slices Asiago cheese
- Paprika, to taste
- Fine sea salt and ground black pepper, to savor
- 12 rashers bacon

Directions

1. Lay out the bacon rashers; place 1 slice of Asiago cheese on each bacon piece.
2. Top with turkey, season with paprika, salt, and pepper, and roll them up; secure with a cocktail stick.
3. Air-fry at 365 degrees F for 13 minutes. Bon appétit!

253. Eggs with Turkey Sausage

Preparation time: 20 minutes

Servings 6

Nutrition Information:290 Calories; 10.1g Fat; 28.5g Carbs; 21.9g Protein; 2.2g Sugars

Ingredients

- 6 English muffins
- 1 teaspoon dried dill weed
- 1 teaspoon mustard seeds
- 6 turkey sausages
- 3 bell peppers, seeded and thinly sliced
- 6 medium-sized eggs
- 1/2 teaspoon fennel seeds
- 1 teaspoon sea salt
- 1/3 teaspoon freshly cracked pink peppercorns

Directions

1. Set your air fryer to cook at 325 degrees F. Cook the sausages and bell peppers in the air fryer cooking basket for 8 minutes.
2. Crack the eggs into the ramekins; sprinkle them with salt, dill weed, mustard seeds, fennel seeds, and peppercorns. Cook an additional 12 minutes at 395 degrees F.
3. Serve on English muffins and enjoy!

254. Turkey with Honey Applesauce

Preparation time: 30 minutes + marinating time

Servings 2

Nutrition Information:378 Calories; 24.1g Fat; 23.7g Carbs; 16g Protein; 18.2g Sugars

Ingredients

- 1/3 teaspoon mustard powder
- 1/3 cup apple cider vinegar
- 1 apple, peeled, cored and diced
- 1/2 pound turkey, sliced
- 1 garlic clove, peeled and halved
- 1/2 teaspoon shallot powder
- 1 tablespoon honey
- 1 tablespoons melted butter
- 1 teaspoon freshly cracked pink peppercorns
- 1 teaspoon onion salt
- 1/3 teaspoon ground allspice

Directions

1. Rub turkey slices with the garlic halves and transfer them to a mixing dish. Now, stir in seasonings and cider vinegar. Allow it to marinate at least 2 hours.
2. After that, roast your turkey for 28 minutes at 395 degrees F.
3. In the meantime, place the apples, honey, and butterin a sauté pan that is preheated over a moderate heat. Cook for 9 minutes or until apples have softened.
4. Pour the apple sauce over warm turkey breasts and serve on a serving platter.

255. Rustic Turkey Breast with Walnuts

Preparation time: 1 hour 30 minutes

Servings 2

Nutrition Information:388 Calories; 20.5g Fat; 16g Carbs; 34.6g Protein; 10.2g Sugars

Ingredients

- 1 ½ tablespoons soy sauce
- 1/2 tablespoon cornstarch
- 2 bay leaves
- 1/3 cup dry sherry
- 1 ½ tablespoons chopped walnuts
- 1 teaspoon shallot powder
- 2 turkey breasts, sliced
- 1 teaspoon garlic powder
- 2 teaspoons olive oil
- 1/2 teaspoon onion salt
- 1/2 teaspoon red pepper flakes, crushed
- 1 teaspoon ground black pepper

Directions

1. Begin by preheating your air fryer to 395 degrees F. Place all ingredients, minus chopped walnuts, in a mixing bowl and let them marinate at least 1 hour.
2. After that, cook the marinated turkey breast approximately 23 minutes or until heated through.
3. Pause the machine, scatter chopped walnuts over the top and air-fry an additional 5 minutes. Bon appétit!

256. Country Turkey and Pepper Frittata

Preparation time: 5 minutes

Servings 1

Nutrition Information:342 Calories; 27.1g Fat; 4g Carbs; 19.4g Protein; 2.2g Sugars

Ingredients

- 1/2 red bell pepper, seeded and chopped
- 1 clove garlic, finely minced
- 1/3 teaspoon parsley flakes
- 1/2 green bell pepper, seeded and chopped
- 3 eggs, whisked
- 2 ounces ground turkey
- 1/2 small-sized leek, finely chopped
- 1 teaspoon garlic pepper
- 1/2 teaspoon fine sea salt

Directions

1. Simply whisk all of the above ingredients in a mixing dish. Now, scrape the mixture into the air fryer baking tray.
2. Set the machine to cook at 355 degrees F; air-fry approximately 8 minutes. Eat warm, garnished with hot sauce, if desired.

257. Lemony Turkey with Mustard Sauce

Preparation time: 1 hour 10 minutes

Servings 4

Nutrition Information:175 Calories; 9.6g Fat; 1.7g Carbs;10.9g Protein; 0.8g Sugars

Ingredients

- ½ teaspoon cumin powder
- 4 turkey breasts, quartered
- 2 cloves garlic, smashed
- ½ teaspoon hot paprika
- 2 tablespoons melted butter
- 1 teaspoon fine sea salt
- Freshly cracked mixed peppercorns, to savor
- Fresh juice of 1 lemon
- For the Mustard Sauce:
- 1 ½ tablespoons mayonnaise
- 1 ½ cups Greek yogurt
- 1/2 tablespoon yellow mustard

Directions

1. Grab a medium-sized mixing dish and combine together the garlic and melted butter; rub this mixture evenly over the surface of the turkey.
2. Add the cumin powder, followed by paprika, salt, peppercorns, and lemon juice. Place in your refrigerator at least 55 minutes.
3. Set your air fryer to cook at 375 degrees F. Roast the turkey for 18 minutes, turning halfway through; roast in batches.
4. In the meantime, make the mustard sauce by mixing all ingredients for the sauce. Serve warm roasted turkey with the mustard sauce. Bon appétit!

258. Turkey Tortilla Wraps

Preparation time: 2 hours + 20 minutes

Servings 4

Nutrition Information:195 Calories; 9.1g Fat; 23.3g Carbs; 6g Protein; 0.4g Sugars

Ingredients

- 8 corn tortillas
- 1/2 tablespoon Dijon mustard
- ½ small-sized red onion, thinly sliced
- 1 ½ tablespoons vegetable oil
- 1/3 cup Mexican blend cheese, shredded

- 1 turkey breasts, halved
- 1/2 teaspoon Tabasco
- 1 teaspoon garlic powder
- 2 teaspoons white vinegar
- 1/3 teaspoon kosher salt
- 1/3 teaspoon black pepper

Directions

1. Combine the turkey, Tabasco, black pepper, kosher salt, garlic powder, white vinegar, and vegetable oil in a mixing bowl. Cover and let it marinate at least 2 hours.
2. After that, preheat the air fryer to 355 degrees F; drain the turkey and air-fry for 23 minutes. Allow it to cool slightly.
3. Shred the turkey with meat claws. To assemble your wraps, microwave the tortillas. Spread the tortillas with Dijon mustard.
4. Divide the turkey filling among warm tortillas; add Mexican blend cheese and red onion; roll them tightly. Bon appétit!

259. Zesty Air Fried Turkey Leg

Preparation time: 30 minutes

Servings 6

Nutrition Information:244 Calories; 16g Fat; 8g Carbs; 11g Protein; 3.9g Sugars

Ingredients

- 1 ½ tablespoons yellow mustard
- 1 ½ tablespoons herb seasoning blend
- 1/3 cup tamari sauce
- 1 ½ tablespoons olive oil
- 1/2 lemon, juiced
- 3 turkey drumsticks
- 1/3 cup pear or apple cider vinegar
- 2 sprigs rosemary, chopped

Directions

1. Dump all ingredients into a mixing dish. Let it marinate overnight.
2. Set your air fryer to cook at 355 degrees F.
3. Season turkey drumsticks with salt and black pepper and roast them at 355 degrees F for 28 minutes. Cook one drumstick at a time.
4. Pause the machine after 14 minutes and flip turkey drumstick. Serve warm with a plum sauce. Bon appétit!

260. Lime Turkey Tortilla Roll-Ups

Preparation time: 2 hours + 25 minutes

Servings 8

Nutrition Information:347 Calories; 14.6g Fat; 19g Carbs; 34.1g Protein; 0.8g Sugars

Ingredients

- 8 corn tortillas
- 1/3 Colby cheese, thinly sliced
- 1/2 large-sized turkey breasts, halved
- 1 teaspoon cumin powder
- 1/3 small-sized onion, chopped
- 1/3 cup lime juice
- 3 cloves garlic, minced

- 1 teaspoon garlic powder
- Kosher salt, to savor
- 1 ½ tablespoons olive oil

Directions

1. Combine the turkey, cumin powder, garlic powder, lime juice, and olive oil in a mixing bowl. Cover and marinate it at least 2 hours.
2. After that, preheat the air fryer to 355 degrees F; discard the marinade, drain the turkey and air-fry for 23 minutes. Allow it to cool slightly.
3. Now, shred the turkey with meat claws. Now, stir in the minced garlic and mix to combine well. To finish, heat your tortillas in a microwave until pliable.
4. Divide the turkey filling among the tortillas; add the cheese, onion, and salt, and roll them tightly; secure with toothpicks. Bon appétit!

261. Curried Turkey Drumsticks

Preparation time: 25 minutes

Servings 2

Nutrition Information:240 Calories; 9.6g Fat; 16.2g Carbs; 19.9g Protein; 2.3g Sugars

Ingredients

- 1 ½ tablespoons red curry paste
- 1/2 teaspoon cayenne pepper
- 1 ½ tablespoons minced ginger
- 2 turkey drumsticks
- 1/3 cup coconut milk
- 1 teaspoon kosher salt, or more to taste
- 1/3 teaspoon ground pepper, to more to taste

Directions

1. First of all, place turkey drumsticks with all ingredients in your refrigerator; let it marinate overnight.
2. Cook turkey drumsticks at 380 degrees F for 23 minutes; make sure to flip them over at half-time. Serve with the salad on the side.

262. Easy Curry Grilled Chicken Wings

Servings: 4

Preparation Time: 35 minutes

Ingredients:

- 2 pounds chicken wings
- ½ cup plain yogurt
- 1 tablespoons curry powder
- Salt and pepper to taste

Directions:

1. Season the chicken wings with yogurt, curry powder, salt and pepper. Toss to combine everything.
2. Allow to marinate in the fridge for at least 2 hours.
3. Preheat the air fryer at 3900F.
4. Place the grill pan accessory in the air fryer.
5. Grill the chicken for 35 minutes and make sure to flip the chicken halfway through the cooking time.

Nutrition information:

Calories:314 ; Carbs: 3.3g; Protein: 51.3g; Fat: 9.2g

263. Spicy Chicken with Lemon

Servings: 4

Preparation Time: 45 minutes

Ingredients:

- 2 pounds chicken thighs
- ¼ cup smoked paprika
- ½ teaspoon liquid smoke seasoning
- Salt and pepper to taste
- 1 ½ tablespoon cayenne pepper
- 4 lemons, halved
- ½ cup parsley leaves

Directions:

1. 1.Preheat the air fryer at 3900F.
2. 2.Place the grill pan accessory in the air fryer.
3. 3.In a large foil, place the chicken and season with paprika, liquid smoke seasoning, salt, pepper, and cayenne pepper.
4. 4.Top with lemon and parsley.
5. 5.Directions:
6. 6.Place on the grill and cook for 45 minutes.

Nutrition information:

Calories: 546; Carbs: 10.4g; Protein: 39.2g; Fat: 39.1g

264. Korean Grilled Chicken

Servings: 4

Preparation Time: 30 minutes

Ingredients:

- 2 pounds chicken wings
- 1 teaspoon salt
- ½ teaspoon fresh ground black pepper
- ½ cup gochujang
- 1 scallion, sliced thinly

Directions:

1. Place in a Ziploc bag the chicken wings, salt, pepper, and gochujang sauce.
2. Allow to marinate in the fridge for at least 2 hours.
3. Preheat the air fryer at 3900F.
4. Place the grill pan accessory in the air fryer.
5. Grill the chicken wings for 30 minutes making sure to flip the chicken every 10 minutes.
6. Top with scallions and serve with more gochujang.

Nutrition information:

Calories: 289; Carbs: 0.8g; Protein: 50.1g; Fat: 8.2g

265. Chicken with Shishito Peppers

Servings: 6

Preparation Time: 30 minutes

Ingredients:

- 3 pounds chicken wings
- Salt and pepper to taste
- 2 tablespoons sesame oil
- 1 ½ cups shishito peppers, pureed

Directions:

1. Place all ingredients in a Ziploc bowl and allow to marinate for at least 2 hours in the fridge.
2. Preheat the air fryer at 3900F.
3. Place the grill pan accessory in the air fryer.
4. Grill for at least 30 minutes flipping the chicken every 5 minutes and basting with the remaining sauce.

Nutrition information:

Calories: 333; Carbs: 1.7g; Protein: 50.2g; Fat: 12.6g

266. Grilled Chicken with Scallions

Servings: 4
Preparation Time: 1 hour

Ingredients:

- 2 pounds whole chicken
- Salt and pepper to taste
- 4 sprigs rosemary
- 2 heads of garlic, peeled and crushed
- 2 bunches scallions

Directions:

1. Season the whole chicken with salt and pepper.
2. Place inside the chicken cavity the rosemary, garlic, and scallions.
3. Preheat the air fryer at 3900F.
4. Place the grill pan accessory in the air fryer.
5. Grill the chicken for 1 hour.

Nutrition information:

Calories: 470; Carbs: 46.2g; Protein: 37.2g;

Fat: 15.9g

267. PiriPiri Chicken

Servings: 6
Preparation Time: 45 minutes

Ingredients:

- 3 pounds chicken breasts
- ½ cup piripiri sauce
- ¼ cup fresh lemon juice
- Salt and pepper to taste
- 1-inch fresh ginger, peeled and sliced thinly
- 1 large shallots, quartered
- 3 cloves of garlic, minced

Directions:

1. Preheat the air fryer at 3900F.
2. Place the grill pan accessory in the air fryer.
3. On a large foil, place the chicken top with the rest of the ingredients.
4. Fold the foil and crimp the edges.
5. Grill for 45 minutes.

Nutrition information:

Calories:404 ; Carbs: 3.4g; Protein: 47.9g; Fat: 21.1g

268. Turmeric and Lemongrass Chicken

Servings: 6
Preparation Time: 40 minutes

Ingredients:

- 3 shallots, chopped
- 3 cloves of garlic, minced
- 2 lemongrass stalks
- 1 teaspoon turmeric
- Salt and pepper to taste
- 2 tablespoons fish sauce
- 3 pounds whole chicken

Directions:

1. Place all ingredients in a Ziploc bag and allow to marinate for at least 2 hours in the fridge.
2. Preheat the air fryer at 3900F.
3. Place the grill pan accessory in the air fryer.
4. Grill the chicken for 40 minutes making sure to flip every 10 minutes for even grilling.

Nutrition information:

Calories: 486; Carbs: 49.1g; Protein: 38.5g; Fat: 16.1g

269. Peruvian Grilled Chicken

Servings: 4

Preparation Time: 40 minutes

Ingredients:

- 1/3 cup soy sauce
- 2 tablespoons fresh lime juice
- 5 cloves of garlic, minced
- 2 teaspoons ground cumin
- 1 teaspoon paprika
- ½ teaspoon dried oregano
- 2 ½ pounds chicken, quartered

Directions:

1. Place all ingredients in a Ziploc bag and shake to mix everything.
2. Allow to marinate for at least 2 hours in the fridge.
3. Preheat the air fryer at 3900F.
4. Place the grill pan accessory in the air fryer.
5. Grill the chicken for 40 minutes making sure to flip the chicken every 10 minutes for even grilling.

Nutrition information:

Calories:389 ; Carbs: 7.9g; Protein: 59.7g; Fat: 11.8g

270. Moroccan Chicken

Servings: 4

Preparation Time: 40 minutes

Ingredients:

- 2 pounds of boneless chicken thighs
- 4 cloves of garlic, chopped
- Salt and pepper to taste
- 2 teaspoons paprika
- ¼ teaspoons crushed red pepper flakes
- 2 teaspoons ground cumin

Directions:

1. On a dish, season the chicken with garlic, salt, pepper, paprika, crushed red pepper flakes, and ground cumin.
2. Preheat the air fryer at 3900F.
3. Place the grill pan accessory in the air fryer.
4. Grill the chicken for 40 minutes.

5. Flip the chicken every 10 minutes to cook evenly.

Nutrition information:

Calories:755; Carbs: 35.6g; Protein: 43.1g; Fat: 51.3g

271. Rotisserie Chicken with Herbes

Servings: 6

Preparation Time: 1 hour

Ingredients:

- 3 pounds chicken, whole
- 2 tablespoons dried herbes de Provence
- 1 tablespoon salt

Directions:

1. Season the whole chicken with dried herbes de Provence and salt. Rub all the seasoning on the chicken including the cavity.
2. Preheat the air fryer at 3900F.
3. Place the grill pan accessory in the air fryer.
4. Place the chicken and grill for 1 hour.

Nutrition information:

Calories: 256; Carbs:1.1 g; Protein: 46.2g; Fat: 6.2g

272. Grilled Oregano Chicken

Servings: 6

Preparation Time: 40 minutes

Ingredients:

- 3 pounds chicken breasts
- 2 tablespoons oregano, chopped
- 4 cloves of garlic, minced
- 1 tablespoon grated lemon zest
- 2 tablespoons fresh lemon juice
- Salt and pepper to taste

Directions:

1. Preheat the air fryer at 3900F.
2. Place the grill pan accessory in the air fryer.
3. Season the chicken with oregano, garlic, lemon zest, lemon juice, salt and pepper.
4. Grill for 40 minutes and flip every 10 minutes to cook evenly.

Nutrition information:

Calories: 398; Carbs: 1.9g; Protein: 47.5g; Fat: 21.2g

273. Honey Sriracha Chicken

Servings: 4

Preparation Time: 40 minutes

Ingredients:

- 3 tablespoons rice vinegar
- 2 tablespoons sriracha
- 1 tablespoon honey
- 1 teaspoon Dijon mustard
- 4 chicken breasts
- ½ teaspoon paprika
- ½ teaspoon garlic powder
- Salt and pepper to taste

Directions:

1. Place all ingredients in a Ziploc bag and allow to marinate for at least 2 hours in the fridge.
2. Preheat the air fryer at 3900F.
3. Place the grill pan accessory in the air fryer.
4. Grill the chicken for at least 40 minutes and flip the chicken every 10 minutes for even cooking.

Nutrition information:

Calories: 525; Carbs: 6.1g; Protein: 60.8g; Fat: 26.9g

274. Tequila Glazed Chicken

Servings: 6

Preparation Time: 40 minutes

Ingredients:

- 2 tablespoons whole coriander seeds
- Salt and pepper to taste
- 3 pounds chicken breasts
- 1/3 cup orange juice
- ¼ cup tequila
- 2 tablespoons brown sugar
- 2 tablespoons honey
- 3 cloves of garlic, minced
- 1 shallot, minced

Directions:

1. Place all ingredients in a Ziploc bag and allow to marinate for at least 2 hours in the fridge.
2. Preheat the air fryer at 3900F.
3. Place the grill pan accessory in the air fryer.
4. Grill the chicken for at least 40 minutes
5. Flip the chicken every 10 minutes for even cooking.
6. Meanwhile, pour the marinade in a saucepan and simmer until the sauce thickens.
7. Brush the chicken with the glaze before serving.

Nutrition information:

Calories: 449; Carbs: 11.2g; Protein: 48.1g; Fat: 22.5g

275. Cider Glazed Chicken

Preparation time: 10 minutes

Cooking time: 14 minutes

Servings: 4

Ingredients:

- 1 sweet potato, cubed
- 2 apples, cored and sliced
- 1 tablespoon olive oil
- 1 tablespoon rosemary, chopped
- Salt and black pepper to the taste
- 6 chicken thighs, bone in and skin on
- 2/3 cup apple cider
- 1 tablespoon mustard
- 2 tablespoons honey
- 1 tablespoon butter

Directions:

1. Heat up a pan that fits your air fryer with half of the oil over medium high heat, add cider, honey, butter and mustard, whisk well, bring to a simmer, take off heat, add chicken and toss really well.

2. In a bowl, mix potato cubes with rosemary, apples, salt, pepper and the rest of the oil, toss well and add to chicken mix.
3. Place pan in your air fryer and cook at 390 degrees F for 14 minutes.
4. Divide everything on plates and serve.
5. Enjoy!

Nutrition information:calories 241, fat 7, fiber 12, carbs 28, protein 22

276. Veggie Stuffed Chicken Breasts

Preparation time: 10 minutes

Cooking time: 15 minutes

Servings: 4

Ingredients:

- 4 chicken breasts, skinless and boneless
- 2 tablespoons olive oil
- Salt and black pepper to the taste
- 1 zucchini, chopped
- 1 teaspoon Italian seasoning
- 2 yellow bell peppers, chopped
- 3 tomatoes, chopped
- 1 red onion, chopped
- 1 cup mozzarella, shredded

Directions:

1. Mix a slit on each chicken breast creating a pocket, season with salt and pepper and rub them with olive oil.
2. In a bowl, mix zucchini with Italian seasoning, bell peppers, tomatoes and onion and stir.
3. Stuff chicken breasts with this mix, sprinkle mozzarella over them, place them in your air fryer's basket and cook at 350 degrees F for 15 minutes.
4. Divide among plates and serve.
5. Enjoy!

Nutrition information:calories 300, fat 12, fiber 7, carbs 22, protein 18

277. Greek Chicken

Preparation time: 10 minutes

Cooking time: 15 minutes

Servings: 4

Ingredients:

- 2 tablespoons olive oil
- Juice from 1 lemon
- 1 teaspoon oregano, dried
- 3 garlic cloves, minced
- 1 pound chicken thighs
- Salt and black pepper to the taste
- ½ pound asparagus, trimmed
- 1 zucchini, roughly chopped
- 1 lemon sliced

Directions:

1. In a heat proof dish that fits your air fryer, mix chicken pieces with oil, lemon juice, oregano, garlic, salt, pepper, asparagus, zucchini and lemon slices, toss, introduce in preheated air fryer and cook at 380 degrees F for 15 minutes.
2. Divide everything on plates and serve.
3. Enjoy!

Nutrition information:calories 300, fat 8,

fiber 12, carbs 20, protein 18

278. Duck Breasts with Red Wine and Orange Sauce

Preparation time: 10 minutes

Cooking time: 35 minutes

Servings: 4

Ingredients:

- ½ cup honey
- 2 cups orange juice
- 4 cups red wine
- 2 tablespoons sherry vinegar
- 2 cups chicken stock
- 2 teaspoons pumpkin pie spice
- 2 tablespoons butter
- 2 duck breasts, skin on and halved
- 2 tablespoons olive oil
- Salt and black pepper to the taste

Directions:

1. Heat up a pan with the orange juice over medium heat, add honey, stir well and cook for 10 minutes.
2. Add wine, vinegar, stock, pie spice and butter, stir well, cook for 10 minutes more and take off heat.
3. Season duck breasts with salt and pepper, rub with olive oil, place in preheated air fryer at 370 degrees F and cook for 7 minutes on each side.
4. Divide duck breasts on plates, drizzle wine and orange juice all over and serve right away.
5. Enjoy!

Nutrition information:calories 300, fat 8, fiber 12, carbs 24, protein 11

279. Duck Breast with Fig Sauce

Preparation time: 10 minutes

Cooking time: 20 minutes

Servings: 4

Ingredients:

- 2 duck breasts, skin on, halved
- 1 tablespoon olive oil
- ½ teaspoon thyme, chopped
- ½ teaspoon garlic powder
- ¼ teaspoon sweet paprika
- Salt and black pepper to the taste
- 1 cup beef stock
- 3 tablespoons butter, melted
- 1 shallot, chopped
- ½ cup port wine
- 4 tablespoons fig preserves
- 1 tablespoon white flour

Directions:

1. Season duck breasts with salt and pepper, drizzle half of the melted butter, rub well, put in your air fryer's basket and cook at 350 degrees F for 5 minutes on each side.
2. Meanwhile, heat up a pan with the olive oil and the rest of the butter over medium high heat, add shallot, stir and cook for 2 minutes.
3. Add thyme, garlic powder, paprika, stock, salt, pepper, wine and figs, stir and cook for 7-8 minutes.
4. Add flour, stir well, cook until sauce thickens a bit and take off heat.
5. Divide duck breasts on plates, drizzle figs sauce all over and serve.
6. Enjoy!

Nutrition information:calories 246, fat 12, fiber 4, carbs 22, protein 3

280. Duck Breasts and Raspberry Sauce

Preparation time: 10 minutes

Cooking time: 15 minutes

Servings: 4

Ingredients:

- 2 duck breasts, skin on and scored
- Salt and black pepper to the taste
- Cooking spray
- ½ teaspoon cinnamon powder
- ½ cup raspberries
- 1 tablespoon sugar
- 1 teaspoon red wine vinegar
- ½ cup water

Directions:

1. Season duck breasts with salt and pepper, spray them with cooking spray, put in preheated air fryer skin side down and cook at 350 degrees F for 10 minutes.
2. Heat up a pan with the water over medium heat, add raspberries, cinnamon, sugar and wine, stir, bring to a simmer, transfer to your blender, puree and return to pan.
3. Add air fryer duck breasts to pan as well, toss to coat, divide among plates and serve right away.
4. Enjoy!

Nutrition information:calories 456, fat 22, fiber 4, carbs 14, protein 45

281. Duck and Cherries

Preparation time: 10 minutes

Cooking time: 20 minutes

Servings: 4

Ingredients:

- ½ cup sugar
- ¼ cup honey
- 1/3 cup balsamic vinegar
- 1 teaspoon garlic, minced
- 1 tablespoon ginger, grated
- 1 teaspoon cumin, ground
- ½ teaspoon clove, ground
- ½ teaspoon cinnamon powder
- 4 sage leaves, chopped
- 1 jalapeno, chopped
- 2 cups rhubarb, sliced
- ½ cup yellow onion, chopped
- 2 cups cherries, pitted
- 4 duck breasts, boneless, skin on and scored
- Salt and black pepper to the taste

Directions:

1. Season duck breast with salt and pepper, put in your air fryer and cook at 350 degrees F for 5 minutes on each side.
2. Meanwhile, heat up a pan over medium heat, add sugar, honey, vinegar, garlic, ginger, cumin, clove, cinnamon, sage, jalapeno, rhubarb, onion and cherries, stir, bring to a simmer and cook for 10 minutes.
3. Add duck breasts, toss well, divide everything on plates and serve.
4. Enjoy!

Nutrition information:calories 456, fat 13, fiber 4, carbs 64, protein 31

282. Easy Duck Breasts

Preparation time: 10 minutes

Cooking time: 15 minutes

Servings: 4

Ingredients:

- 4 duck breasts, skinless and boneless
- 4 garlic heads, peeled, tops cut off and quartered
- 2 tablespoons lemon juice
- Salt and black pepper to the taste
- ½ teaspoon lemon pepper
- 1 and ½ tablespoon olive oil

Directions:

1. In a bowl, mix duck breasts with garlic, lemon juice, salt, pepper, lemon pepper and olive oil and toss everything.
2. Transfer duck and garlic to your air fryer and cook at 350 degrees F for 15 minutes.
3. Divide duck breasts and garlic on plates and serve.
4. Enjoy!

Nutrition information:calories 200, fat 7, fiber 1, carbs 11, protein 17

283. Duck and Tea Sauce

Preparation time: 10 minutes

Cooking time: 20 minutes

Servings: 4

Ingredients:

- 2 duck breast halves, boneless
- 2 and ¼ cup chicken stock
- ¾ cup shallot, chopped
- 1 and ½ cup orange juice
- Salt and black pepper to the taste
- 3 teaspoons earl gray tea leaves
- 3 tablespoons butter, melted
- 1 tablespoon honey

Directions:

1. Season duck breast halves with salt and pepper, put in preheated air fryer and cook at 360 degrees F for 10 minutes.
2. Meanwhile, heat up a pan with the butter over medium heat, add shallot, stir and cook for 2-3 minutes.
3. Add stock, stir and cook for another minute.
4. Add orange juice, tea leaves and honey, stir, cook for 2-3 minutes more and strain into a bowl.
5. Divide duck on plates, drizzle tea sauce all over and serve.
6. Enjoy!

Nutrition information:calories 228, fat 11, fiber 2, carbs 20, protein 12

284. Marinated Duck Breasts

Preparation time: 1 day

Cooking time: 15 minutes

Servings: 2

Ingredients:

- 2 duck breasts
- 1 cup white wine

- ¼ cup soy sauce
- 2 garlic cloves, minced
- 6 tarragon springs
- Salt and black pepper to the taste
- 1 tablespoon butter
- ¼ cup sherry wine

Directions:

1. In a bowl, mix duck breasts with white wine, soy sauce, garlic, tarragon, salt and pepper, toss well and keep in the fridge for 1 day.
2. Transfer duck breasts to your preheated air fryer at 350 degrees F and cook for 10 minutes, flipping halfway.
3. Meanwhile, pour the marinade in a pan, heat up over medium heat, add butter and sherry, stir, bring to a simmer, cook for 5 minutes and take off heat.
4. Divide duck breasts on plates, drizzle sauce all over and serve.
5. Enjoy!

Nutrition information:calories 475, fat 12, fiber 3, carbs 10, protein 48

285. Chicken Breasts with Passion Fruit Sauce

Preparation time: 10 minutes

Cooking time: 10 minutes

Servings: 4

Ingredients:

- 4 chicken breasts
- Salt and black pepper to the taste
- 4 passion fruits, halved, deseeded and pulp reserved
- 1 tablespoon whiskey
- 2 star anise
- 2 ounces maple syrup
- 1 bunch chives, chopped

Directions:

1. Heat up a pan with the passion fruit pulp over medium heat, add whiskey, star anise, maple syrup and chives, stir well, simmer for 5-6 minutes and take off heat.
2. Season chicken with salt and pepper, put in preheated air fryer and cook at 360 degrees F for 10 minutes, flipping halfway.
3. Divide chicken on plates, heat up the sauce a bit, drizzle it over chicken and serve.
4. Enjoy!

Nutrition information:calories 374, fat 8, fiber 22, carbs 34, protein 37

286. Chicken Breasts and BBQ Chili Sauce

Preparation time: 10 minutes

Cooking time: 20 minutes

Servings: 6

Ingredients:

- 2 cups chili sauce
- 2 cups ketchup
- 1 cup pear jelly
- ¼ cup honey
- ½ teaspoon liquid smoke
- 1 teaspoon chili powder
- 1 teaspoon mustard powder
- 1 teaspoon sweet paprika

- Salt and black pepper to the taste
- 1 teaspoon garlic powder
- 6 chicken breasts, skinless and boneless

Directions:

1. Season chicken breasts with salt and pepper, put in preheated air fryer and cook at 350 degrees F for 10 minutes.
2. Meanwhile, heat up a pan with the chili sauce over medium heat, add ketchup, pear jelly, honey, liquid smoke, chili powder, mustard powder, sweet paprika, salt, pepper and the garlic powder, stir, bring to a simmer and cook for 10 minutes.
3. Add air fried chicken breasts, toss well, divide among plates and serve.
4. Enjoy!

Nutrition information:calories 473, fat 13, fiber 7, carbs 39, protein 33

287. Duck Breasts And Mango Mix

Preparation time: 1 hour

Cooking time: 10 minutes

Servings: 4

Ingredients:

- 4 duck breasts
- 1 and ½ tablespoons lemongrass, chopped
- 3 tablespoons lemon juice
- 2 tablespoons olive oil
- Salt and black pepper to the taste
- 3 garlic cloves, minced
- For the mango mix:
- 1 mango, peeled and chopped
- 1 tablespoon coriander, chopped
- 1 red onion, chopped
- 1 tablespoon sweet chili sauce
- 1 and ½ tablespoon lemon juice
- 1 teaspoon ginger, grated
- ¾ teaspoon sugar

Directions:

1. In a bowl, mix duck breasts with salt, pepper, lemongrass, 3 tablespoons lemon juice, olive oil and garlic, toss well, keep in the fridge for 1 hour, transfer to your air fryer and cook at 360 degrees F for 10 minutes, flipping once.
2. Meanwhile, in a bowl, mix mango with coriander, onion, chili sauce, lemon juice, ginger and sugar and toss well.
3. Divide duck on plates, add mango mix on the side and serve.
4. Enjoy!

Nutrition information:calories 465, fat 11, fiber 4, carbs 29, protein 38

288. Quick Creamy Chicken Casserole

Preparation time: 10 minutes

Cooking time: 12 minutes

Servings: 4

Ingredients:

- 10 ounces spinach, chopped
- 4 tablespoons butter
- 3 tablespoons flour
- 1 and ½ cups milk

- ½ cup parmesan, grated
- ½ cup heavy cream
- Salt and black pepper to the taste
- 2 cup chicken breasts, skinless, boneless and cubed
- 1 cup bread crumbs

Directions:

1. Heat up a pan with the butter over medium heat, add flour and stir well.
2. Add milk, heavy cream and parmesan, stir well, cook for 1-2 minutes more and take off heat.
3. In a pan that fits your air fryer, spread chicken and spinach.
4. Add salt and pepper and toss.
5. Add cream mix and spread, sprinkle bread crumbs on top, introduce in your air fryer and cook at 350 for 12 minutes.
6. Divide chicken and spinach mix on plates and serve.
7. Enjoy!

Nutrition information:calories 321, fat 9, fiber 12, carbs 22, protein 17

289. Chicken and Peaches

Preparation time: 10 minutes

Cooking time: 30 minutes

Servings: 6

Ingredients:

- 1 whole chicken, cut into medium pieces
- ¾ cup water
- 1/3 cup honey
- Salt and black pepper to the taste
- ¼ cup olive oil
- 4 peaches, halved

Directions:

1. Put the water in a pot, bring to a simmer over medium heat, add honey, whisk really well and leave aside.
2. Rub chicken pieces with the oil, season with salt and pepper, place in your air fryer's basket and cook at 350 degrees F for 10 minutes.
3. Brush chicken with some of the honey mix, cook for 6 minutes more, flip again, brush one more time with the honey mix and cook for 7 minutes more.
4. Divide chicken pieces on plates and keep warm.
5. Brush peaches with what's left of the honey marinade, place them in your air fryer and cook them for 3 minutes.
6. Divide among plates next to chicken pieces and serve.
7. Enjoy!

Nutrition information:calories 430, fat 14, fiber 3, carbs 15, protein 20

290. Tea Glazed Chicken

Preparation time: 10 minutes

Cooking time: 30 minutes

Servings: 6

Ingredients:

- ½ cup apricot preserves
- ½ cup pineapple preserves
- 6 chicken legs
- 1 cup hot water

- 6 black tea bags
- 1 tablespoon soy sauce
- 1 onion, chopped
- ¼ teaspoon red pepper flakes
- 1 tablespoon olive oil
- Salt and black pepper to the taste
- 6 chicken legs

Directions:

1. Put the hot water in a bowl, add tea bags, leave aside covered for 10 minutes, discard bags at the end and transfer tea to another bowl.
2. Add soy sauce, pepper flakes, apricot and pineapple preserves, whisk really well and take off heat.
3. Season chicken with salt and pepper, rub with oil, put in your air fryer and cook at 350 degrees F for 5 minutes.
4. Spread onion on the bottom of a baking dish that fits your air fryer, add chicken pieces, drizzle the tea glaze on top, introduce in your air fryer and cook at 320 degrees F for 25 minutes.
5. Divide everything on plates and serve.
6. Enjoy!

Nutrition information:calories 298, fat 14, fiber 1, carbs 14, protein 30

291. Chicken and Radish Mix

Preparation time: 10 minutes

Cooking time: 30 minutes

Servings: 4

Ingredients:

- 4 chicken things, bone-in
- Salt and black pepper to the taste
- 1 tablespoon olive oil
- 1 cup chicken stock
- 6 radishes, halved
- 1 teaspoon sugar
- 3 carrots, cut into thin sticks
- 2 tablespoon chives, chopped

Directions:

1. Heat up a pan that fits your air fryer over medium heat, add stock, carrots, sugar and radishes, stir gently, reduce heat to medium, cover pot partly and simmer for 20 minutes.
2. Rub chicken with olive oil, season with salt and pepper, put in your air fryer and cook at 350 degrees F for 4 minutes.
3. Add chicken to radish mix, toss, introduce everything in your air fryer, cook for 4 minutes more, divide among plates and serve.
4. Enjoy!

Nutrition information: calories 237, fat 10, fiber 4, carbs 19, protein 29

292. Hot & Spicy Buffalo Wings

Preparation Time:26 minutes

Servings: 4

Ingredients:

- 2 lbs. chicken wings
- 6 tablespoons melted butter, divided
- Salt to taste
- ½ cup hot & spicy sauce, divided

Directions:

1. In a bowl, mix ¼ cup hot and spicy sauce and 3 tablespoons of melted butter. Cover chicken pieces with the mixture and marinate for 2-hours in the fridge. Preheat your air fryer to 400°Fahrenheit. Split the wings into 2 batches. Place the first batch into air fryer and cook for 12-minutes, shaking halfway through cook time. Repeat with the second batch. Place all the wings into air fryer for additional 2-minute cook time. Finish preparing sauce by mixing the remaining 3 tablespoons of butter and ¼ cup of hot sauce. Dip cooked wings in sauce and enjoy!

Nutrition Information: Calories: 303, Total Fat: 11.2g, Carbs: 9.4g, Protein: 14.6g

293. Chinese Chicken Wings

Preparation Time:20 minutes

Servings: 4

Ingredients:

8 chicken wings

- Salt and pepper to taste
- 1 tablespoon mixed spices
- 2 tablespoon soy sauce
- 2 tablespoons five spice

Directions:

1. Mix all ingredients in a bowl. Line baking pan with aluminum foil and preheat your air fryer to 360°Fahrenheit. Cook the chicken in oil for 15-minutes. Raise the temperature to 390°Fahrenheit, flip chicken pieces over and cook for an additional 5-minutes.

Nutrition Information: Calories: 302, Total Fat: 11.2g, Carbs: 8.7g, Protein: 14.3g

294. Herb Chicken Wings

Preparation Time:30 minutes

Servings: 6

Ingredients:

- 4 lbs. of chicken wings
- 6 tablespoons lime juice
- 6 tablespoons wine vinegar
- 1 teaspoon fresh ginger, minced
- 1 teaspoon liquid Stevia
- 1 teaspoon thyme, chopped
- ½ teaspoon white pepper
- ¼ teaspoon cinnamon
- 6 garlic cloves, chopped
- 2 tablespoons soy sauce
- 2 tablespoons olive oil
- ¼ teaspoon sea salt

Directions:

1. Toss ingredients into a large bowl and mix well. Place marinated chicken in the fridge for an hour. Preheat air fryer to 390°Fahrenheit. Add half of the marinated chicken into air fryer and cook for 15-minutes. Shake halfway through cook time. Cook the remaining chicken in at the same time and temperature. Serve hot!

Nutrition Information: Calories: 301, Total Fat: 12.2g, Carbs: 9.2g, Protein: 14.2g

295. Yummy Sweet Mustard Chicken

Preparation Time:12 minutes

Servings: 4

Ingredients:

- 12-ounce chicken breast, diced
- ¼ cup milk
- ½ teaspoon white pepper
- 1 cup cornstarch
- 6-ounces Sweet Mustard sauce

Directions:

1. Add milk and chicken to a mixing bowl and set aside for 2-minutes. Drain the milk from chicken and toss chicken with cornstarch. Place the chicken in the air fryer at 350°Fahrenheit for 12-minutes. Place chicken in serving dish and sprinkle with white pepper along with a dish of sauce for dipping chicken pieces in.

Nutrition Information: Calories: 301, Total Fat: 11.8g, Carbs: 9.5g, Protein: 14.7g

296. Crispy Chicken Strips

Preparation Time:15 minutes

Servings: 4

Ingredients:

- 1 cup breadcrumbs
- 2 lbs. chicken breast, skinless, boneless
- ½ cup almond flour
- 1 teaspoon sea salt
- ¼ teaspoon black pepper
- 6 tablespoons skimmed milk
- 3 large eggs
- 2 tablespoons olive oil

Directions:

1. In a bowl, mix breadcrumbs and olive oil. Mix well and set aside. Whisk the eggs and milk in a different bowl, adding salt and pepper. In a third bowl, add the flour. Cut the chicken breast into strips about 1-inch long. Dip the strips into flour, then egg mixture, and finally into breadcrumbs. Preheat your air fryer to 380°Fahrenheit. Cook the coated chicken strips for 15-minutes. Shake a couple of times during cook time.

Nutrition Information: Calories: 298, Total Fat: 11.2g, Carbs: 9.5g, Protein: 15.3g

297. Crispy Popcorn Chicken

Preparation Time:10 minutes

Servings: 12

Ingredients:

- 1 chicken breast, boneless
- Salt and pepper to taste
- 1 cup breadcrumbs
- 2 teaspoons mix spice
- ¼ cup almond flour
- 1 egg, beaten

Directions:

1. Add the chicken to your food processor and process it until it is minced. In a bowl, add the beaten

egg. In another bowl, add the flour. In a third shallow dish add the breadcrumbs, mix spice, pepper, and salt and stir to combine. Make small chicken balls from minced chicken. Roll chicken balls in flour, then dip into egg, then coat with breadcrumbs. Place coated chicken balls into air fryer and air fry at 350°Fahrenheit for 10-minutes. Serve hot!

Nutrition Information: Calories: 297, Total Fat: 11.3g, Carbs: 8.9g, Protein: 14.2g

298. Tasty Chicken Tenderloins

Preparation Time:12 minutes

Servings: 4

Ingredients:

- 8 chicken tenderloins
- Salt and pepper to taste
- 1 egg, beaten
- 2 tablespoons olive oil
- 1 cup breadcrumbs

Directions:

1. Preheat your air fryer to 350°Fahrenheit. Mix olive oil, breadcrumbs, pepper and salt in a bowl. Add the beaten egg in another dish. Dip chicken into egg then coat with breadcrumbs and place into air fryer basket and cook for 12-minutes.

Nutrition Information: Calories: 289, Total Fat: 11.3g, Carbs: 10.4g, Protein: 13.2g

299. Orange Herb Chicken Wings

Preparation Time:35 minutes

Servings: 6

Ingredients:

- 6 chicken wings
- 1 ½ tablespoons Worcestershire sauce
- 1 orange juice and zest
- ½ teaspoon dried thyme
- 1 teaspoon mint
- 1 teaspoon basil
- 1 teaspoon rosemary
- 1 teaspoon parsley
- Salt and pepper to taste
- ½ teaspoon sage

Directions:

1. Add the chicken and all the remaining ingredients in a bowl. Place marinated chicken in the fridge for 30-minutes. Preheat your air fryer to 350°Fahrenheit. Wrap chicken in aluminum foil with juices. Place wrapped the chicken in air fryer basket and cooked at 350°Fahrenheit for 20-minutes. Open the foil wrapped chicken and discard orange zest. Air fry chicken wings at 350°Fahrenheit for another 15-minutes. Serve hot!

Nutrition Information: Calories: 301, Total Fat: 11.6g, Carbs: 9.3g, Protein: 14.2g

300. Crunchy Chicken Strips

Preparation Time:12 minutes

Servings: 8

Ingredients:

- 1 chicken breast, cut into strips
- ¾ cup breadcrumbs
- 1 teaspoon mix spice
- 1 tablespoon plain oats
- Salt and pepper to taste
- 1 tablespoon dried coconut
- ¼ cup almond flour
- 1 egg, beaten

Directions:

1. In a bowl, mix oats, mix spice, coconut, pepper, salt, and breadcrumbs. Add beaten egg to another bowl. Add the flour to a third dish. Take the flour and coat chicken strips with it, then dip in egg and roll in breadcrumb mixture. Place the coated chicken strips in air fryer basket and air fry at 350°Fahrenheit and cook for 4-minutes. Serve hot!

Nutrition Information: Calories: 286, Total Fat: 10.8g, Carbs: 8.7g, Protein: 13.2g

301. Rosemary Lemon Chicken

Preparation Time:19 minutes

Servings: 2

Ingredients:

- ¾ lb. chicken
- ½ fresh lemon, cut into wedges
- 1 tablespoon oyster sauce
- 1 teaspoon liquid stevia
- 1 tablespoon rosemary, fresh, chopped
- 1 tablespoon soy sauce
- ½ tablespoon olive oil
- 1 teaspoon fresh ginger, minced

Directions:

1. In a bowl, mix chicken, soy sauce, oil, and ginger. Put the marinated chicken inside of fridge for 30-minutes. Preheat your air fryer to 390°Fahrenheit for 3 minutes. Add marinated chicken into baking pan and set inside air fryer and cook for 6-minutes. In a small bowl, mix stevia, rosemary and oyster sauce. Pour the rosemary mixture over the chicken, then place lemon wedges over chicken. Continue to cook for an additional 13-minutes and flip the chicken over halfway through the cook time.

Nutrition Information: Calories: 285, Total Fat: 10.3g, Carbs: 8.2g, Protein: 14.2g

302. Roasted Whole Chicken with Herbs

Preparation Time:40 minutes

Servings: 4

Ingredients:

- 5 lb. whole chicken with skin
- 2 tablespoons extra-virgin olive oil
- ½ teaspoon rosemary
- ½ teaspoon basil
- ½ teaspoon thyme
- 1 teaspoon onion powder
- 1 teaspoon garlic powder
- Salt and black pepper to taste

Directions:

1. Rub the chicken with salt, herbs, pepper and olive oil. Set aside for 30-minutes. Preheat your air fryer to 340°Fahrenheit. Cook chicken for 20 minutes then turn. Cook for another 20-minutes. Set aside for 10-minutes, then slice and serve.

Nutrition Information: Calories: 298, Total Fat: 11.3g, Carbs: 8.9g, Protein: 16.2g

303. Spicy & Sweet Chicken Wings

Preparation Time:16 minutes

Servings: 6

Ingredients:

- 6 chicken wings
- Salt and pepper to taste
- 2 tablespoons Worcestershire sauce
- 1 teaspoon red chili flakes
- 2 garlic cloves, chopped
- 1 tablespoon honey

Directions:

1. Mix in a bowl, garlic, red chili flakes, honey, Worcestershire sauce, salt, and pepper. Toss chicken wings in mixture and place into fridge for an hour. Place the marinated chicken wings in the air fryer basket and spray them with cooking spray. Air fry chicken wings at 320°Fahrenheit for 8-minutes. After 8-minutes, turn the heat to 350°Fahrenheit for another 4-minutes. Serve hot!

304. Parmesan Crusted Chicken Fillet

Preparation Time:6 minutes

Servings: 3

Ingredients:

- 8 chicken fillets
- 1 egg, beaten
- 1-ounce garlic powder
- ½ cup parmesan cheese
- 1 cup breadcrumbs
- 1 teaspoon Italian herbs
- 1-ounce salted butter, melted

Directions:

1. Mix in a bowl, egg, melted butter, garlic powder and Italian herbs. Marinate chicken fillets in egg mixture. Mix breadcrumbs and parmesan and cover fillets with it. Set chicken aside for 10-minutes. Place aluminum foil in air fryer basket. Preheat your air fryer to 390°Fahrenheit for 3-minutes. Layer 4 pieces of chicken on foil in basket. Cook for 6-minutes without flipping. Repeat the procedure for remaining chicken pieces. Serve hot!

Nutrition Information: Calories: 289, Total Fat: 11.2g, Carbs: 8.6g, Protein: 13.6g

305. Bacon Wrapped Herb Chicken

Preparation Time:15 minutes

Servings: 6

Ingredients:

- 1 chicken breast, cut into 6 pieces
- 6 slices of bacon
- ½ teaspoon basil, dried
- ½ teaspoon parsley, dried
- ½ teaspoon paprika
- Salt and pepper to taste
- 1 tablespoon soft cheese

Directions:

1. In a bowl, mix basil, parsley, salt, pepper, and paprika. Place the bacon slices on a dish and spread them with soft cheese. Place the chicken pieces into basil mix and cover with seasoning. Place the chicken pieces on top of bacon slices. Roll up and secure with toothpick. Place into air fryer and cook at 350°Fahrenheit and cook for 15-minutes.

Nutrition Information: Calories: 298, Total Fat: 11.4g, Carbs: 8.9g, Protein: 13.6g

306. Lemon Chicken & Peppercorns

Preparation Time:15 minutes

Servings: 1

Ingredients:

- 1 chicken breast
- Salt and pepper to taste
- 1 tablespoon chicken seasoning
- Handful of peppercorns
- 1 lemon juice
- 1 teaspoon garlic, minced

Directions:

1. Preheat your air fryer to 350°Fahrenheit. Season the chicken with salt and pepper. Rub chicken seasoning all over the chicken. Place the seasoned chicken onto aluminum foil sheet. Add garlic, lemon juice, black peppercorns on top of chicken and seal the foil. Place chicken in air fryer and cook for 15-minutes.

Nutrition Information: Calories: 300, Total Fat: 10.8g, Carbs: 9.4g, Protein: 14.6g

307. Chicken Sandwich

Preparation Time:15 minutes

Servings: 2

Ingredients:

- 2 chicken breasts, boneless, skinless
- 6 tablespoons soy sauce
- 4 hamburger buns
- 1 tablespoon olive oil
- 1 cup almond flour
- 2 large eggs
- ½ cup skimmed milk
- ½ teaspoon garlic powder
- Salt and black pepper to taste
- 1 teaspoon smoked paprika

Directions:

1. Cut the chicken breast into 2-3 pieces, depending on size. Transfer to a bowl and sprinkle with soy sauce. Season with garlic powder, smoked paprika, salt, and pepper. Set aside. Combine eggs and milk in another bowl. In a third shallow dish add flour. Dip marinated chicken into egg mixture and then into flour. Preheat your air fryer to 380°Fahrenheit.

Sprinkle with olive oil and place chicken pieces into air fryer and cook for 15-minutes. Toast hamburger buns and assemble sandwiches.

Nutrition Information: Calories: 296, Total Fat: 11.8g, Carbs: 9.2g, Protein: 13.6g

308. Curry Chicken Thighs

Preparation Time:30 minutes

Servings: 2

Ingredients:

- 2 chicken thighs
- 2 garlic cloves, minced
- 1 small zucchini, cut into small chunks
- 6 dried apricots
- 1 long turnip, cut into small chunks
- 1 tablespoon whole pistachios
- 1 tablespoon olive oil
- Salt and black pepper to taste
- 6 basil leaves
- 1 teaspoon curry powder

Directions:

1. Preheat your air fryer to 320°Fahrenheit. Cut chicken up into 2 pieces. Cut the vegetables up into bite-sized chunks. Add all the ingredients except basil in dish and mix well. Cook for 30 minutes. Sprinkle top with basil and serve.

Nutrition Information: Calories: 287, Total Fat: 10.2g, Carbs: 8.7g, Protein: 13.8g

309. Chicken Drumsticks

Preparation Time:20 minutes

Servings: 4

Ingredients:

- 8 chicken drumsticks
- 1 large egg, lightly beaten
- Salt and pepper to taste
- 1/3 cup oats
- 1/3 cup cauliflower
- 2 tablespoons thyme
- 2 tablespoons oregano
- 2 tablespoons mustard powder
- 1 teaspoon cayenne pepper
- 3 tablespoons coconut milk

Directions:

1. Preheat your oven to 350°Fahrenheit. Season chicken drumsticks with salt and pepper. Rub coconut milk all over chicken drumsticks. Add cayenne pepper, mustard powder, oregano, oats, thyme, cauliflower, into food processor and mix until you have a consistency of breadcrumbs. In a small bowl, add beaten egg. Dip the chicken into breadcrumb mixture then into egg and dip again into breadcrumbs. Place coated chicken drumsticks inside air fryer and cook for 20-minutes. Serve hot.

Nutrition Information: Calories: 299, Total Fat: 11.3g, Carbs: 8.5g, Protein: 13.9g

310. Garlic Chicken Nuggets

Preparation Time:10 minutes

Servings: 4

Ingredients:

- ¾ cup breadcrumbs
- 9-ounce chicken breast, thinly chopped
- 1 teaspoon parsley
- 2 eggs, divided
- 1 teaspoon tomato ketchup
- 1 tablespoon olive oil
- Salt and pepper to taste
- 1 teaspoon garlic, minced
- 1 teaspoon paprika

Directions:

1. Mix breadcrumbs, salt, pepper, paprika, and oil. Mix well to make a thick paste. Mix chopped chicken, ketchup, one egg, parsley in a bowl. Shape the chicken mixture into little nugget shapes and dip into other beaten egg. Coat the nuggets with breadcrumbs. Cook at 390°Fahrenheit for 10-minutes in air fryer.

Nutrition Information: Calories: 285, Total Fat: 11.3g, Carbs: 8.2g, Protein: 13.9g

MEAT

311. Crispy Lamb Recipe

Preparation Time:40 Minutes

Servings: 4

Ingredients:

- 1 tbsp. bread crumbs
- 1 garlic clove; minced
- 28 oz. rack of lamb
- 2 tbsp. macadamia nuts; toasted and crushed
- 1 tbsp. olive oil
- 1 egg;
- 1 tbsp. rosemary; chopped.
- Salt and black pepper to the taste

Directions:

2. In a bowl; mix oil with garlic and stir well.
3. Season lamb with salt, pepper and brush with the oil.
4. In another bowl, mix nuts with breadcrumbs and rosemary.
5. Put the egg in a separate bowl and whisk well.
6. Dip lamb in egg, then in macadamia mix, place them in your air fryer's basket, cook at 360 °F and cook for 25 minutes; increase heat to 400 °F and cook for 5 minutes more. Divide among plates and serve right away.

Nutrition information:Calories: 230; Fat: 2; Fiber: 2; Carbs: 10; Protein: 12

312. Lamb Ribs Recipe

Preparation Time:55 Minutes

Servings: 8

Ingredients:

- 8 lamb ribs
- 4 garlic cloves; minced
- 2 carrots; chopped
- 3 tbsp. white flour
- 2 cups veggie stock
- 1 tbsp. rosemary; chopped
- 2 tbsp. extra virgin olive oil
- Salt and black pepper to the taste

Directions:

1. Season lamb ribs with salt and pepper, rub with oil and garlic, put in preheated air fryer and cook at 360 °F, for 10 minutes.
2. In a heat proof dish that fits your fryer, mix stock with flour and whisk well.
3. Add rosemary, carrots and lamb ribs, place in your air fryer and cook at 350 °F, for 30 minutes. Divide lamb mix on plates and serve hot.

Nutrition information:Calories: 302; Fat: 7; Fiber: 2; Carbs: 22; Protein: 27

313. Lamb and Spinach Mix Recipe

Preparation Time:45 Minutes

Servings: 6

Ingredients:

- 2 tbsp. ginger; grated
- 2 garlic cloves; minced
- 2 tsp. cardamom; ground
- 1/2 tsp. chili powder
- 1 tsp. turmeric
- 2 tsp. coriander; ground
- 1 lb. spinach
- 1 red onion; chopped
- 1 lb. lamb meat; cubed
- 2 tsp. cumin powder
- 1 tsp. garam masala
- 14 oz. canned tomatoes; chopped.

Directions:

1. In a heat proof dish that fits your air fryer, mix lamb with spinach, tomatoes, ginger, garlic, onion, cardamom, cloves, cumin, garam masala, chili, turmeric and coriander; stir, introduce in preheated air fryer and cook at 360 °F, for 35 minutes Divide into bowls and serve.

Nutrition information:Calories: 160; Fat: 6; Fiber: 3; Carbs: 17; Protein: 20

314. Simple Fried Pork Shoulder Recipe

Preparation Time:1 hour and 50 minutes

Servings: 6

Ingredients:

- 3 tbsp. garlic; minced
- 4 lbs. pork shoulder
- 3 tbsp. olive oil
- Salt and black pepper to the taste

Directions:

2. In a bowl; mix olive oil with salt, pepper and oil, whisk well and brush pork shoulder with this mix.
3. Place in preheated air fryer and cook at 390 °F, for 10 minutes.
4. Reduce heat to 300 °F and roast pork for 1 hour and 10 minutes. Slice pork shoulder, divide among plates and serve with a side salad.

Nutrition information:Calories: 221; Fat: 4; Fiber: 4; Carbs: 7; Protein: 10

315. Marinated Lamb and Veggies Recipe

Preparation Time:40 Minutes

Servings: 4

Ingredients:

- 1 carrot; chopped
- 1/2 tbsp. olive oil
- 3 oz. bean sprouts
- 1 onion; sliced
- 8 oz. lamb loin; sliced
- For the marinade:
- 1 garlic clove; minced
- 1/2 apple; grated
- 1 tbsp. ginger; grated
- 5 tbsp. soy sauce
- 1 tbsp. sugar
- Salt and black pepper to the taste
- 1 small yellow onion; grated
- 2 tbsp. orange juice

Directions:

1. In a bowl; mix 1 grated onion with

the apple, garlic, 1 tbsp. ginger, soy sauce, orange juice, sugar and black pepper, whisk well, add lamb and leave aside for 10 minutes.

2. Heat up a pan that fits your air fryer with the olive oil over medium high heat, add 1 sliced onion, carrot and bean sprouts; stir and cook for 3 minutes.
3. Add lamb and the marinade, transfer pan to your preheated air fryer and cook at 360 °F, for 25 minutes. Divide everything into bowls and serve.

Nutrition information:Calories: 265; Fat: 3; Fiber: 7; Carbs: 18; Protein: 22

316. Lamb and Creamy Brussels Sprouts Recipe

Preparation Time:1 hour and 20 minutes

Servings: 4

Ingredients:

- 2 lbs. leg of lamb; scored
- 1 ½ lbs. Brussels sprouts; trimmed
- 2 tbsp. olive oil
- 1 tbsp. rosemary; chopped
- 1 tbsp. lemon thyme; chopped.
- 1 tbsp. butter; melted
- 1/2 cup sour cream
- 1 garlic clove; minced
- Salt and black pepper to the taste

Directions:

1. Season leg of lamb with salt, pepper, thyme and rosemary, brush with oil, place in your air fryer's basket, cook at 300 °F, for 1 hour, transfer to a plate and keep warm.
2. In a pan that fits your air fryer, mix Brussels sprouts with salt, pepper, garlic, butter and sour cream, toss, put in your air fryer and cook at 400 °F, for 10 minutes. Divide lamb on plates, add Brussels sprouts on the side and serve.

Nutrition information:Calories: 440; Fat: 23; Fiber: 0; Carbs: 2; Protein: 49

317. Garlic and Bell Pepper Beef Recipe

Preparation Time:60 Minutes

Servings: 4

Ingredients:

- 11 oz. steak fillets; sliced
- 4 garlic cloves; minced
- 2 tbsp. olive oil
- 1 tbsp. sugar
- 2 tbsp. fish sauce
- 2 tsp. corn flour
- 1/2 cup beef stock
- 1 red bell pepper; cut into strips
- Black pepper to the taste
- 4 green onions; sliced

Directions:

1. In a pan that fits your air fryer mix beef with oil, garlic, black pepper and bell pepper; stir, cover and keep in the fridge for 30 minutes.
2. Put the pan in your preheated air fryer and cook at 360 °F, for 14 minutes.
3. In a bowl; mix sugar with fish sauce; stir well, pour over beef and cook at 360 °F, for 7 minutes more.

4. Add stock mixed with corn flour and green onions, toss and cook at 370 °F, for 7 minutes more. Divide everything on plates and serve.

Nutrition information:Calories: 343; Fat: 3; Fiber: 12; Carbs: 26; Protein: 38

318. Beef Medallions Mix Recipe

Preparation Time:2 hours 10 Minutes

Servings: 4

Ingredients:

- 2 tsp. chili powder
- 1 cup tomatoes; crushed
- 4 beef medallions
- 2 tsp. onion powder
- 2 tbsp. soy sauce
- 1 tbsp. hot pepper
- 2 tbsp. lime juice
- Salt and black pepper to the taste

Directions:

1. In a bowl; mix tomatoes with hot pepper, soy sauce, chili powder, onion powder, a pinch of salt, black pepper and lime juice and whisk well
2. Arrange beef medallions in a dish, pour sauce over them, toss and leave them aside for 2 hours.
3. Discard tomato marinade, put beef in your preheated air fryer and cook at 360 °F, for 10 minutes. Divide steaks on plates and serve with a side salad

Nutrition information:Calories: 230; Fat: 4; Fiber: 1; Carbs: 13; Protein: 14

319. Sirloin Steaks and Pico De Gallo Recipe

Preparation Time:20 Minutes

Servings: 4

Ingredients:

- 2 tbsp. chili powder
- 1 tsp. onion powder
- 1 tsp. garlic powder
- 4 medium sirloin steaks
- 1 tsp. cumin; ground
- 1/2 tbsp. sweet paprika
- Salt and black pepper to the taste
- For the Pico de gallo:
- 1 small red onion; chopped
- 1 small green bell pepper; chopped.
- 1 jalapeno; chopped.
- 2 tomatoes; chopped
- 2 garlic cloves; minced
- 2 tbsp. lime juice
- 1/4 cup cilantro; chopped
- 1/4 tsp. cumin; ground

Directions:

1. In a bowl; mix chili powder with a pinch of salt, black pepper, onion powder, garlic powder, paprika and 1 tsp. cumin; stir well, season steaks with this mix, put them in your air fryer and cook at 360 °F, for 10 minutes.
2. In a bowl; mix red onion with tomatoes, garlic, lime juice, bell pepper, jalapeno, cilantro, black pepper to the taste and 1/4 tsp. cumin and toss. Top steaks with this mix and serve right away

Nutrition information:Calories: 200; Fat:

12; Fiber: 4; Carbs: 15; Protein: 18

320. Short Ribs and Beer Sauce Recipe

Preparation Time:60 Minutes

Servings: 6

Ingredients:

- 4 lbs. short ribs; cut into small pieces
- 1 yellow onion; chopped.
- 1 cup chicken stock
- 1 bay leaf
- 6 thyme springs; chopped
- Salt and black pepper to the taste
- 1/4 cup tomato paste
- 1 cup dark beer
- 1 Portobello mushroom; dried

Directions:

1. Heat up a pan that fits your air fryer over medium heat, add tomato paste, onion, stock, beer, mushroom, bay leaves and thyme and bring to a simmer.
2. Add ribs, introduce in your air fryer and cook at 350 °F, for 40 minutes. Divide everything on plates and serve.

Nutrition information:Calories: 300; Fat: 7; Fiber: 8; Carbs: 18; Protein: 23

321. Beef Kabobs Recipe

Preparation Time:20 Minutes

Servings: 4

Ingredients:

- 2 red bell peppers; chopped
- 2 lbs. sirloin steak; cut into medium pieces
- 1/2 tbsp. cumin; ground
- 1/4 cup olive oil
- 1/4 cup salsa
- 1 red onion; chopped
- 1 zucchini; sliced
- Juice form 1 lime
- 2 tbsp. chili powder
- 2 tbsp. hot sauce
- Salt and black pepper to the taste

Directions:

1. In a bowl; mix salsa with lime juice, oil, hot sauce, chili powder, cumin, salt and black pepper and whisk well.
2. Divide meat bell peppers, zucchini and onion on skewers, brush kabobs with the salsa mix you made earlier, put them in your preheated air fryer and cook them for 10 minutes at 370 °F, flipping kabobs halfway. Divide among plates and serve with a side salad.

Nutrition information:Calories: 170; Fat: 5; Fiber: 2; Carbs: 13; Protein: 16

322. Fryer Lamb Shanks Recipe

Preparation Time:55 Minutes

Servings: 4

Ingredients:

- 4 lamb shanks
- 1 yellow onion; chopped
- 1 tbsp. olive oil

- 2 tsp. honey
- 5 oz. dry sherry
- 2 ½ cups chicken stock
- 4 tsp. coriander seeds; crushed
- 2 tbsp. white flour
- 4 bay leaves
- Salt and pepper to the taste

Directions:

1. Season lamb shanks with salt and pepper, rub with half of the oil, put in your air fryer and cook at 360 °F, for 10 minutes.
2. Heat up a pan that fits your air fryer with the rest of the oil over medium high heat, add onion and coriander; stir and cook for 5 minutes.
3. Add flour, sherry, stock, honey and bay leaves, salt and pepper; stir, bring to a simmer, add lamb, introduce everything in your air fryer and cook at 360 °F, for 30 minutes. Divide everything on plates and serve.

Nutrition information:Calories: 283; Fat: 4; Fiber: 2; Carbs: 17; Protein: 26

323. Lamb and Green Pesto Recipe

Preparation Time:1 hour 45 Minutes

Servings: 4

Ingredients:

- 1 cup parsley
- 1 cup mint
- 1 small yellow onion; roughly chopped
- 1/3 cup pistachios; chopped.
- 1 tsp. lemon zest; grated
- 5 tbsp. olive oil
- 2 lbs. lamb riblets
- 1/2 onion; chopped.
- 5 garlic cloves; minced
- Juice from 1 orange
- Salt and black pepper to the taste

Directions:

1. In your food processor, mix parsley with mint, onion, pistachios, lemon zest, salt, pepper and oil and blend very well.
2. Rub lamb with this mix, place in a bowl; cover and leave in the fridge for 1 hour.
3. Transfer lamb to a baking dish that fits your air fryer, also add garlic, drizzle orange juice and cook in your air fryer at 300 °F, for 45 minutes.

Nutrition information:Calories: 200; Fat: 4; Fiber: 6; Carbs: 15; Protein: 7

324. Garlic Lamb Chops Recipe

Preparation Time:20 Minutes

Servings: 4

Ingredients:

- 8 lamb chops
- 3 tbsp. olive oil
- 4 garlic cloves; minced
- 1 tbsp. oregano; chopped.
- 1 tbsp. coriander; chopped.
- Salt and black pepper to the taste

Directions:

1. In a bowl; mix oregano with salt,

pepper, oil, garlic and lamb chops and toss to coat.

2. Transfer lamb chops to your air fryer and cook at 400 °F, for 10 minutes. Divide lamb chops on plates and serve with a side salad.

Nutrition information:Calories: 231; Fat: 7; Fiber: 5; Carbs: 14; Protein: 23

325. Filet Mignon and Mushrooms Sauce Recipe

Preparation Time:35 Minutes

Servings: 4

Ingredients:

- 12 mushrooms; sliced
- 1/4 cup Dijon mustard
- 1/4 cup wine
- 1¼ cup coconut cream
- 2 tbsp. parsley; chopped.
- 1 shallot; chopped
- 4 fillet mignons
- 2 garlic cloves; minced
- 2 tbsp. olive oil
- Salt and black pepper to the taste

Directions:

1. Heat up a pan with the oil over medium high heat, add garlic and shallots; stir and cook for 3 minutes.
2. Add mushrooms; stir and cook for 4 minutes more.
3. Add wine; stir and cook until it evaporates.
4. Add coconut cream, mustard, parsley, a pinch of salt and black pepper to the taste; stir, cook for 6 minutes more and take off heat.
5. Season fillets with salt and pepper, put them in your air fryer and cook at 360 °F, for 10 minutes. Divide fillets on plates and serve with the mushroom sauce on top.

Nutrition information:Calories: 340; Fat: 12; Fiber: 1; Carbs: 14; Protein: 23

326. Short Ribs and Sauce Recipe

Preparation Time:46 Minutes

Servings: 4

Ingredients:

- 2 green onions; chopped.
- 1 tsp. vegetable oil
- 1/2 cup soy sauce
- 1/4 cup rice wine
- 1/4 cup pear juice
- 3 garlic cloves; minced
- 3 ginger slices
- 4 lbs. short ribs
- 1/2 cup water
- 2 tsp. sesame oil

Directions:

1. Heat up a pan that fits your air fryer with the oil over medium heat, add green onions, ginger and garlic; stir and cook for 1 minute.
2. Add ribs, water, wine, soy sauce, sesame oil and pear juice; stir, introduce in your air fryer and cook at 350 °F, for 35 minutes. Divide ribs and sauce on plates and serve.

Nutrition information:Calories: 321; Fat: 12; Fiber: 4; Carbs: 20; Protein: 14

327. Roasted Pork Belly and Apple Sauce Recipe

Preparation Time:50 Minutes

Servings: 6

Ingredients:

- 2 tbsp. sugar
- 1 tbsp. lemon juice
- 1-quart water
- 17 oz. apples; cored and cut into wedges
- 2 lbs. pork belly; scored
- A drizzle of olive oil
- Salt and black pepper to the taste

Directions:

1. In your blender, mix water with apples, lemon juice and sugar, pulse well, transfer to a bowl, add meat, toss well, drain, put in your air fryer and cook at 400 °F, for 40 minutes.
2. Pour the sauce in a pot, heat up over medium heat and simmer for 15 minutes. Slice pork belly, divide among plates, drizzle the sauce all over and serve.

Nutrition information:Calories: 456; Fat: 34; Fiber: 4; Carbs: 10; Protein: 25

328. Burgundy Beef Mix Recipe

Preparation Time:1 hour 10 Minutes

Servings: 7

Ingredients:

- 2 lbs. beef chuck roast; cubed
- 15 oz. canned tomatoes; chopped
- 4 carrots; chopped.
- 1/2 lbs. mushrooms; sliced
- 2 celery ribs; chopped
- 2 yellow onions; chopped
- 1/2 tsp. mustard powder
- 3 tbsp. almond flour
- 1 tbsp. thyme; chopped
- 1 cup water
- 1 cup beef stock
- Salt and black pepper to the taste

Directions:

1. Heat up a heat proof pot that fits your air fryer over medium high heat, add beef; stir and brown them for a couple of minutes.
2. Add tomatoes, mushrooms, onions, carrots, celery, salt, pepper mustard, stock and thyme and stir.
3. In a bowl mix water with flour; stir well, add this to the pot, toss, introduce in your air fryer and cook at 300 °F, for 1 hour. Divide into bowls and serve.

Nutrition information:Calories: 275; Fat: 13; Fiber: 4; Carbs: 17; Protein: 28

329. Beef Roast and Grapes

Preparation time: 10 minutes

Cooking time: 40 minutes

Servings: 4

Ingredients:

- 1 pound beef roast meat, cubed
- 3 tablespoons olive oil
- Salt and black pepper to taste
- 1½ cups chicken stock
- ½ cup dry white wine

- 2 garlic cloves, minced
- 1 teaspoon thyme, chopped
- ½ red onion, chopped
- ½ pound red grapes

Directions:

1. Heat up the oil in a pan that fits your air fryer over medium-high heat.
2. Add the beef, salt, and pepper; toss, and brown for 5 minutes.
3. Add the stock, wine, garlic, thyme, and onions; toss and cook for 5 minutes more.
4. Transfer the pan to your air fryer and cook at 390 degrees F for 25 minutes.
5. Add the grapes, toss gently, and cook everything for 5-6 minutes more.
6. Divide between plates and serve right away.

Nutrition information:calories 290, fat 12, fiber 5, carbs 19, protein 28

330. Sage Pork Mix

Preparation time: 10 minutes

Cooking time: 50 minutes

Servings: 6

Ingredients:

- 2½ pounds pork loin, boneless and cubed
- ¾ cup beef stock
- 2 tablespoons olive oil
- ½ tablespoon smoked paprika
- 3 teaspoons sage, dried
- ½ tablespoon garlic powder
- 1 teaspoon basil, dried
- 1 teaspoon oregano, dried
- Salt and black pepper to taste

Directions:

1. In a pan that fits your air fryer, heat up the oil over medium heat.
2. Add the pork, toss, and brown for 5 minutes.
3. Add the paprika, sage, garlic powder, basil, oregano, salt, and pepper; toss and cook for 2 more minutes.
4. Next add the stock and toss.
5. Place the pan in the fryer and cook at 360 degrees F for 40 minutes.
6. Divide everything between plates and serve.

Nutrition information:calories 290, fat 11, fiber 6, carbs 20, protein 29

331. Beef Roast

Preparation time: 10 minutes

Cooking time: 55 minutes

Servings: 4

Ingredients:

- 3 tablespoons garlic, minced
- 1 tablespoon smoked paprika
- 3 tablespoons olive oil
- 2 pounds beef roast
- Salt and black pepper to taste

Directions:

1. In a bowl, combine all the ingredients and coat the roast well.
2. Place the roast in your air fryer and cook at 390 degrees F for 55 minutes.
3. 2.Slice the roast, divide it between plates, and serve with a side salad.

Nutrition information:calories 291, fat 12, fiber 9, carbs 20, protein 26

332. Tarragon Pork Loin

Preparation time: 10 minutes

Cooking time: 55 minutes

Servings: 6

Ingredients:

- 3 pounds pork loin roast, trimmed
- Salt and black pepper to taste
- 3 garlic cloves, minced
- 2 tablespoons tarragon, chopped
- 2 teaspoons sweet paprika
- ¼ cup olive oil

Directions:

1. In a bowl, mix the roast with all the other ingredients and rub well.
2. Transfer the roast to your air fryer and cook at 390 degrees F for 55 minutes.
3. Slice the roast, divide it between plates, and serve.

Nutrition information:calories 290, fat 14, fiber 9, carbs 19, protein 22

333. Beef and Celery Mix

Preparation time: 10 minutes

Cooking time: 55 minutes

Servings: 6

Ingredients:

- 1 pound yellow onion, chopped
- 3 pounds beef roast
- 1 pound celery, chopped
- Salt and black pepper to taste
- 3 cups beef stock
- 16 ounces canned tomatoes, chopped
- 2 tablespoons olive oil

Directions:

1. Place all the ingredients into a baking dish that fits your air fryer and mix well.
2. Put the pan in the fryer and cook at 390 degrees F for 55 minutes.
3. Slice the roast, and then divide it and the celery mix between plates.
4. Serve, and enjoy!

Nutrition information:calories 300, fat 12, fiber 4, carbs 18, protein 20

334. Chinese Beef Mix

Preparation time: 5 minutes

Cooking time: 20 minutes

Servings: 4

Ingredients:

- 1 cup green onion, chopped
- 1 cup soy sauce
- ¼ cup sesame seeds, toasted
- 5 garlic cloves, minced
- Black pepper to taste
- 1 pound beef stew meat, cut into strips

Directions:

1. In a pan that fits your air fryer, place all ingredients and mix well.
2. Place the pan in the fryer and cook at

390 degrees F for 20 minutes.

3. Divide everything into bowls and serve.

Nutrition information:calories 289, fat 8, fiber 12, carbs 20, protein 19

335. Pork and Bell Pepper Mix

Preparation time: 5 minutes

Cooking time: 20 minutes

Servings: 4

Ingredients:

- 1 pound pork, cut into strips
- 4 garlic cloves, minced
- 2 tablespoons olive oil
- 2 red bell peppers, cut in strips
- A pinch of salt and black pepper
- 2 tablespoons fish sauce
- ½ cup beef stock
- 4 shallots, chopped

Directions:

1. In a pan that fits your air fryer, place all the ingredients and toss.
2. Place the pan in the fryer and cook at 400 degrees F for 20 minutes, shaking the fryer halfway.
3. Divide everything between plates and serve.

Nutrition information:calories 293, fat 12, fiber 12, carbs 20, protein 29

336. Lamb and Beans

Preparation time: 5 minutes

Cooking time: 30 minutes

Servings: 4

Ingredients:

- 1 carrot, chopped
- 1 yellow onion, sliced
- ½ tablespoon olive oil
- 3 ounces canned kidney beans, drained
- 8 ounces lamb loin, cubed
- 1 garlic clove, minced
- Salt and black pepper to taste
- 1 tablespoon ginger, grated
- 3 tablespoons soy sauce

Directions:

1. In baking dish that fits your air fryer, place all of the ingredients and mix well.
2. Place the dish in the fryer and cook at 390 degrees F for 30 minutes.
3. Divide everything into bowls and serve.

Nutrition information:calories 275, fat 3, fiber 7, carbs 20, protein 18

337. Pork Chops and Spinach Mix

Preparation time: 5 minutes

Cooking time: 15 minutes

Servings: 4

Ingredients:

- 2 pork chops
- Salt and black pepper to taste
- 2 cups baby spinach
- 3 tablespoons spinach pesto

- ¼ cup beef stock

Directions:

1. Place the pork chops, salt, pepper, and spinach pesto in a bowl; toss well.
2. Place the pork chops in the air fryer and cook at 400 degrees F for 4 minutes on each side.
3. Transfer the chops to a pan that fits your air fryer, and add the stock and the baby spinach.
4. Put the pan in the fryer and cook at 400 degrees F for 7 minutes more.
5. Divide everything between plates and serve.

Nutrition information:calories 290, fat 11, fiber 9, carbs 22, protein 19

338. Ground Beef Mix

Preparation time: 5 minutes

Cooking time: 20 minutes

Servings: 4

Ingredients:

- 1 tablespoon olive oil
- 1 pound ground beef
- 1 yellow onion, chopped
- Salt and black pepper to taste
- 2 garlic cloves, minced
- ½ teaspoon cumin
- ¼ cup tomato salsa
- 1 green bell pepper, chopped

Directions:

1. Heat up the oil in a pan that fits your air fryer over medium heat.
2. Add the onion, garlic, bell peppers, and the cumin; stir, and sauté for 3 minutes.
3. Add the meat, toss, cook for 3 minutes more, and take off the heat.
4. Add the salsa, toss, and place the pan in the fryer; cook at 380 degrees F for 14 minutes more.
5. Divide everything into bowls and serve.

Nutrition information:calories 264, fat 11, fiber 4, carbs 20, protein 16

339. Smoked Pork Roast

Preparation time: 5 minutes

Cooking time: 55 minutes

Servings: 4

Ingredients:

- 2 pounds pork loin roast
- Salt and black pepper to taste
- 1 tablespoon olive oil
- 3 tablespoons smoked paprika
- 1 teaspoon liquid smoke
- 1 tablespoon brown sugar
- 2 tablespoons oregano, chopped

Directions:

1. Place all ingredients into a bowl, mix well, and be sure the pork is thoroughly coated.
2. Transfer the roast to your air fryer and cook at 370 degrees F for 55 minutes.
3. Slice the roast, divide it between plates, and serve.

Nutrition information:calories 300, fat

12, fiber 9, carbs 22, protein 18

340. Pork and Cauliflower Mix

Preparation time: 5 minutes

Cooking time: 22 minutes

Servings: 4

Ingredients:

- 1 pound pork stew meat, cubed
- 1 cauliflower head, florets separated
- 2 tablespoons olive oil
- 1 teaspoon soy sauce
- 1 teaspoon sugar
- ⅓ cup balsamic vinegar
- 1 garlic clove, minced

Directions:

1. Place all the ingredients in a pan that fits your air fryer and mix well.
2. Put the pan into the fryer and cook at 390 degrees F for 22 minutes.
3. Divide into bowls, serve, and enjoy.

Nutrition information:calories 270, fat 9, fiber 7, carbs 23, protein 20

341. Hearty Pork with Vegetables

Preparation time: 20 minutes

Servings 2

Nutrition Information:147 Calories; 3.7g Fat; 11.9g Carbs; 17g Protein; 1.2g Sugars

Ingredients

- ½ cup cream of onion soup
- ½ bell pepper, seeded and diced
- Fine sea salt and black pepper, to taste
- 1/3 cup carrots, chopped
- 4 ounces pork tenderloin, diced
- 1/3 cup onions, chopped
- 2 teaspoons cayenne pepper
- 2 garliccloves, halved

Directions

1. Begin by preheating your air fryer to 385 degrees F.
2. Add all ingredients to a baking dish that is previously greased with a thin layer of canola oil; cook about 5 minutes.
3. Gently stir the ingredients and cook an additional 12 minutes. Bon appétit!

342. Pork Sausage with Eggs and Peppers

Preparation time: 24 minutes

Servings 6

Nutrition Information:400 Calories; 21.6g Fat; 2.8g Carbs; 45.6g Protein; 1.2g Sugars

Ingredients

- 1 green bell pepper, seeded and thinly sliced
- 6 medium-sized eggs
- 1 Habanero pepper, seeded and minced
- 1/2 teaspoon sea salt
- 2 teaspoons fennel seeds
- 1 red bell pepper, seeded and thinly

sliced

- 1 teaspoon tarragon
- 1/2 teaspoon freshly cracked black pepper
- 6 pork sausages

Directions

1. Place the sausages and all peppers in the air fryer cooking basket. Cook at 335 degrees F for 9 minutes.
2. Divide the eggs among 6 ramekins; sprinkle each egg with the seasonings. Cook for 11 more minutes at 395 degrees F. Serve warm.

343. Saucy Pork Meatballs with Fennel

Preparation time: 25 minutes

Servings 4

Nutrition Information:372 Calories; 24g Fat; 12.7g Carbs; 25g Protein; 6.9g Sugars

Ingredients

- 10 ounces ground pork
- ½ cup tomato paste
- 1/2 tablespoon fresh chopped thyme
- 2 fennels, thinly sliced
- 2 eggs
- 1 ½ cups fresh scallions, chopped
- 3 tablespoons breadcrumbs, preferably homemade
- 1 ½ tablespoon vegetable oil
- 1 teaspoon freshly ground black pepper
- 1 teaspoon fine sea salt

Directions

1. In a saucepan that is placed over a moderate heat, cook the sliced fennel in the hot vegetable oil. Sauté the fennel until tender and reserve.
2. Mix the other ingredients, except for the tomato paste. Shape the mixture into 10 small balls.
3. Now, cook the meatballs in the air fryer for 6 minutes at 395 degrees F. Arrange the cooked meatballs in the bottom of an oven proof dish; pour in the tomato paste.
4. Add the reserved fennel and cook in your air fryer at 335 degrees F for an additional 4 more minutes. Bon appétit!

344. Sautéed Mixed Greens with Bacon

Preparation time: 7 minutes

Servings 2

Nutrition Information:259 Calories; 16.4g Fat; 9.8g Carbs; 18.5g Protein; 2.7g Sugars

Ingredients

- 7 ounces mixed greens
- 8 thick slices pork bacon
- 2 shallots, peeled and diced
- Nonstick cooking spray

Directions

1. Begin by preheating the air fryer to 345 degrees F.
2. Now, add the shallot and bacon to the air fryer cooking basket; set the timer for 2 minutes. Spritz with a nonstick cooking spray.

3. After that, pause the air fryer; throw in the mixed greens; give it a good stir and cook an additional 5 minutes. Serve warm.

345. Easy Family Dinner Rolls

Preparation time: 14 minutes

Servings 5

Nutrition Information:284 Calories; 17.4g Fat; 15.4g Carbs; 17.2g Protein; 1.3g Sugars

Ingredients

- 5 slices Colby cheese
- 1 teaspoon ground black pepper
- ½ pound ground pork
- 5 dinner rolls
- 1/2 teaspoon shallot powder
- 1 teaspoon fine sea salt
- ½ teaspoon smoked cayenne pepper
- 1/3 teaspoon porcini powder
- 3 cloves garlic

Directions

1. Start by preheating your air fryer to 405 degrees F. Mix the ground pork with the garlic, shallot powder, porcini powder, fine sea salt, smoked cayenne pepper, and black pepper.
2. Form the ground pork mixture into 5 patties and transfer to the air fryer cooking basket. Now, cook for 8 minutes in the preheated air fryer.
3. Next, pause your machine; immediately place the cheese slices on top of the warm burgers; return them to the air fryer and continue to cook for 2 more minutes.
4. Place the cheeseburgers in dinner rolls, add your favorite toppings and eat warm!

346. Chinese-Style Pork Bites

Preparation time: 14 minutes

Servings 4

Nutrition Information:147 Calories; 7.9g Fat; 8g Carbs; 10.7g Protein; 4.2g Sugars

Ingredients

- 1 teaspoon five-spice powder
- 1/2 onion, peeled and finely chopped
- 1/2 teaspoon fine sea salt
- 1 ½ tablespoons Worcester sauce
- 1/2 teaspoon ground black pepper, to taste
- 1/2 tablespoon apple cider vinegar
- 1/3 pound ground pork
- 3 cloves garlic, minced

Directions

1. Firstly, mix all of the above ingredients in a large-sized bowl.
2. Shape into bite-sized balls and cook in your air fryer for 13 minutes at 365 degrees F. Serve on a nice platter with cocktail picks and enjoy!

347. Old-Fashioned Pork Pasta Sauce

Preparation time: 19 minutes

Servings 4

Nutrition Information:394 Calories; 25.3g Fat; 10.1g Carbs; 31g Protein; 5.5g Sugars

Ingredients

- 1 teaspoon kosher salt
- 1/2 tablespoon tomato ketchup
- 1/3 teaspoon cayenne pepper
- 1½ pounds ground pork
- 1/3 cup tomato paste
- 3 cloves garlic, minced
- 1/2 medium-sized white onion, peeled and chopped
- 1/3 tablespoon fresh cilantro, chopped
- 1/2 tablespoon extra-virgin olive oil
- 1/3 teaspoon freshly cracked black pepper
- 1/2 teaspoon grated fresh ginger

Directions

1. Begin by preheating your air fryer to 395 degrees F.
2. Then, thoroughly combine all the ingredients until the mixture is uniform.
3. Transfer the meat mixture to the air fryer baking dish and cook for about 14 minutes. Serve with the cooked pasta and enjoy.

348. Rosemary Pork Sausage Balls

Preparation time: 19 minutes

Servings 4

Nutrition Information:192 Calories; 9.2g Fat; 17.9g Carbs; 11.6g Protein; 3g Sugars

Ingredients

- 3 garlic cloves, peeled and minced
- 2 tablespoons fresh or dried rosemary
- 3 cups scallions, finely chopped
- 7 ounces sausage meat
- 1/3 cup seasoned breadcrumbs
- Salt and ground black pepper, to taste

Directions

1. Place all of the above ingredients in a mixing dish; mix until everything is thoroughly combined.
2. Roll into small balls and air-fry at 355 degrees F for 13 minutes. Serve with toothpicks and your favorite sauce.Bon appétit!

349. Potato and Ground Pork Casserole

Preparation time: 37 minutes

Servings 6

Nutrition Information:429 Calories; 8g Fat; 67g Carbs; 21.9g Protein; 4.2g Sugars

Ingredients

- 2 eggs
- 1/3 cup Cheddar cheese, grated
- 5 potatoes, peeled and shredded
- 1/3 cup cream
- 1/2 shallot, peeled and chopped
- 11 ounces lean ground pork
- 1/2 tablespoon fresh cilantro leaves
- 3 tablespoons seasoned breadcrumbs
- 1/2 teaspoon ground black pepper
- 1/3 teaspoon ground allspice
- 1 teaspoon fresh thyme leaves

- 1 teaspoon fine sea salt

Directions

1. Start by preheating your air fryer to 395 degrees F. Prepare two mixing bowls.
2. Now, mix the shallot, ground pork, thyme, cilantro, and the egg; then, stir in the seasoned breadcrumbs, salt and black pepper. Mix well, shapeinto mini meatballs and reserve.
3. In another bowl, toss the potatoes with the cream and allspice. Now, cook the potato mixture for 23 minutes in the preheated air fryer.
4. Once the cooking is done, place the reserved mini meatballs in a single layer on top of the potato mixture.
5. Top with Cheddar cheese and cook an additional 9 minutes or until the cheese has browned. Serve warm in individual plates.

350. Mediterranean-Style Pork Chops with Petite Potatoes

Preparation time: 33 minutes

Servings 4

Nutrition Information:512 Calories; 12g Fat; 65.7g Carbs; 49g Protein; 2.9g Sugars

Ingredients

- 11 petite potatoes, quartered into wedges
- 1/2 teaspoon fine sea salt
- 3 garlic cloves, pressed
- 1 tablespoon fresh rosemary,chopped
- 1/2 tablespoon fresh thyme, chopped
- Zest of 1 medium-sized orange
- 3 boneless pork chops
- 2 tablespoons canola oil, divided
- 1/2 teaspoon dried basil
- 1 teaspoon ground black pepper, divided

Directions

1. Rub the pork with canola oil; add the thyme, rosemary, basil, black pepper, salt, and orange zest; toss to combine. Set aside.
2. Now, combine the potatoes and minced garlic; add the salt and ground black pepper to taste.
3. Add the potatoes to a baking dish. Place the chops on top of the potatoes.
4. Bake at 365 degrees F for 27 minutes, turning halfway through.

351. Barbeque Pork Strips

Preparation time: 30 minutes

Servings 4

Nutrition Information:141 Calories; 5.3g Fat; 6.3g Carbs; 16.1g Protein; 5.1g Sugars

Ingredients

- 2 tablespoons tomato purée
- 2 tablespoons brown sugar
- 2 teaspoons ground ginger
- 2 teaspoons soy sauce
- 2 tablespoons dry white wine
- ½ pound pork loin steak, cut into strips
- 2 teaspoons crushed red pepper flakes

- 2 teaspoons sesame oil
- A few drops liquid smoke
- Salt and ground black pepper, to taste

Directions

1. Start by preheating your air fryer to 385 degrees F.
2. Toss the pork with other ingredients; let it marinate at least 20 minutes in a fridge.
3. Then, air-fry the pork strips for 7 minutes. Bon appétit!

352. Morning Bubble & Squeak with Pork

Preparation time: 31 minutes

Servings 4

Nutrition Information:219 Calories; 12.9g Fat; 3.2g Carbs; 21.6g Protein; 1g Sugars

Ingredients

- 1/3 cup Colby cheese, grated
- 1 teaspoon fine sea salt
- 2 cups pulled pork
- 1/3 teaspoon marjoram
- 1/2 large-sized shallot, thinly sliced
- 3 cloves garlic, finely minced
- 3 eggs, whisked
- 1/2 teaspoon thyme
- 1/3 teaspoon ground black pepper
- Leftover stuffing or vegetables
- A pinch of grated nutmeg

Directions

1. Begin by preheating your air fryer to 345 degrees F.
2. In a mixing dish, thoroughly combine all the ingredients using a wide spatula.
3. Dump the mixture into a baking dish. Then, bake in the preheated air fryer for about 26 minutes or until it's bubbling. Work in batches as needed. Bon appétit!

353. Delicious Red Gold Potatoes with Bacon

Preparation time: 17 minutes

Servings 6

Nutrition Information:400 Calories; 14.3g Fat; 60.4g Carbs; 10.5g Protein; 5g Sugars

Ingredients

- 1 teaspoon onion powder
- 1 ½ tablespoons canola oil
- 4 garlic cloves, peeled and smashed
- 6 Red Gold potatoes, peeled and diced
- 1/2 teaspoon caraway seeds
- 1 teaspoon sea salt
- 6 slices bacon, diced
- 1/2 teaspoon whole grain mustard
- 1 teaspoon ground black pepper

Directions

1. Begin by preheating your air fryer to 365 degrees F. Then, throw diced potatoes into a baking pan. Now, cook them for 8 minutes, checking for doneness and stirring once.
2. Add the rest of the above ingredients;

cook an additional 4-5 minutes. Serve and enjoy!

354. Pork Chops with Kale

Preparation time: 25 minutes

Serving 6

Nutrition Information:440 Calories; 16.2g Fat; 13.4g Carbs; 56g Protein; 10g Sugars

Ingredients

- 3 center-cut loin pork chops
- 1/2 teaspoon fresh thyme
- 1/3 tablespoon honey
- 1/2 apple, cored and cut into
- 1/3 teaspoon dried basil
- 3 cups kale leaves, torn into pieces
- 1 1/2 teaspoons olive oil
- 1/3 cup pear cider vinegar
- 1/2 teaspoon yellow mustard
- Ground black pepper and fine sea salt, to your liking

Directions

1. To make the dressing, combine the olive oil, pear cider vinegar, yellow mustard, and honey. Now, stir in ground black pepper and fine sea salt.
2. In another bowl, mix the kale and apple; toss with the dressing to coat well. Season the pork chops on all sides with thyme and basil.
3. Roast the pork chops at 405 degrees F for 18 minutes, turning halfway through. Serve warm.

355. Herbed and Breaded Pork Schnitzel

Preparation time: 15 minutes

Servings 2

Nutrition Information:275 Calories; 18.6g Fat; 2.7g Carbs; 22.9g Protein; 1.2g Sugars

Ingredients

- 1 pork schnitzel, halved
- 1 teaspoon garlic salt
- 1/2 heaping tablespoon fresh parsley
- 1 cup breadcrumbs of choice, preferably homemade
- 1/3 tablespoon pear cider vinegar
- 1/2 teaspoon mustard
- 2 eggs, beaten
- 1/2 teaspoon fennel seed
- 1/3 teaspoon ground black pepper

Directions

1. Blitz the breadcrumbs, vinegar, black pepper, garlic salt, mustard, fennel seeds, and fresh parsley in your food processor until uniform and smooth. Dump the blended mixture into a shallow bowl.
2. Add the beaten egg to another shallow bowl.
3. Coat the pork with the beaten egg; then, dredge them in the herb mixture.
4. Bake at 355 degrees F for about 14 minutes. Bon appétit!

Spicy Pork Kebabs

Preparation time: 22 minutes

Servings 3

Nutrition Information:330 Calories; 16.9g Fat; 3g Carbs; 39.3g Protein; 1.3g Sugars

Ingredients

- 5 tablespoons breadcrumbs
- 2 tablespoons tomato puree
- 1/2 fresh serrano,minced
- 1/3 teaspoon paprika
- 1/2 pound pork,ground
- ½ cup green onions, finely chopped
- 3 cloves garlic, peeled and finely minced
- 1 teaspoon ground black pepper, or more to taste
- 1 teaspoon salt, or more to taste

Directions

1. Thoroughly combine all ingredients in a mixing dish. Then, form your mixture into sausage shapes.
2. Cook for 18 minutes at 355 degrees F. Mound salad on a serving platter, top with air fried kebabs and serve warm.

356. Pork Sausage with Vidalia Onions and Celery

Preparation time: 28 minutes

Servings 6

Nutrition Information:216 Calories; 5.6g Fat; 31.6g Carbs; 11.3g Protein; 3.5g Sugars

Ingredients

- 6 English muffins
- 1 teaspoon red pepper flakes, crushed
- 6 pork sausages
- 3 Vidalia onions, peeled and cleaned
- 3 celery stalks, thinly sliced
- 6 medium-sized eggs
- 2 teaspoons cumin seeds
- 1 teaspoon sea salt

Directions

1. Place the sausages, celery, and Vidalia onions in an air fryer cooking basket. Cook at 325
2. degrees F for 10 minutes; taste for doneness and cook for 3 more minutes as needed.
3. Divide the eggs among 6 ramekins; sprinkle them with red pepper, cumin seeds and sea salt. Now, turn the temperature to 395 degrees F; cook for 12 more minutes.
4. Serve with English muffins and some extra toppings of choice. Enjoy!

357. Saucy Hoisin Pork

Preparation time: 30 minutes

Servings 4

Nutrition Information:219 Calories; 8.1g Fat; 19.5g Carbs; 17.1g Protein; 14.5g Sugars

Ingredients

- 2 tablespoons honey
- 2 tablespoons dry white wine
- 1/3 cup hoisin sauce
- 2 teaspoons smoked cayenne pepper
- 3 potatoes, peeled and cubed
- 3 garlic cloves, pressed

- 1/2 pound pork loin steak, cut into strips
- 3 teaspoons fresh lime juice
- Salt and ground black pepper, to taste

Directions

1. Start by preheating your air fryer to 395 degrees F.
2. Toss the pork with other ingredients; let it marinate at least 20 minutes in a fridge.
3. Then, air-fry the pork strips for 5 minutes. Bon appétit!

358. Bubble & Squeak with Pork Sausage

Preparation time: 30 minutes

Servings 6

Nutrition Information:485 Calories; 27.6g Fat; 8.2g Carbs; 49g Protein; 1.2g Sugars

Ingredients

- 1 ½ cup potato mash
- 1/2 teaspoon tarragon
- 1/3 cup Colby cheese
- 1/2 teaspoon ground black pepper
- 1/2 onion, peeled and sliced
- 1 teaspoon cumin powder
- 1/2 teaspoon sea salt
- 3 beaten eggs
- 6 pork sausages, chopped

Directions

1. Grab a mixing dish and mix all ingredients in the order listed above.
2. Divide the prepared mixture among 6 ramekins; now, place ramekins in your air fryer.
3. Cook for 27 minutes at 365 degrees F. Eat warm.

359. Basil-Vermouth Pork Chops

Preparation time: 22 minutes

Servings 6

Nutrition Information:393 Calories; 15.4g Fat; 2.6g Carbs; 56g Protein; 0.2g Sugars

Ingredients

- 2 tablespoons vermouth
- 6 center-cut loin pork chops
- 1/2 tablespoon fresh basil, minced
- 1/3 teaspoon freshly ground black pepper, or more to taste
- 2 tablespoons whole grain mustard
- 1 teaspoon fine kosher salt

Directions

1. Toss pork chops with other ingredients until they are well coated on both sides.
2. Air-fry your chops for 18 minutes at 405 degrees F, turning once or twice.
3. Mound your favorite salad on a serving plate; top with pork chops and enjoy.

360. Pork and Bell Peppers

Preparation time: 10 minutes

Cooking time: 22 minutes

Servings: 2

Ingredients:

- 1 sweet onion, chopped
- 1 red bell pepper, cut into strips
- 1 green bell pepper, cut into strips
- 1 yellow bell pepper, cut in strips
- Salt and black pepper to taste
- 1 tablespoon olive oil
- 7 ounces pork tenderloin, cut into strips

Directions:

1. Place all of the ingredients into a pan that fits your air fryer, and toss well.
2. Put the pan in the fryer and cook at 390 degrees F for 22 minutes.
3. Divide the mix between plates and serve.

Nutrition information:calories 280, fat 13, fiber 7, carbs 21, protein 19

361. Beef and Peas

Preparation time: 5 minutes

Cooking time: 25 minutes

Servings: 2

Ingredients:

- 2 beef steaks, cut into strips
- Salt and black pepper to taste
- 14 ounces snow peas
- 2 tablespoons soy sauce
- 1 tablespoon olive oil

Directions:

1. Put all of the ingredients into a pan that fits your air fryer; toss well.
2. Place the pan in the fryer and cook at 390 degrees F for 25 minutes.
3. Divide everything between plates and serve.

Nutrition information:calories 265, fat 11, fiber 4, carbs 22, protein 19

362. Fennel Pork Mix

Preparation time: 5 minutes

Cooking time: 15 minutes

Servings: 4

Ingredients:

- 3 tablespoons olive oil
- 2 pork chops
- Salt and black pepper to taste
- 1 teaspoon fennel seeds, roasted
- 1 tablespoon rosemary, chopped

Directions:

1. In a bowl, mix the pork chops with the oil, salt, pepper, fennel, and the rosemary; toss and make sure the pork chops are coated well.
2. Transfer the chops to your air fryer and cook at 400 degrees F for 15 minutes.
3. Divide the chops between plates and serve.

Nutrition information:calories 281, fat 11, fiber 8, carbs 17, protein 20

363. Lamb Meatballs

Preparation time: 10 minutes

Cooking time: 12 minutes

Servings: 8

Ingredients:

- 4 ounces lamb meat, minced
- Salt and black pepper to taste
- 1 egg, whisked
- ½ tablespoon lemon zest
- 1 tablespoon oregano, chopped
- Cooking spray

Directions:

1. In a bowl, combine all of the ingredients except the cooking spray and stir well.
2. Shape medium-sized meatballs out of this mix.
3. Place the meatballs in your air fryer's basket, grease them with cooking spray, and cook at 400 degrees F for 12 minutes.
4. Divide between plates and serve.

Nutrition information:calories 294, fat 12, fiber 2, carbs 22, protein 19

364. Pork Meatloaf

Preparation time: 5 minutes

Cooking time: 20 minutes

Servings: 4

Ingredients:

- 1 pound ground pork meat
- 3 tablespoons breadcrumbs
- Cooking spray
- 1 egg, whisked
- 1 ounce chorizo, chopped
- Salt and black pepper to taste
- 1 tablespoon thyme, chopped
- 1 yellow onion, chopped

Directions:

1. Place all of the ingredients (except the cooking spray) in a bowl and stir / combine well.
2. Transfer the mixture to a loaf pan, greased with cooking spray, that fits your air fryer.
3. Place the pan in the fryer and cook at 390 degrees F for 20 minutes.
4. Slice and serve.

Nutrition information:calories 290, fat 12, fiber 1, carbs 19, protein 26

365. Lamb and Lemon Sauce

Preparation time: 10 minutes

Cooking time: 30 minutes

Servings: 4

Ingredients:

- 2 lamb shanks
- Salt and black pepper to the taste
- 2 garlic cloves, minced
- 4 tablespoons olive oil
- Juice from ½ lemon
- Zest from ½ lemon
- ½ teaspoon oregano, dried

Directions:

1. Season lamb with salt, pepper, rub with garlic, put in your air fryer and cook at 350 degrees F for 30 minutes.
2. Meanwhile, in a bowl, mix lemon juice with lemon zest, some salt and pepper, the olive oil and oregano and

whisk very well.

3. Shred lamb, discard bone, divide among plates, drizzle the lemon dressing all over and serve.
4. Enjoy!

Nutrition information:calories 260, fat 7, fiber 3, carbs 15, protein 12

366. Lamb and Green Pesto

Preparation time: 1 hour

Cooking time: 45 minutes

Servings: 4

Ingredients:

- 1 cup parsley
- 1 cup mint
- 1 small yellow onion, roughly chopped
- 1/3 cup pistachios, chopped
- 1 teaspoon lemon zest, grated
- 5 tablespoons olive oil
- Salt and black pepper to the taste
- 2 pounds lamb riblets
- ½ onion, chopped
- 5 garlic cloves, minced
- Juice from 1 orange

Directions:

1. In your food processor, mix parsley with mint, onion, pistachios, lemon zest, salt, pepper and oil and blend very well.
2. Rub lamb with this mix, place in a bowl, cover and leave in the fridge for 1 hour.
3. Transfer lamb to a baking dish that fits your air fryer, also add garlic, drizzle orange juice and cook in your air fryer at 300 degrees F for 45 minutes.
4. Divide lamb on plates and serve.
5. Enjoy!

Nutrition information:calories 200, fat 4, fiber 6, carbs 15, protein 7

367. Lamb Racks and Fennel Mix

Preparation time: 10 minutes

Cooking time: 16 minutes

Servings: 4

Ingredients:

- 12 ounces lamb racks
- 2 fennel bulbs, sliced
- Salt and black pepper to the taste
- 2 tablespoons olive oil
- 4 figs, cut into halves
- 1/8 cup apple cider vinegar
- 1 tablespoon brown sugar

Directions:

1. In a bowl, mix fennel with figs, vinegar, sugar and oil, toss to coat well, transfer to a baking dish that fits your air fryer, introduce in your air fryer and cook at 350 degrees F for 6 minutes.
2. Season lamb with salt and pepper, add to the baking dish with the fennel mix and air fry for 10 minutes more.
3. Divide everything on plates and serve.
4. Enjoy!

Nutrition information:calories 240, fat 9, fiber 3, carbs 15, protein 12

368. Burgundy Beef Mix

Preparation time: 10 minutes

Cooking time: 1 hour

Servings: 7

Ingredients:

- 2 pounds beef chuck roast, cubed
- 15 ounces canned tomatoes, chopped
- 4 carrots, chopped
- Salt and black pepper to the taste
- ½ pounds mushrooms, sliced
- 2 celery ribs, chopped
- 2 yellow onions, chopped
- 1 cup beef stock
- 1 tablespoon thyme, chopped
- ½ teaspoon mustard powder
- 3 tablespoons almond flour
- 1 cup water

Directions:

1. Heat up a heat proof pot that fits your air fryer over medium high heat, add beef, stir and brown them for a couple of minutes.
2. Add tomatoes, mushrooms, onions, carrots, celery, salt, pepper mustard, stock and thyme and stir.
3. In a bowl mix water with flour, stir well, add this to the pot, toss, introduce in your air fryer and cook at 300 degrees F for 1 hour.
4. Divide into bowls and serve.
5. Enjoy!

Nutrition information:calories 275, fat 13, fiber 4, carbs 17, protein 28

369. Mexican Beef Mix

Preparation time: 10 minutes

Cooking time: 1 hour and 10 minutes

Servings: 8

Ingredients:

- 2 yellow onions, chopped
- 2 tablespoons olive oil
- 2 pounds beef roast, cubed
- 2 green bell peppers, chopped
- 1 habanero pepper, chopped
- 4 jalapenos, chopped
- 14 ounces canned tomatoes, chopped
- 2 tablespoons cilantro, chopped
- 6 garlic cloves, minced
- ½ cup water
- Salt and black pepper to the taste
- 1 and ½ teaspoons cumin, ground
- ½ cup black olives, pitted and chopped
- 1 teaspoon oregano, dried

Directions:

1. In a pan that fits your air fryer, combine beef with oil, green bell peppers, onions, jalapenos, habanero pepper, tomatoes, garlic, water, cilantro, oregano, cumin, salt and pepper, stir, put in your air fryer and cook at 300 degrees F for 1 hour and 10 minutes.
2. Add olives, stir, divide into bowls and serve.
3. Enjoy!

Nutrition information:calories 305, fat

14, fiber 4, carbs 18, protein 25

370. Creamy Ham and Cauliflower Mix

Preparation time: 10 minutes

Cooking time: 4 hours

Servings: 6

Ingredients:

- 8 ounces cheddar cheese, grated
- 4 cups ham, cubed
- 14 ounces chicken stock
- ½ teaspoon garlic powder
- ½ teaspoon onion powder
- Salt and black pepper to the taste
- 4 garlic cloves, minced
- ¼ cup heavy cream
- 16 ounces cauliflower florets

Directions:

1. In a pot that fits your air fryer, mix ham with stock, cheese, cauliflower, garlic powder, onion powder, salt, pepper, garlic and heavy cream, stir, put in your air fryer and cook at 300 degrees F for 1 hour.
2. Divide into bowls and serve.
3. Enjoy!

Nutrition information:calories 320, fat 20, fiber 3, carbs 16, protein 23

371. Air Fried Sausage and Mushrooms

Preparation time: 10 minutes

Cooking time: 40 minutes

Servings: 6

Ingredients:

- 3 red bell peppers, chopped
- 2 pounds pork sausage, sliced
- Salt and black pepper to the taste
- 2 pounds Portobello mushrooms, sliced
- 2 sweet onions, chopped
- 1 tablespoon brown sugar
- 1 teaspoon olive oil

Directions:

1. In a baking dish that fits your air fryer, mix sausage slices with oil, salt, pepper, bell pepper, mushrooms, onion and sugar, toss, introduce in your air fryer and cook at 300 degrees F for 40 minutes.
2. Divide among plates and serve right away.
3. Enjoy!

Nutrition information:calories 130, fat 12, fiber 1, carbs 13, protein 18

372. Sausage and Kale

Preparation time: 10 minutes

Cooking time: 20 minutes

Servings: 4

Ingredients:

- 1 cup yellow onion, chopped
- 1 and ½ pound Italian pork sausage, sliced
- ½ cup red bell pepper, chopped
- Salt and black pepper to the taste
- 5 pounds kale, chopped

- 1 teaspoon garlic, minced
- ¼ cup red hot chili pepper, chopped
- 1 cup water

Directions:

1. In a pan that fits your air fryer, mix sausage with onion, bell pepper, salt, pepper, kale, garlic, water and chili pepper, toss, introduce in preheated air fryer and cook at 300 degrees F for 20 minutes.
2. Divide everything on plates and serve.
3. Enjoy!

Nutrition information:calories 150, fat 4, fiber 1, carbs 12, protein 14

373. Sirloin Steaks and Pico De Gallo

Preparation time: 10 minutes

Cooking time: 10 minutes

Servings: 4

Ingredients:

- 2 tablespoons chili powder
- 4 medium sirloin steaks
- 1 teaspoon cumin, ground
- ½ tablespoon sweet paprika
- 1 teaspoon onion powder
- 1 teaspoon garlic powder
- Salt and black pepper to the taste
- For the Pico de gallo:
- 1 small red onion, chopped
- 2 tomatoes, chopped
- 2 garlic cloves, minced
- 2 tablespoons lime juice
- 1 small green bell pepper, chopped
- 1 jalapeno, chopped
- ¼ cup cilantro, chopped
- ¼ teaspoon cumin, ground

Directions:

1. In a bowl, mix chili powder with a pinch of salt, black pepper, onion powder, garlic powder, paprika and 1 teaspoon cumin, stir well, season steaks with this mix, put them in your air fryer and cook at 360 degrees F for 10 minutes.
2. In a bowl, mix red onion with tomatoes, garlic, lime juice, bell pepper, jalapeno, cilantro, black pepper to the taste and ¼ teaspoon cumin and toss.
3. Top steaks with this mix and serve right away
4. Enjoy!

Nutrition information:calories 200, fat 12, fiber 4, carbs 15, protein 18

374. Coffee Flavored Steaks

Preparation time: 10 minutes

Cooking time: 15 minutes

Servings: 4

Ingredients:

- 1 and ½ tablespoons coffee, ground
- 4 rib eye steaks
- ½ tablespoon sweet paprika
- 2 tablespoons chili powder
- 2 teaspoons garlic powder
- 2 teaspoons onion powder
- ¼ teaspoon ginger, ground

- ¼ teaspoon, coriander, ground
- A pinch of cayenne pepper
- Black pepper to the taste

Directions:

1. In a bowl, mix coffee with paprika, chili powder, garlic powder, onion powder, ginger, coriander, cayenne and black pepper, stir, rub steaks with this mix, put in preheated air fryer and cook at 360 degrees F for 15 minutes.
2. Divide steaks on plates and serve with a side salad.
3. Enjoy!

Nutrition information:calories 160, fat 10, fiber 8, carbs 14, protein 12

375. Filet Mignon and Mushrooms Sauce

Preparation time: 10 minutes

Cooking time: 25 minutes

Servings: 4

Ingredients:

- 12 mushrooms, sliced
- 1 shallot, chopped
- 4 fillet mignons
- 2 garlic cloves, minced
- 2 tablespoons olive oil
- ¼ cup Dijon mustard
- ¼ cup wine
- 1 and ¼ cup coconut cream
- 2 tablespoons parsley, chopped
- Salt and black pepper to the taste

Directions:

1. Heat up a pan with the oil over medium high heat, add garlic and shallots, stir and cook for 3 minutes.
2. Add mushrooms, stir and cook for 4 minutes more.
3. Add wine, stir and cook until it evaporates.
4. Add coconut cream, mustard, parsley, a pinch of salt and black pepper to the taste, stir, cook for 6 minutes more and take off heat.
5. Season fillets with salt and pepper, put them in your air fryer and cook at 360 degrees F for 10 minutes.
6. Divide fillets on plates and serve with the mushroom sauce on top.
7. Enjoy!

Nutrition information:calories 340, fat 12, fiber 1, carbs 14, protein 23

376. Beef Kabobs

Preparation time: 10 minutes

Cooking time: 10 minutes

Servings: 4

Ingredients:

- 2 red bell peppers, chopped
- 2 pounds sirloin steak, cut into medium pieces
- 1 red onion, chopped
- 1 zucchini, sliced
- Juice form 1 lime
- 2 tablespoons chili powder
- 2 tablespoon hot sauce
- ½ tablespoons cumin, ground
- ¼ cup olive oil
- ¼ cup salsa

- Salt and black pepper to the taste

Directions:

1. In a bowl, mix salsa with lime juice, oil, hot sauce, chili powder, cumin, salt and black pepper and whisk well.
2. Divide meat bell peppers, zucchini and onion on skewers, brush kabobs with the salsa mix you made earlier, put them in your preheated air fryer and cook them for 10 minutes at 370 degrees F flipping kabobs halfway.
3. Divide among plates and serve with a side salad.
4. Enjoy!

Nutrition information:calories 170, fat 5, fiber 2, carbs 13, protein 16

377. Mediterranean Steaks and Scallops

Preparation time: 10 minutes

Cooking time: 14 minutes

Servings: 2

Ingredients:

- 10 sea scallops
- 2 beef steaks
- 4 garlic cloves, minced
- 1 shallot, chopped
- 2 tablespoons lemon juice
- 2 tablespoons parsley, chopped
- 2 tablespoons basil, chopped
- 1 teaspoon lemon zest
- ¼ cup butter
- ¼ cup veggie stock
- Salt and black pepper to the taste

Directions:

1. Season steaks with salt and pepper, put them in your air fryer, cook at 360 degrees F for 10 minutes and transfer to a pan that fits the fryer.
2. Add shallot, garlic, butter, stock, basil, lemon juice, parsley, lemon zest and scallops, toss everything gently and cook at 360 degrees F for 4 minutes more.
3. Divide steaks and scallops on plates and serve.
4. Enjoy!

Nutrition information:calories 150, fat 2, fiber 2, carbs 14, protein 17

378. Beef Medallions Mix

Preparation time: 2 hours

Cooking time: 10 minutes

Servings: 4

Ingredients:

- 2 teaspoons chili powder
- 1 cup tomatoes, crushed
- 4 beef medallions
- 2 teaspoons onion powder
- 2 tablespoons soy sauce
- Salt and black pepper to the taste
- 1 tablespoons hot pepper
- 2 tablespoons lime juice

Directions:

1. In a bowl, mix tomatoes with hot pepper, soy sauce, chili powder, onion powder, a pinch of salt, black pepper and lime juice and whisk well.
2. Arrange beef medallions in a dish,

pour sauce over them, toss and leave them aside for 2 hours.

3. Discard tomato marinade, put beef in your preheated air fryer and cook at 360 degrees F for 10 minutes.
4. Divide steaks on plates and serve with a side salad.
5. Enjoy!

Nutrition information:calories 230, fat 4, fiber 1, carbs 13, protein 14

379. Balsamic Beef

Preparation time: 10 minutes

Cooking time: 1 hour

Servings: 6

Ingredients:

- 1 medium beef roast
- 1 tablespoon Worcestershire sauce
- ½ cup balsamic vinegar
- 1 cup beef stock
- 1 tablespoons honey
- 1 tablespoon soy sauce
- 4 garlic cloves, minced

Directions:

1. In a heat proof dish that fits your air fryer, mix roast with roast with Worcestershire sauce, vinegar, stock, honey, soy sauce and garlic, toss well, introduce in your air fryer and cook at 370 degrees F for 1 hour.
2. Slice roast, divide among plates, drizzle the sauce all over and serve.
3. Enjoy!

Nutrition information:calories 311, fat 7, fiber 12, carbs 20, protein 16

380. Pork Chops and Roasted Peppers

Preparation time: 10 minutes

Cooking time: 16 minutes

Servings: 4

Ingredients:

- 3 tablespoons olive oil
- 3 tablespoons lemon juice
- 1 tablespoon smoked paprika
- 2 tablespoons thyme, chopped
- 3 garlic cloves, minced
- 4 pork chops, bone in
- Salta and black pepper to the taste
- 2 roasted bell peppers, chopped

Directions:

1. In a pan that fits your air fryer, mix pork chops with oil, lemon juice, smoked paprika, thyme, garlic, bell peppers, salt and pepper, toss well, introduce in your air fryer and cook at 400 degrees F for 16 minutes.
2. Divide pork chops and peppers mix on plates and serve right away.
3. Enjoy!

Nutrition information:calories 321, fat 6, fiber 8, carbs 14, protein 17

381. Pork Chops and Green Beans

Preparation time: 10 minutes

Cooking time: 15 minutes

Servings: 4

Ingredients:

- 4 pork chops, bone in
- 2 tablespoons olive oil
- 1 tablespoon sage, chopped
- Salt and black pepper to the taste
- 16 ounces green beans
- 3 garlic cloves, minced
- 2 tablespoons parsley, chopped

Directions:

1. In a pan that fits your air fryer, mix pork chops with olive oil, sage, salt, pepper, green beans, garlic and parsley, toss, introduce in your air fryer and cook at 360 degrees F for 15 minutes.
2. Divide everything on plates and serve.
3. Enjoy!

Nutrition information:calories 261, fat 7, fiber 9, carbs 14, protein 20

382. Pork Chops and Sage Sauce

Preparation time: 10 minutes

Cooking time: 15 minutes

Servings: 2

Ingredients:

- 2 pork chops
- Salt and black pepper to the taste
- 1 tablespoon olive oil
- 2 tablespoons butter
- 1 shallot, sliced
- 1 handful sage, chopped
- 1 teaspoon lemon juice

Directions:

1. Season pork chops with salt and pepper, rub with the oil, put in your air fryer and cook at 370 degrees F for 10 minutes, flipping them halfway.
2. Meanwhile, heat up a pan with the butter over medium heat, add shallot, stir and cook for 2 minutes.
3. Add sage and lemon juice, stir well, cook for a few more minutes and take off heat.
4. Divide pork chops on plates, drizzle sage sauce all over and serve.
5. Enjoy!

Nutrition information:calories 265, fat 6, fiber 8, carbs 19, protein 12

383. Tasty Ham and Greens

Preparation time: 10 minutes

Cooking time: 16 minutes

Servings: 8

- **Ingredients:**

- 2 tablespoons olive oil
- 4 cups ham, chopped
- 2 tablespoons flour
- 3 cups chicken stock
- 5 ounces onion, chopped
- 16 ounces collard greens, chopped
- 14 ounces canned black eyed peas, drained
- ½ teaspoon red pepper, crushed

Directions:

1. Drizzle the oil in a pan that fits your air fryer, add ham, stock and flour and whisk.
2. Also add onion, black eyed peas, red

pepper and collard greens, introduce in your air fryer and cook at 390 degrees F for 16 minutes.
3. Divide everything on plates and serve.
4. Enjoy!

Nutrition information:calories 322, fat 6, fiber 8, carbs 12, protein 5

384. Ham and Veggie Air Fried Mix

Preparation time: 10 minutes

Cooking time: 20 minutes

Servings: 6

Ingredients:

- ¼ cup butter
- ¼ cup flour
- 3 cups milk
- ½ teaspoon thyme, dried
- 2 cups ham, chopped
- 6 ounces sweet peas
- 4 ounces mushrooms, halved
- 1 cup baby carrots

Directions:

1. Heat up a large pan that fits your air fryer with the butter over medium heat, melt it, add flour and whisk well.
2. Add milk and, well again and take off heat.
3. Add thyme, ham, peas, mushrooms and baby carrots, toss, put in your air fryer and cook at 360 degrees F for 20 minutes.
4. Divide everything on plates and serve.
5. Enjoy!

Nutrition information:calories 311, fat 6, fiber 8, carbs 12, protein 7

SIDE DISH

385. Simple Eggplant Mix

Preparation time: 10 minutes

Cooking time: 10 minutes

Servings: 4

Ingredients:

- 8 baby eggplants, cubed
- Salt and black pepper to taste
- 1 green bell pepper, chopped
- 1 tablespoon tomato sauce
- 1 bunch coriander, chopped
- ½ teaspoon garlic powder
- 1 tablespoon olive oil
- 1 yellow onion, chopped

Directions:

1. In a pan that fits your air fryer, combine all the ingredients and toss.
2. Place the pan in the fryer and cook at 370 degrees F for 10 minutes.
3. Divide between plates and serve as a side dish.

Nutrition information:calories 210, fat 5, fiber 7, carbs 12, protein 5

386. Creamy Tomatoes

Preparation time: 5 minutes

Cooking time: 6 minutes

Servings: 4

Ingredients:

- 1 pound cherry tomatoes, halved
- Salt and black pepper to taste
- A drizzle of olive oil
- 1 cup heavy cream
- ½ tablespoon Creole seasoning

Directions:

1. In a pan that fits your air fryer, combine all the ingredients and toss.
2. Place the pan in the fryer and cook at 400 degrees F for 6 minutes.
3. Divide between plates and serve.

Nutrition information:calories 174, fat 5, fiber 7, carbs 11, protein 4

387. Brussels Sprouts Side Dish Delight

Preparation time: 10 minutes

Cooking time: 25 minutes

Servings: 8

Ingredients:

- 3 pounds Brussels sprouts, halved
- 1 teaspoon olive oil
- 1 pound bacon, chopped
- Salt and black pepper to taste
- 4 tablespoons butter, melted
- 3 shallots, chopped
- 1 cup milk
- 2 cups heavy cream
- ¼ teaspoon nutmeg, ground
- 3 tablespoons prepared horseradish

Directions:

1. Preheat your air fryer at 370 degrees

F, and add oil, bacon, salt, pepper, and Brussels sprouts; toss.

2. Then add butter, shallots, heavy cream, milk, nutmeg, and horseradish; toss again and cook for 25 minutes.
3. Divide between plates and serve as a side dish.
4. Enjoy!

Nutrition information:calories 214, fat 5, fiber 8, carbs 12, protein 5

388. Simple Zucchini Fries

Preparation time: 10 minutes

Cooking time: 12 minutes

Servings: 4

Ingredients:

- 2 small zucchinis, cut into fries
- 2 teaspoons olive oil
- Salt and black pepper to taste
- 2 eggs, whisked
- 1 cup breadcrumbs
- ½ cup white flour

Directions:

1. In a bowl, mix the flour, salt, and pepper; stir.
2. Put the breadcrumbs in another bowl and whisk the eggs in a third bowl.
3. Dredge the zucchini fries in the flour, then in the eggs, and then in the breadcrumbs.
4. Use the oil to grease your air fryer and heat to 400 degrees F.
5. Add the zucchini fries and cook for 12 minutes; serve as a side dish.

Nutrition information:calories 182, fat 6, fiber 3, carbs 11, protein 5

389. Mixed Peppers Side Dish

Preparation time: 5 minutes

Cooking time: 20 minutes

Servings: 4

Ingredients:

- 1 tablespoon smoked paprika
- 1 tablespoon olive oil
- 4 red bell peppers, cut into medium strips
- 4 green bell peppers, cut in medium strips
- 1 red onion, chopped
- Salt and black pepper to taste

Directions:

1. In your air fryer, mix all ingredients, toss, and cook at 360 degrees F for 20 minutes.
2. Divide the peppers between plates and serve as a side dish.

Nutrition information:calories 172, fat 5, fiber 4, carbs 7, protein 4

390. French Carrots Mix

Preparation time: 5 minutes

Cooking time: 20 minutes

Servings: 4

Ingredients:

- 1 pound baby carrots, trimmed
- 2 teaspoons olive oil

- 1 teaspoon herbs de Provence
- 2 tablespoons lime juice

Directions:

1. In a bowl, mix all ingredients well and then transfer to your air fryer's basket.
2. Cook at 320 degrees F for 20 minutes.
3. Divide between plates and serve as a side dish.

Nutrition information:calories 132, fat 4, fiber 3, carbs 11, protein 4

391. Maple Parsnips Mix

Preparation time: 5 minutes
Cooking time: 40 minutes
Servings: 6

Ingredients:

- 2 pounds parsnips, roughly cubed
- 2 tablespoons maple syrup
- 1 tablespoon cilantro, chopped
- 1 tablespoon olive oil

Directions:

1. Preheat your air fryer at 360 degrees F, then add the oil and heat it up.
2. Add the other ingredients, toss, and cook for 40 minutes.
3. Divide between plates and serve as a side dish.

Nutrition information:calories 174, fat 5, fiber 3, carbs 11, protein 4

392. Simple Air Fried Beets

Preparation time: 5 minutes
Cooking time: 35 minutes
Servings: 6

Ingredients:

- 3 pounds small beets, trimmed and halved
- 4 tablespoons maple syrup
- 1 tablespoon olive oil

Directions:

1. Heat up your air fryer at 360 degrees F, then add the oil and heat it up.
2. Add the beets and maple syrup, toss, and cook for 35 minutes.
3. Divide the beets between plates and serve as a side dish.

Nutrition information:calories 171, fat 4, fiber 2, carbs 13, protein 3

393. Cauliflower and Mushroom Risotto

Preparation time: 10 minutes
Cooking time: 40 minutes
Servings: 6

Ingredients:

- 2 tablespoons olive oil
- 4 tablespoons soy sauce
- 3 garlic cloves, minced
- 1 tablespoon ginger, grated
- Juice of 1 lime
- 1 cauliflower head, riced
- 10 ounces water chestnuts, drained
- 15 ounces mushrooms, chopped
- 1 egg, whisked

Directions:

1. In your air fryer, mix the cauliflower rice, oil, soy sauce, garlic, ginger, lime juice, chestnuts, and mushrooms.
2. Stir, cover, and cook at 350 degrees F for 20 minutes.
3. Add the egg, toss, and cook at 360 degrees F for 20 minutes more.
4. Divide between plates and serve.

Nutrition information:calories 182, fat 3, fiber 2, carbs 8, protein 4

394. Moroccan Eggplant Side Dish

Preparation time: 5 minutes

Cooking time: 20 minutes

Servings: 6

Ingredients:

- 1½ pounds eggplant, cubed
- 1 tablespoon olive oil
- 1 teaspoon onion powder
- 1 teaspoon sumac
- 2 teaspoons za'atar
- Juice of 1 lime

Directions:

1. Place all ingredients in your air fryer and mix well.
2. Cook at 370 degrees F for 20 minutes.
3. Divide between plates and serve as a side dish.

Nutrition information:calories 182, fat 4, fiber 7, carbs 12, protein 4

395. Air Fried Cauliflower Mix

Preparation time: 5 minutes

Cooking time: 20 minutes

Servings: 4

Ingredients:

- 1 tablespoon olive oil
- 1 cauliflower head, florets separated
- 3 garlic cloves, minced
- Juice of 1 lime
- 1 tablespoon black sesame seeds

Directions:

1. Heat up your air fryer at 350 degrees F, then add the oil and heat it up.
2. Add the cauliflower, garlic, and lime juice; toss and then cook for 20 minutes.
3. Divide between plates, sprinkle the sesame seeds on top, and serve as a side dish.

Nutrition information:calories 182, fat 4, fiber 3, carbs 11, protein 4

396. Simple Rosemary Potatoes

Preparation time: 10 minutes

Cooking time: 30 minutes

Servings: 4

Ingredients:

- 4 potatoes, thinly sliced
- Salt and black pepper to taste
- 1 tablespoon olive oil
- 2 teaspoons rosemary, chopped

Directions:

1. Place all the ingredients in a bowl, mix well, and then transfer to your air fryer's basket.
2. Cook at 370 degrees F for 30 minutes.
3. Divide between plates and serve as a side dish.

Nutrition information:calories 190, fat 4, fiber 4, carbs 14, protein 4

397. Parsnips and Carrots Fries

Preparation time: 5 minutes

Cooking time: 15 minutes

Servings: 4

Ingredients:

- 4 parsnips, cut into medium sticks
- 4 carrots, cut into medium sticks
- Salt and black pepper to taste
- 2 tablespoons thyme, chopped
- 2 tablespoons olive oil
- ½ teaspoon onion powder

Directions:

1. In a bowl, mix all ingredients and toss.
2. Transfer the fries to your air fryer's basket and cook at 350 degrees F for 15 minutes.
3. Divide between plates and serve as a side dish.

Nutrition information:calories 160, fat 3, fiber 4, carbs 7, protein 3

398. Easy Mushroom Mix

Preparation time: 5 minutes

Cooking time: 15 minutes

Servings: 6

Ingredients:

- 15 ounces mushrooms, roughly sliced
- 1 red onion, chopped
- Salt and black pepper to taste
- ½ teaspoon nutmeg, ground
- 2 tablespoons olive oil
- 6 ounces canned tomatoes, chopped

Directions:

1. Place all ingredients in a pan that fits your air fryer and mix well.
2. Put the pan in the fryer and cook at 380 degrees F for 15 minutes.
3. Divide the mix between plates and serve as a side dish.

Nutrition information:calories 202, fat 6, fiber 1, carbs 16, protein 4

399. Yellow Squash and Zucchini Mix

Preparation time: 10 minutes

Cooking time: 35 minutes

Servings: 4

Ingredients:

- 5 teaspoons olive oil
- 1 pound zucchinis, sliced
- 1 yellow squash, halved, deseeded, and cut in chunks
- Salt and white pepper to taste

- 1 tablespoon cilantro, chopped

Directions:

1. In a bowl, mix all the ingredients, toss well, and transfer them to your air fryer's basket.
2. Cook for 35 minutes at 400 degrees.
3. Divide everything between plates and serve as a side dish.

Nutrition information:calories 200, fat 4, fiber 1, carbs 15, protein 4

400. Cheesy Mushroom Salad

Preparation time: 5 minutes

Cooking time: 15 minutes

Servings: 3

Ingredients:

- 10 large mushrooms, halved
- 1 tablespoon mixed herbs, dried
- 1 tablespoon cheddar cheese, grated
- 1 tablespoon mozzarella cheese, grated
- A drizzle of olive oil
- 2 teaspoons parsley flakes
- Salt and black pepper to taste

Directions:

1. Use the oil to grease a pan that fits your air fryer.
2. Add all other ingredients and toss.
3. Place the pan in the fryer and cook at 380 degrees F for 15 minutes.
4. Divide between plates and serve as a side dish.

Nutrition information:calories 161, fat 7, fiber 1, carbs 12, protein 6

401. Lime Corn

Preparation time: 5 minutes

Cooking time: 15 minutes

Servings: 2

Ingredients:

- 2 ears of corn, shucked and silk removed
- Salt and black pepper to taste
- 2 teaspoons olive oil
- Juice of 2 limes
- 2 teaspoons smoked paprika

Directions:

1. In a bowl, mix the salt with the pepper, oil, lime juice, and paprika and stir well.
2. Rub the corn with this mix and put it in your air fryer's basket.
3. Cook at 400 degrees F for 15 minutes.
4. Divide between plates and serve.

Nutrition information:calories 180, fat 7, fiber 2, carbs 12, protein 6

402. Garlic Potatoes

Preparation time: 5 minutes

Cooking time: 40 minutes

Servings: 4

Ingredients:

- 4 large potatoes, pricked with a fork
- Salt and black pepper to taste

- 2 tablespoons olive oil
- 1 tablespoon garlic, minced

Directions:

1. Place all of the ingredients in a bowl and mix well, ensuring the potatoes are coated.
2. Put the potatoes in your air fryer's basket and cook at 400 degrees F for 40 minutes.
3. Peel the potatoes (if desired), cut up, divide between plates, and serve as a side dish.

Nutrition information:calories 173, fat 3, fiber 2, carbs 16, protein 4

403. Creamy Cabbage Mix

Preparation time: 10 minutes

Cooking time: 20 minutes

Servings: 2

Ingredients:

- 1 green cabbage head, shredded
- 1 yellow onion, chopped
- Salt and black pepper to taste
- 4 bacon slices, chopped
- 1 cup whipped cream

Directions:

1. In a pan that fits your air fryer, mix all the ingredients and stir.
2. Place the pan in the fryer and cook at 400 degrees F for 20 minutes.
3. Divide between plates and serve as a side dish.

Nutrition information:calories 208, fat 10, fiber 4, carbs 12, protein 4

404. Veggie Fries

Preparation time: 10 minutes

Cooking time: 30 minutes

Servings: 4

Ingredients:

- 4 parsnips, cut into medium sticks
- 2 sweet potatoes cut into medium sticks
- 4 mixed carrots cut into medium sticks
- Salt and black pepper to the taste
- 2 tablespoons rosemary, chopped
- 2 tablespoons olive oil
- 1 tablespoon flour
- ½ teaspoon garlic powder

Directions:

1. Put veggie fries in a bowl, add oil, garlic powder, salt, pepper, flour and rosemary and toss to coat.
2. Put sweet potatoes in your preheated air fryer, cook them for 10 minutes at 350 degrees F and transfer them to a platter.
3. Put parsnip fries in your air fryer, cook for 5 minutes and transfer over potato fries.
4. Put carrot fries in your air fryer, cook for 15 minutes at 350 degrees F and transfer to the platter with the other fries.
5. Divide veggie fries on plates and serve them as a side dish.
6. Enjoy!

Nutrition information:calories 100, fat 0, fiber 4, carbs 7, protein 4

405. Air Fried Creamy Cabbage

Preparation time: 10 minutes

Cooking time: 20 minute

Servings: 4

Ingredients:

- 1 green cabbage head, chopped
- 1 yellow onion, chopped
- Salt and black pepper to the taste
- 4 bacon slices, chopped
- 1 cup whipped cream
- 2 tablespoons cornstarch

Directions:

1. Put cabbage, bacon and onion in your air fryer.
2. In a bowl, mix cornstarch with cream, salt and pepper, stir and add over cabbage.
3. Toss, cook at 400 degrees F for 20 minutes, divide among plates and serve as a side dish.
4. Enjoy!

Nutrition information:calories 208, fat 10, fiber 3, carbs 16, protein 5

406. Tortilla Chips

Preparation time: 10 minutes

Cooking time: 6 minutes

Servings: 4

Ingredients:

- 8 corn tortillas, cut into triangles
- Salt and black pepper to the taste
- 1 tablespoon olive oil
- A pinch of garlic powder
- A pinch of sweet paprika

Directions:

1. In a bowl, mix tortilla chips with oil, add salt, pepper, garlic powder and paprika, toss well, place them in your air fryer's basket and cook them at 400 degrees F for 6 minutes.
2. Serve them as a side for a fish dish.
3. Enjoy!

Nutrition information:calories 53, fat 1, fiber 1, carbs 6, protein 4

407. Zucchini Croquettes

Preparation time: 10 minutes

Cooking time: 10 minutes

Servings: 4

Ingredients:

- 1 carrot, grated
- 1 zucchini, grated
- 2 slices of bread, crumbled
- 1 egg
- Salt and black pepper to the taste
- ½ teaspoon sweet paprika
- 1 teaspoon garlic, minced
- 2 tablespoons parmesan cheese, grated
- 1 tablespoon corn flour

Directions:

1. Put zucchini in a bowl, add salt, leave aside for 10 minutes, squeeze excess water and transfer them to another bowl.
2. Add carrots, salt, pepper, paprika,

garlic, flour, parmesan, egg and bread crumbs, stir well, shape 8 croquettes, place them in your air fryer and cook at 360 degrees F for 10 minutes.
3. Divide among plates and serve as a side dish
4. Enjoy!

Nutrition information:calories 100, fat 3, fiber 1, carbs 7, protein 4

408. Creamy Potatoes

Preparation time: 10 minutes

Cooking time: 20 minutes

Servings: 4

Ingredients:

- 1 an ½ pounds potatoes, peeled and cubed
- 2 tablespoons olive oil
- Salt and black pepper to the taste
- 1 tablespoon hot paprika
- 1 cup Greek yogurt

Directions:

1. Put potatoes in a bowl, add water to cover, leave aside for 10 minutes, drain, pat dry them, transfer to another bowl, add salt, pepper, paprika and half of the oil and toss them well.
2. Put potatoes in your air fryer's basket and cook at 360 degrees F for 20 minutes.
3. In a bowl, mix yogurt with salt, pepper and the rest of the oil and whisk.
4. Divide potatoes on plates, drizzle yogurt dressing all over, toss them and serve as a side dish.
5. Enjoy!

Nutrition information:calories 170, fat 3, fiber 5, carbs 20, protein 5

409. Mushroom Cakes

Preparation time: 10 minutes

Cooking time: 8 minutes

Servings: 8

Ingredients:

- 4 ounces mushrooms, chopped
- 1 yellow onion, chopped
- Salt and black pepper to the taste
- ½ teaspoon nutmeg, ground
- 2 tablespoons olive oil
- 1 tablespoon butter
- 1 and ½ tablespoon flour
- 1 tablespoon bread crumbs
- 14 ounces milk

Directions:

1. Heat up a pan with the butter over medium high heat, add onion and mushrooms, stir, cook for 3 minutes, add flour, stir well again and take off heat.
2. Add milk gradually, salt, pepper and nutmeg, stir and leave aside to cool down completely.
3. In a bowl, mix oil with bread crumbs and whisk.
4. Take spoonfuls of the mushroom filling, add to breadcrumbs mix, coat well, shape patties out of this mix, place them in your air fryer's basket and cook at 400 degrees F for 8 minutes.
5. Divide among plates and serve as a

side for a steak

6. Enjoy!

Nutrition information:calories 192, fat 2, fiber 1, carbs 16, protein 6

410. Creamy Roasted Peppers Side Dish

Preparation time: 10 minutes

Cooking time: 10 minutes

Servings: 4

Ingredients:

- 1 tablespoon lemon juice
- 1 red bell pepper
- 1 green bell pepper
- 1 yellow bell pepper
- 1 lettuce head, cut into strips
- 1 ounce rocket leaves
- Salt and black pepper to the taste
- 3 tablespoons Greek yogurt
- 2 tablespoons olive oil

Directions:

1. Place bell peppers in your air fryer's basket, cook at 400 degrees F for 10 minutes, transfer to a bowl, leave aside for 10 minutes, peel them, discard seeds, cut them in strips, transfer to a larger bowl, add rocket leaves and lettuce strips and toss.
2. In a bowl, mix oil with lemon juice, yogurt, salt and pepper and whisk well.
3. Add this over bell peppers mix, toss to coat, divide among plates and serve as a side salad.
4. Enjoy!

Nutrition information:calories 170, fat 1, fiber 1, carbs 2, protein 6

411. Greek Veggie Side Dish

Preparation time: 10 minutes

Cooking time: 45 minutes

Servings: 4

Ingredients:

- 1 eggplant, sliced
- 1 zucchini, sliced
- 2 red bell peppers, chopped
- 2 garlic cloves, minced
- 3 tablespoons olive oil
- 1 bay leaf
- 1 thyme spring, chopped
- 2 onions, chopped
- 4 tomatoes, cut into quarters
- Salt and black pepper to the taste

Directions:

1. In your air fryer's pan, mix eggplant slices with zucchini ones, bell peppers, garlic, oil, bay leaf, thyme, onions, tomatoes, salt and pepper, toss and cook them at 300 degrees F for 35 minutes.
2. Divide among plates and serve as a side dish.
3. Enjoy!

Nutrition information:calories 200, fat 1, fiber 3, carbs 7, protein 6

412. Yellow Squash and Zucchinis Side Dish

Preparation time: 10 minutes

Cooking time: 35 minutes

Servings: 4

Ingredients:

- 6 teaspoons olive oil
- 1 pound zucchinis, sliced
- ½ pound carrots, cubed
- 1 yellow squash, halved, deseeded and cut into chunks
- Salt and white pepper to the taste
- 1 tablespoon tarragon, chopped

Directions:

1. In your air fryer's basket, mix zucchinis with carrots, squash, salt, pepper and oil, toss well and cook at 400 degrees F for 25 minutes.
2. Divide them on plates and serve as a side dish with tarragon sprinkled on top.
3. Enjoy!

Nutrition information:calories 160, fat 2, fiber 1, carbs 5, protein 5

413. Flavored Cauliflower Side Dish

Preparation time: 10 minutes

Cooking time: 10 minutes

Servings: 4

Ingredients:

- 12 cauliflower florets, steamed
- Salt and black pepper to the taste
- ¼ teaspoon turmeric powder
- 1 and ½ teaspoon red chili powder
- 1 tablespoon ginger, grated
- 2 teaspoons lemon juice
- 3 tablespoons white flour
- 2 tablespoons water
- Cooking spray
- ½ teaspoon corn flour

Directions:

1. In a bowl, mix chili powder with turmeric powder, ginger paste, salt, pepper, lemon juice, white flour, corn flour and water, stir, add cauliflower, toss well and transfer them to your air fryer's basket.
2. Coat them with cooking spray, cook them at 400 degrees F for 10 minutes, divide among plates and serve as a side dish.
3. Enjoy!

Nutrition information:calories 70, fat 1, fiber 2, carbs 12, protein 3

414. Coconut Cream Potatoes

Preparation time: 10 minutes

Cooking time: 20 minutes

Servings: 4

Ingredients:

- 2 eggs, whisked
- Salt and black pepper to the taste
- 1 tablespoon cheddar cheese, grated
- 1 tablespoon flour
- 2 potatoes, sliced
- 4 ounces coconut cream

Directions:

1. Place potato slices in your air fryer's basket and cook at 360 degrees F for

10 minutes.

2. Meanwhile, in a bowl, mix eggs with coconut cream, salt, pepper and flour.
3. Arrange potatoes in your air fryer's pan, add coconut cream mix over them, sprinkle cheese, return to air fryer's basket and cook at 400 degrees F for 10 minutes more.
4. Divide among plates and serve as a side dish.
5. Enjoy!

Nutrition information:calories 170, fat 4, fiber 1, carbs 15, protein 17

415. Cajun Onion Wedges

Preparation time: 10 minutes

Cooking time: 15 minutes

Servings: 4

Ingredients:

- 2 big white onions, cut into wedges
- Salt and black pepper to the taste
- 2 eggs
- ¼ cup milk
- 1/3 cup panko
- A drizzle of olive oil
- 1 and ½ teaspoon paprika
- 1 teaspoon garlic powder
- ½ teaspoon Cajun seasoning

Directions:

1. In a bowl, mix panko with Cajun seasoning and oil and stir.
2. In another bowl, mix egg with milk, salt and pepper and stir.
3. Sprinkle onion wedges with paprika and garlic powder, dip them in egg mix, then in bread crumbs mix, place in your air fryer's basket, cook at 360 degrees F for 10 minutes, flip and cook for 5 minutes more.
4. Divide among plates and serve as a side dish.
5. Enjoy!

Nutrition information:calories 200, fat 2, fiber 2, carbs 14, protein 7

416. Wild Rice Pilaf

Preparation time: 10 minutes

Cooking time: 25 minutes

Servings: 12

Ingredients:

- 1 shallot, chopped
- 1 teaspoon garlic, minced
- A drizzle of olive oil
- 1 cup farro
- ¾ cup wild rice
- 4 cups chicken stock
- Salt and black pepper to the taste
- 1 tablespoon parsley, chopped
- ½ cup hazelnuts, toasted and chopped
- ¾ cup cherries, dried
- Chopped chives for serving

Directions:

1. In a dish that fits your air fryer, mix shallot with garlic, oil, faro, wild rice, stock, salt, pepper, parsley, hazelnuts and cherries, stir, place in your air fryer's basket and cook at 350 degrees F for 25 minutes.
2. Divide among plates and serve as a

side dish.

3. Enjoy!

Nutrition information:calories 142, fat 4, fiber 4, carbs 16, protein 4

417. Pumpkin Rice

Preparation time: 5 minutes

Cooking time: 30 minutes

Servings: 4

Ingredients:

- 2 tablespoons olive oil
- 1 small yellow onion, chopped
- 2 garlic cloves, minced
- 12 ounces white rice
- 4 cups chicken stock
- 6 ounces pumpkin puree
- ½ teaspoon nutmeg
- 1 teaspoon thyme, chopped
- ½ teaspoon ginger, grated
- ½ teaspoon cinnamon powder
- ½ teaspoon allspice
- 4 ounces heavy cream

Directions:

1. In a dish that fits your air fryer, mix oil with onion, garlic, rice, stock, pumpkin puree, nutmeg, thyme, ginger, cinnamon, allspice and cream, stir well, place in your air fryer's basket and cook at 360 degrees F for 30 minutes.
2. Divide among plates and serve as a side dish.
3. Enjoy!

Nutrition information:calories 261, fat 6, fiber 7, carbs 29, protein 4

418. Colored Veggie Rice

Preparation time: 10 minutes

Cooking time: 25 minutes

Servings: 4

Ingredients:

- 2 cups basmati rice
- 1 cup mixed carrots, peas, corn and green beans
- 2 cups water
- ½ teaspoon green chili, minced
- ½ teaspoon ginger, grated
- 3 garlic cloves, minced
- 2 tablespoons butter
- 1 teaspoon cinnamon powder
- 1 tablespoon cumin seeds
- 2 bay leaves
- 3 whole cloves
- 5 black peppercorns
- 2 whole cardamoms
- 1 tablespoon sugar
- Salt to the taste

Directions:

1. Put the water in a heat proof dish that fits your air fryer, add rice, mixed veggies, green chili, grated ginger, garlic cloves, cinnamon, cloves, butter, cumin seeds, bay leaves, cardamoms, black peppercorns, salt and sugar, stir, put in your air fryer's basket and cook at 370 degrees F for 25 minutes.
2. Divide among plates and serve as a side dish.

3. Enjoy!

Nutrition information:calories 283, fat 4, fiber 8, carbs 34, protein 14

419. Potato Casserole

Preparation time: 15 minutes

Cooking time: 40 minutes

Servings: 4

Ingredients:

- 3 pounds sweet potatoes, scrubbed
- ¼ cup milk
- ½ teaspoon nutmeg, ground
- 2 tablespoons white flour
- ¼ teaspoon allspice, ground
- Salt to the taste
- For the topping:
- ½ cup almond flour
- ½ cup walnuts, soaked, drained and ground
- ¼ cup pecans, soaked, drained and ground
- ¼ cup coconut, shredded
- 1 tablespoon chia seeds
- ¼ cup sugar
- 1 teaspoon cinnamon powder
- 5 tablespoons butter

Directions:

1. Place potatoes in your air fryer's basket, prick them with a fork and cook at 360 degrees F for 30 minutes.
2. Meanwhile, in a bowl, mix almond flour with pecans, walnuts, ¼ cup coconut, ¼ cup sugar, chia seeds, 1 teaspoon cinnamon and the butter and stir everything.
3. Transfer potatoes to a cutting board, cool them, peel and place them in a baking dish that fits your air fryer.
4. Add milk, flour, salt, nutmeg and allspice and stir
5. Add crumble mix you've made earlier on top, place dish in your air fryer's basket and cook at 400 degrees F for 8 minutes.
6. Divide among plates and serve as a side dish.
7. Enjoy!

Nutrition information:calories 162, fat 4, fiber 8, carbs 18, protein 4

420. Lemony Artichokes

Preparation time: 10 minutes

Cooking time: 15 minutes

Servings: 4

Ingredients:

- 2 medium artichokes, trimmed and halved
- Cooking spray
- 2 tablespoons lemon juice
- Salt and black pepper to the taste

Directions:

1. Grease your air fryer with cooking spray, add artichokes, drizzle lemon juice and sprinkle salt and black pepper and cook them at 380 degrees F for 15 minutes.
2. Divide them on plates and serve as a side dish.
3. Enjoy!

Nutrition information:calories 121, fat 3, fiber 6, carbs 9, protein 4

421. Cauliflower and Broccoli Delight

Preparation time: 10 minutes

Cooking time: 7 minutes

Servings: 4

Ingredients:

- 2 cauliflower heads, florets separated and steamed
- 1 broccoli head, florets separated and steamed
- Zest from 1 orange, grated
- Juice from 1 orange
- A pinch of hot pepper flakes
- 4 anchovies
- 1 tablespoon capers, chopped
- Salt and black pepper to the taste
- 4 tablespoons olive oil

Directions:

1. In a bowl, mix orange zest with orange juice, pepper flakes, anchovies, capers salt, pepper and olive oil and whisk well.
2. Add broccoli and cauliflower, toss well, transfer them to your air fryer's basket and cook at 400 degrees F for 7 minutes.
3. Divide among plates and serve as a side dish with some of the orange vinaigrette drizzled on top.
4. Enjoy!

Nutrition information:calories 300, fat 4, fiber 7, carbs 28, protein 4

422. Garlic Beet Wedges

Preparation time: 10 minutes

Cooking time: 15 minutes

Servings: 4

Ingredients:

- 4 beets, washed, peeled and cut into large wedges
- 1 tablespoon olive oil
- Salt and black to the taste
- 2 garlic cloves, minced
- 1 teaspoon lemon juice

Directions:

1. In a bowl, mix beets with oil, salt, pepper, garlic and lemon juice, toss well, transfer to your air fryer's basket and cook them at 400 degrees F for 15 minutes.
2. Divide beets wedges on plates and serve as a side dish.
3. Enjoy!

Nutrition information:calories 182, fat 6, fiber 3, carbs 8, protein 2

423. Fried Red Cabbage

Preparation time: 10 minutes

Cooking time: 15 minutes

Servings: 4

Ingredients:

- 4 garlic cloves, minced
- ½ cup yellow onion, chopped
- 1 tablespoon olive oil
- 6 cups red cabbage, chopped
- 1 cup veggie stock
- 1 tablespoon apple cider vinegar
- 1 cup applesauce

- Salt and black pepper to the taste

Directions:

1. In a heat proof dish that fits your air fryer, mix cabbage with onion, garlic, oil, stock, vinegar, applesauce, salt and pepper, toss really well, place dish in your air fryer's basket and cook at 380 degrees F for 15 minutes.
2. Divide among plates and serve as a side dish.
3. Enjoy!

Nutrition information:calories 172, fat 7, fiber 7, carbs 14, protein 5

424. Artichokes and Tarragon Sauce

Preparation time: 10 minutes

Cooking time: 18 minutes

Servings: 4

Ingredients:

- 4 artichokes, trimmed
- 2 tablespoons tarragon, chopped
- 2 tablespoons chicken stock
- Lemon zest from 2 lemons, grated
- 2 tablespoons lemon juice
- 1 celery stalk, chopped
- ½ cup olive oil
- Salt to the taste

Directions:

1. In your food processor, mix tarragon, chicken stock, lemon zest, lemon juice, celery, salt and olive oil and pulse very well.
2. In a bowl, mix artichokes with tarragon and lemon sauce, toss well, transfer them to your air fryer's basket and cook at 380 degrees F for 18 minutes.
3. Divide artichokes on plates, drizzle the rest of the sauce all over and serve as a side dish.
4. Enjoy!

Nutrition information:calories 215, fat 3, fiber 8, carbs 28, protein 6

425. Brussels Sprouts and Pomegranate Seeds Side Dish

Preparation time: 5 minutes

Cooking time: 10 minutes

Servings: 4

Ingredients:

- 1 pound Brussels sprouts, trimmed and halved
- Salt and black pepper to the taste
- 1 cup pomegranate seeds
- ¼ cup pine nuts, toasted
- 1 tablespoons olive oil
- 2 tablespoons veggie stock

Directions:

1. In a heat proof dish that fits your air fryer, mix Brussels sprouts with salt, pepper, pomegranate seeds, pine nuts, oil and stock, stir, place in your air fryer's basket and cook at 390 degrees F for 10 minutes.
2. Divide among plates and serve as a side dish.
3. Enjoy!

Nutrition information: calories 152, fat 4, fiber 7, carbs 12, protein 3

426. Crispy Brussels Sprouts and Potatoes

Preparation time: 10 minutes

Cooking time: 8 minutes

Servings: 4

Ingredients:

- 1 and ½ pounds Brussels sprouts, washed and trimmed
- 1 cup new potatoes, chopped
- 1 and ½ tablespoons bread crumbs
- Salt and black pepper to the taste
- 1 and ½ tablespoons butter

Directions:

1. Put Brussels sprouts and potatoes in your air fryer's pan, add bread crumbs, salt, pepper and butter, toss well and cook at 400 degrees F for 8 minutes.
2. Divide among plates and serve as a side dish.
3. Enjoy!

Nutrition information: calories 152, fat 3, fiber 7, carbs 17, protein 4

427. Tomato Vegetable Curry

Preparation Time:25 minutes

Servings: 4

Ingredients:

- 1 teaspoon oregano
- 1 tablespoon basil leaves, chopped
- 1 tablespoon cilantro leaves, chopped
- 2 teaspoons curry powder
- 2 cloves garlic, minced
- 1 large onion, diced
- ¼ cup chickpeas
- ½ cup water
- ½ cup coconut milk
- ¼ cup potatoes, diced
- ½ cup tomatoes, chopped

Directions:

1. Cut washed veggies into small cubes. Chop the herbs into small pieces and save for later use. Soak and rinse chickpeas with water. Drain and set aside. Add ½ cup coconut milk and ½ cup water to your air-fryer. Add the garlic, onions and cubed vegetables. Season with curry powder, pepper, and oregano. Cook for 20-minutes. Add the basil and cilantro leaves. Cook for another 5-minutes until the soup thickens. Serve warm with Jasmine rice.

Nutrition Information: Calories: 53,Total Fat: 0.82g, Carbs: 9.7g, Protein: 1.9g

428. Crispy Air-Fried Gourd

Preparation Time:15 minutes

Servings: 6

Ingredients:

- 2 medium size bitter gourd (sliced)
- 1 tablespoon rice vinegar
- 1 teaspoon salt
- 1 teaspoon turmeric powder
- 1 teaspoon sugar-free maple syrup
- 2 teaspoons liquid stevia
- 2 tablespoons cornstarch
- 2 teaspoons of coconut oil cooking spray

Directions:

1. Remove the pit from a bitter gourd, cut in half length-wise. Place the sliced bitter gourd into a mixing bowl. Add stevia, maple syrup, rice vinegar, turmeric powder to the bowl. Season with salt and stir with wooden spoon. Let the bitter gourd soak in the mixture for about an hour before cooking. In another bowl, add cornstarch. Coat the marinated bitter gourd with cornstarch and set aside. Preheat your air-fryer to 380°Fahrenheit for 2-minutes. Place the bitter gourd into the air-fryer basket and spray it with coconut oil spray. Cook for 15-minutes or until crispy, shake the basket every 5-minutes during cook time.

Nutrition Information: Calories: 34, Total Fat: 0.2g, Carbs: 7g, Protein: 3.6g

429. Air-Fried Vegan Noodles

Preparation Time:11 minutes

Servings: 4

Ingredients:

- 1 large green bell pepper
- 4 cups of rice noodles
- 1 large red bell pepper
- 1 tablespoon white sesame seeds
- 2 teaspoons sesame oil
- 1 tablespoon basil leaves, minced
- 2 teaspoons rice vinegar
- 1 teaspoon vegan oyster sauce
- 1 teaspoon pepper
- 2 teaspoons ketchup
- ½ teaspoon chili powder

Directions:

1. Allow noodles to soak in a pot of hot water for 3-minutes and then allow them to dry. Preheat your air-fryer to 400°Fahrenheit for 2-minutes. Place noodles into the air-fryer basket and drizzle them with sesame oil, toss to coat. Cook noodles for 8-minutes, toss after 4-minutes of cooking. Once noodles are cooked transfer them to a bowl and set aside. Cut bell peppers into strips, mince spring onions and basil leaves. Place veggies in a mixing bowl. Add soy sauce, vegan oyster sauce, rice vinegar, and ketchup. Add cooked noodles into bowl with veggies and toss to combine. Sprinkle with pepper and chili powder and garnish with sesame seeds. Serve warm.

Nutrition Information: Calories: 235, Total Fat: 10.9, Carbs: 34.7g, Protein: 13.9g

430. Sweet & Spicy Tofu with Steamed Spinach

Preparation Time:24 minutes

Servings: 6

Ingredients:

- 6 cups of spinach, chopped
- 2 teaspoons rice vinegar
- 1 teaspoon agave syrup
- 1 teaspoon salt
- 2-inches ginger, minced
- 1 teaspoon sesame oil
- 1 tablespoon vegan oyster sauce
- 1 teaspoon red pepper flakes
- 1 lb. tofu cubed

Directions:

1. Rinse and drain the tofu. Make sure to press the tofu to remove excess water. Cut tofu into small cubes and place them in a mixing bowl. Add minced ginger to bowl with tofu. Add agave syrup, season with salt, red pepper flakes and stir. Let mixture stand for 30-minutes before frying.
2. Prepare spinach by steaming for 4-minutes, then transfer spinach to bowl. Add vegan oyster sauce and rice vinegar and toss and save for later use. Preheat air-fryer to 370°Fahrenheit. Add the marinated tofu and spray with a teaspoon of sesame oil. Cook for 20-minutes and shake the air-fryer basket every 5-minutes during cook time. Once cooked, transfer the tofu to bowl with steamed spinach mix. Toss all ingredients and serve warm.

Nutrition Information: Calories: 169, Total Fat: 10.8g, Carbs: 6.8g, Protein: 15.2g

431. Air-Fried Walnuts & Green Beans

Preparation Time:20 minutes

Servings: 5

Ingredients:

- ½ teaspoon chili powder
- 4 cups green beans, cut into 3-inch long pieces
- ¼ cup walnuts, roasted
- 4 garlic cloves, chopped
- 1 tablespoon light soy sauce
- 1 teaspoon sugar-free maple syrup
- 1 teaspoon sesame oil
- Salt and pepper to taste

Directions:

1. After washing and chopping vegetable place into a bowl. Prepare by using a mortar and pestle, pound walnuts lightly and then transfer to a bowl of vegetables. Add remaining ingredients to a bowl, except sesame oil. Preheat your air-fryer to 390°Fahrenheit. Add marinated beans and walnuts to air-fryer and spray them with sesame oil. Cook for 20-minutes and shake the basket a couple of times during the cook time. Serve warm.

Nutrition Information: Calories: 155, Total Fat: 12.41g, Carbs: 9.18g, Protein: 4.68g

432. Air-Fried Avocado & Yellow Pepper Salad

Preparation Time:10 minutes

Servings: 6

Ingredients:

- 2 tablespoons potato starch
- 3 large avocados, diced
- ½ cup sweet corn kernels
- 6 lettuce leaves
- 3 large tomatoes, cut into wedges
- 3 yellow pepper, seeded and sliced into small pieces
- 2 teaspoons lemon zest
- 2 tablespoons basil leaves, chopped
- Salt and pepper to taste
- 1 tablespoon vinegar

- 2 tablespoons flaxseed mixed with 3 tablespoons water
- 1 tablespoon olive oil

Directions:

2. Cut avocado in half and remove seed. Scoop the avocado flesh and cut into cubes. Chop tomatoes, yellow peppers, and basil into small pieces and set aside. Slice yellow peppers into thin slices. In blender ad flax seed and water and blend until fluffy. Transfer to a bowl and mix with potato starch. Season with salt and pepper. Mix all the ingredients and coat cubed avocado. In another mixing bowl, combine lettuce leaves with sweet corn kernels, and chopped tomatoes, yellow peppers, and basil leaves. Add vinegar and lemon zest. Whisk all ingredients and save for later.
3. Preheat your air-fryer to 390°Fahrenheit. Spray olive oil over the avocados. Place avocados into air-fryer and cook for 10-minutes. Shake basket halfway through cook time. Once cooked transfer avocados to bowl with lettuce salad and toss with two large salad spoons. Serve right away.

433. Onion Strings

Preparation Time:7 minutes

Serving: 6

Ingredients:

- 8 large onions, shredded
- 2 tablespoons cornstarch
- ½ teaspoon cayenne powder
- 1 teaspoon pepper
- 1 teaspoon apple cider vinegar
- 1 teaspoon olive oil
- 1 teaspoon baking soda

Directions:

1. Remove outer skin from onions, using a vegetable shredder, cut onions into thin strips and set aside. Add baking soda, apple cider vinegar and blend until it becomes fluffy. Transfer mixture to a bowl. Add salt and pepper. Season with cayenne pepper. Add shredded onions into a bowl and toss to combine. In another bowl, add cornstarch. Mix the marinated onions in the bowl of cornstarch, coating them well. Preheat your air-fryer to 390°Fahrenheit. Add onions to the air-fryer basket and spray with olive oil. Cook for 7-minutes, shake halfway through cook time. Once cooked, transfer to plate. Serve warm.

Nutrition Information: Calories: 22, Total Fat: 1.3g, Carbs: 5.6g, Protein: 1.2g

434. Air-Fried Banana Turmeric Chips

Preparation Time:8 minutes

Servings: 4

Ingredients:

- 1 teaspoon of sesame oil
- ½ teaspoon pepper
- 1 teaspoon turmeric
- 4 large bananas, sliced
- ½ teaspoon salt
- 2 teaspoons agave syrup

Directions:

1. In a bowl, mix agave syrup, and turmeric. Season with salt and pepper. Add sliced bananas and toss to combine. Set aside. Preheat your air-fryer to 370°Fahrenheit. Spray sesame oil over sliced bananas and place into the air-fryer basket. Cook bananas for 8-minutes, shake basket halfway through cook time. Serve warm.

Nutrition Information: Calories: 176, Total Fat: 9.9g, Carbs: 23.4g, Protein: 1.13g

435. Spicy Air-Fried Eggplant

Preparation Time:20 minutes

Servings: 4

Ingredients:

- 2 garlic cloves, minced
- 2 large eggplants, sliced
- 2 red chili peppers, chopped
- 2 green chili peppers, minced
- 1 teaspoon sesame oil
- 1 tablespoon light soy sauce
- Pepper and salt to taste

Directions:

1. Cut eggplants and set aside. Chop chilies and mince garlic and save for later use. In a bowl, mix garlic, green and red chili peppers. Add soy sauce and sprinkle with pepper, add eggplant slices, toss and set aside. Preheat your air-fryer to 350°Fahrenheit. Add eggplant slices and spray with sesame oil. Cook for 20-minutes, shake basket every 5-minutes during cook time. Once cooked garnish eggplant slices with chili peppers and garlic. Serve warm.

Nutrition Information: Calories: 223, Total Fat: 6.4g, Carbs: 11.8g, Protein: 3.2g

436. Air-Fried Carrots with Lemon

Preparation Time:18 minutes

Servings: 4

Ingredients:

- 2 cups carrots (julienned)
- 1 tablespoon parsley, chopped
- 1 teaspoon paprika
- 2 teaspoon lemon juice
- ½ teaspoon pepper
- 1 teaspoon salt
- 2 teaspoons olive oil
- 1 tablespoon lemon zest

Directions:

2. In a bowl, combine lemon zest, lemon juice, paprika, salt, pepper, olive oil, carrots, and toss. Combine ingredients and allow to stand for 30-minutes before air-frying.
3. Preheat air-fryer to 390°Fahrenheit. Add carrots to the air-fryer basket and cook for 18-minutes. Give the basket a shake a couple of times during the cook time. Serve warm.

Nutrition Information: Calories: 201, Total Fat: 11.48g, Carbs: 25.3g, Protein: 1.08

437. Air-Fried Radish Cake

Preparation Time:15 minutes

Servings: 4

Ingredients:

- 2 cups radish, cut into big strips
- ¼ cup potato flour
- 1 tablespoon Sriracha sauce
- 1 teaspoon black pepper
- ½ teaspoon salt
- 1 teaspoon olive oil
- 1 tablespoon flax seed combined with 3 tablespoons water

Directions:

1. In a blender add the flax seed and water and blend until smooth. In a mixing bowl, add Sriracha sauce, salt, and pepper. Stir, add strips of radish. Add flax seed mix to the bowl and mix well. Add the potato flour to another bowl. Coat the radish sticks with flour and set aside.
2. Preheat your air-fryer to 350°Fahrenheit. Add coated radish to air-fryer and spray with olive oil. Cook for 15-minutes, shake a couple of times during cook time. Serve warm.

Nutrition Information: Calories: 78, Total Fat: 6.07g, Carbs: 7.14g, Protein: 1.3g

438. Air-Fried Roasted Potatoes with Rosemary

Preparation Time:30 minutes

Servings: 4

Ingredients:

- 2 cups potatoes, diced
- 2 teaspoons rosemary, dried
- 1 teaspoon sesame oil
- 1 teaspoon black pepper

Directions:

1. Preheat your air-fryer to 370°Fahrenheit. Add potatoes and spray them with sesame oil. Heat for 30-minutes and shake air-fryer basket a couple of times during cook time. Garnish with rosemary and serve warm.

Nutrition Information: Calories: 203, Total Fat: 9.53g, Carbs: 27.28g, Protein: 3.11g

439. Potato Fries with Bean Sprouts & Peanut Herb Salad

Preparation Time:20 minutes

Servings: 4

Ingredients:

- 2 cups potato (cut into strips)
- ¾ cup bean sprouts
- 2 tablespoons parsley leaves, chopped
- 2 tablespoons basil leaves, chopped
- 1 teaspoon, pepper
- 1 teaspoon salt
- 1 tablespoon Sriracha sauce
- ½ cup roasted peanuts
- 1 tablespoon rice vinegar
- 2 teaspoons olive oil

Directions:

1. Preheat your air-fryer to 390°Fahrenheit and then place

potato fries into the air-fryer basket. Spray a teaspoon of olive oil and season with salt. Cook for 15-minutes and shake basket a few times during cook time. After potato fries are cooked, save them for later use.

2. Prepare half a cup of peanuts. Preheat your air-fryer to 400°Fahrenheit and put half a cup of peanuts in the basket. Spray a teaspoon of olive oil and cook for 5-minutes. Once roasted, set aside.
3. Now, get a large mixing bowl, combine bean sprouts, chopped parsley, basil leaves in a bowl. Add the potato fries and roasted into a bowl. Season with Sriracha sauce and rice vinegar. Sprinkle with pepper. Toss and serve right away.

Nutrition Information: Calories: 163, Total Fat: 0.7g, Carbs: 34.2g, Protein: 5.03g

440. Tuna with Roast Yams

Preparation Time:30 minutes

Servings: 2

Ingredients:

- 2 large yams
- 1 green onion, finely sliced into rings
- 1 can tuna, in oil, drained
- 2 tablespoons Greek plain yogurt
- ½ tablespoon olive oil
- 1 teaspoon chili powder
- 1 tablespoon capers
- 2 tablespoons red onion diced for garnish

Directions:

1. Preheat your air-fryer to 300°Fahrenheit and brush the yams with olive oil and place them into the air-fryer basket. Cook yams for 20-minutes. Finely mash the tuna in a bowl, add yogurt, chili powder, and half of the green onions. Add salt and pepper to taste.
2. Place the yams on plates and cut them lengthwise. Place the fish blend onto the open yams. Sprinkle filling with capers and leftover green onion. Serve topped with diced red onion and with a crisp salad of your choice.

Nutrition Information: Calories: 214, Total Fat: 3.2g, Carbs: 36.4g, Protein: 3.4

441. Air-Fried Ratatouille

Preparation Time:15 minutes

Servings: 4

Ingredients:

- 1 onion, peeled, cubed
- 1 clove garlic, crushed
- 1 tablespoon olive oil
- 2 tomatoes, chopped
- Fresh ground pepper
- 2 teaspoons Provencal herbs
- 1 large zucchini, sliced
- 1 yellow bell pepper, chopped

Directions:

1. Preheat your air-fryer to 300°Fahrenheit. In an oven-proof bowl, add vegetables, salt, pepper and olive oil and mix well. Put the bowl in the basket in air fryer. Cook for 15-minutes, stirring halfway through cook time. Serve with

fricasseed meat.

Nutritional Values per serving:Calories: 154, Total Fat: 12.05g, Carbs: 11.94g, Protein: 1.69g

442. Toad in the Hole

Preparation Time:30 minutes
Servings: 4

Ingredients:

- 1 cup milk
- ½ cup cold water
- 1 tablespoon basil, fresh sprigs
- 1 red onion, finely sliced
- 1 ½ cups almond flour
- 8 small sausages
- 1 tablespoon olive oil
- 1 clove of garlic, pressed

Directions:

1. Use an ovenproof dish that fits in your air-fryer and coat with oil. Sift the flour in a medium-sized bowl and beat the eggs into it. Gradually include the milk, water, the hacked onion and garlic and season to taste with salt and pepper. Combine everything. Pierce and stick the sprigs of basil into sausages and place into a dish. Pour the batter over sausages. Preheat your air-fryer to 300°Fahrenheit and cook for 30-minutes.

443. Glass Noodle & Tiger Shrimp Salad

Preparation Time:8 minutes
Servings: 4

Ingredients:

- 12 tiger shrimps, butterflied
- Zest of one lemon
- Zest of one lime
- ¼ cup olive oil
- 2 tablespoons mixed spice
- 2 tablespoons olive oil
- A handful of basil, fried for garnish

For the salad:

- 4 baby yellow bell peppers, sliced
- 4 baby red bell peppers, sliced
- 2 scallions, bias cut
- 2 cups green papaya, peeled, seeded, julienned
- ½ cup mint leaves
- ½ cup cilantro leaves
- 16-ounces of glass noodles, cooked and chilled
- 1 English cucumber, peeled, seeded, sliced
- 1 carrot, peeled and julienned
- 2 tablespoons basil leaves, julienned

For dressing:

- 4-ounces of honey
- 2 cups grapeseed oil
- 1 cup soy sauce
- 4-ounces ginger, peeled and grated
- 1 bunch scallions, sliced
- 2 tablespoons of sweet chili sauce

Directions:

1. Preheat your air-fryer to 390°Fahrenheit for 10-minutes. Mix

olive oil and mixed spice and brush mixture over shrimp. Sprinkle the lemon and lime juice over the shrimps. Season with salt and pepper. Place the shrimp in the basket and cook for 4-minutes. Chill shrimps on a plate and repeat cooking process with remaining shrimp. Whisk lemon juice, soy sauce, honey, ginger, scallion and sweet chili sauce in a bowl. Whisk in oil. Add mixture to blend and mix to get a puree consistency. Season to taste. In a bowl, toss mixed greens and salad dressing mix, along with noodles, then divide it between serving plates. Top each plate of salad with 3 shrimps. Garnish with cilantro and basil.

Nutrition Information: Calories: 258, Total Fat: 15.89g, Carbs: 4.41g, Protein: 23.59g

444. Air-Fried Fingerling Potatoes

Preparation Time:30 minutes

Servings: 4

Ingredients:

- 2 lbs. Fingerling potatoes, peeled, cubed
- 2 tablespoons chives, minced
- 2 tablespoons parsley leaves, minced
- 2 garlic cloves, smashed
- 2 tablespoons butter, melted
- 1 shallot, quartered

Directions:

1. Add cubed potatoes to an oven-proof dish. Brush potatoes with melted butter. Sprinkle with cubed potatoes the rest of ingredients. Set your air-fryer for 320°Fahrenheit and cook for 30-minutes. Stir a few times during cook time. Serve warm.

Nutrition Information: Calories: 213, Total Fat: 5.2g, Carbs: 32.1g, Protein: 4.68g

445. Parmesan Chicken Meatballs

Preparation Time:10 minutes

Servings: 4

Ingredients:

- ½ cup whole-wheat breadcrumbs
- Pepper and salt to taste
- ½ lime, zested
- 1/3 cup parmesan cheese, grated
- ½ teaspoon paprika
- 1 teaspoon basil, dried
- 3 garlic cloves, minced
- ½ lb. ground chicken
- 1/3 teaspoon mustard seeds
- 1 ½ tablespoons melted butter
- 2 eggs, beaten

Directions:

1. In a non-stick skillet that is preheated over medium heat, place ground chicken, garlic and cook until chicken is no longer pink, about 5-minutes.
2. Throw the remaining ingredients into skillet. Remove from heat. Allow to cool down and roll into balls. Roll each ball into beaten eggs, then roll them in breadcrumbs and transfer

them into the air-fryer basket. Cook for 8-minutes at 385°Fahrenheit.

Nutrition Information: Calories: 52, Total Fat: 2.46g, Carbs: 2.94g, Protein: 7.8g

446. Meatballs with Mediterranean Dipping Sauce

Preparation Time:15 minutes

Servings: 4

Ingredients:

For the meatballs:

- 1 ½ tablespoons melted butter
- 2 eggs
- ½ tablespoon red pepper flakes, crushed
- 2 tablespoons fresh mint leaves, finely chopped
- 4 garlic cloves, finely minced
- ½ lb. ground pork
- 2 tablespoons capers

For the Mediterranean dipping sauce:

- 1/3 cup black olives, pitted, chopped finely
- 2 tablespoons fresh rosemary
- ½ teaspoon dill, dried
- 1/3 cup Greek yogurt
- ½ teaspoon lemon zest
- 2 tablespoons parsley

Directions:

1. Start the preheating of your air-fryer at 395°Fahrenheit. In a large bowl, add meatball ingredients and combine well. Shape into golf ball size balls. Cook the meatballs for about 9-minutes. Meanwhile, prepare your dipping sauce, by whisking all the ingredients. Serve meatballs warm with Mediterranean sauce.

Nutrition Information: Calories: 52, Total Fat: 2.32g, Carbs: 3.04g, Protein: 7.45g

447. Mayo-Cheddar Jacket Potatoes

Preparation Time:10 minutes

Servings: 8

Ingredients:

- 1/3 cup cheddar cheese, grated
- 3 tablespoons mayonnaise
- Sea salt, ground black pepper and cayenne pepper to taste
- 2 tablespoons chives, chopped
- 1 ½ tablespoons olive oil
- 8 Russet potatoes
- ½ cup soft cheese, softened

Directions:

1. Stab potatoes with a fork. Preheat your air-fryer to 360°Fahrenheit. Bake the potatoes for 10-minutes in the air-fryer basket. Meanwhile, prepare your filling by mixing the rest of the above ingredients. Stuff potatoes with the prepared filling. Serve immediately!

Nutrition Information: Calories: 327, Total Fat: 7g, Carbs: 59g, Protein: 9.4g

448. Pork & Brie Meatballs

Preparation Time:17 minutes

Servings: 8

Ingredients:

- 1 teaspoon cayenne pepper
- 2 teaspoons mustard
- Sea salt and black pepper to taste
- 1 ½ lbs. ground pork
- 2 small yellow onions, chopped
- 5 garlic cloves, minced
- 2 tablespoons Brie cheese, grated

Directions:

1. Mix all the above ingredients until all is well combined. Form into golf ball size balls. Cook at 375°Fahrenheit for 17-minutes.

Nutrition information:Calories: 275, Total Fat: 18.6g, Carbs: 2.7g, Protein: 22.9g

449. Potato Chips & Tangy Dipping Sauce

Preparation Time:18 minutes

Servings: 6

Ingredients:

- 1/3 teaspoon marjoram, dried
- 2 tablespoons garlic paste
- 1/3 cup sour cream
- 5 Russet potatoes, cut into fries
- 2 ½ tablespoons olive oil
- 1 teaspoon seasoned salt
- 1 ½ tablespoons mayonnaise
- 1/3 teaspoon red pepper flakes, crushed

Directions:

1. Soak the potatoes in water for 35-minutes; change the water a few times to remove the starch. Preheat your air-fryer to 325°Fahrenheit and cook fries for 18-minutes. Meanwhile, combine remaining ingredients to make a dipping sauce and enjoy it on the side!

Nutrition Information: Calories: 326, Total Fat: 8.4g, Carbs: 57.5g, Protein: 7.5g

450. Beef Meatballs in Blueberry Chipotle Sauce

Preparation Time:20 minutes

Servings: 4

Ingredients:

- 2 tablespoons Dijon mustard
- Salt and black pepper to taste
- 1 tablespoon herb vinegar
- ½ teaspoon cumin
- 1 teaspoon liquid stevia
- 1 ½ teaspoons garlic, minced
- ½ lb. ground beef
- 1/3 cup blueberry chipotle ketchup
- 2 tablespoons scallions, minced
- 1 ½ Worcestershire sauce

Directions:

1. In a large dish mix meat, cumin, scallions, salt, pepper, combine well. Form meatballs and cook them in your air-fryer at 375°Fahrenheit for 15-minutes. Meanwhile, add the other ingredients into a pan over medium heat and cook for 5-minutes. Add the meatballs to pan and stir,

cook for an additional 5-minutes.

Nutrition Information: Calories: 112, Total Fat: 8.28g, Carbs: 2.4g, Protein: 9.75g

451. Cherry Tomatoes Mix

Preparation time: 10 minutes

Cooking time: 15 minutes

Servings: 4

Ingredients:

- 1 tablespoon shallot, chopped
- 1 garlic clove, minced
- ¾ cup cashews, soaked for a couple of hours and drained
- 2 tablespoons nutritional yeast
- ½ cup veggie stock
- Salt and black pepper to the taste
- 2 teaspoons lemon juice
- 1 cup cherry tomatoes, halved
- 5 teaspoons olive oil
- ¼ teaspoon garlic powder

Directions:

1. Place tomatoes in a pan that fits your air fryer, drizzle the oil over them, season with salt, black pepper and garlic powder, toss to coat and cook in your air fryer at 350 degrees F for 15 minutes.
2. Meanwhile, in a food processor, mix garlic with shallots, cashews, veggie stock, nutritional yeast, lemon juice, a pinch of sea salt and black pepper to the taste and blend well.
3. Divide tomatoes between plates, drizzle the sauce over them and serve as a side dish.
4. Enjoy!

Nutrition information:calories 160, fat 2, fiber 5, carbs 10, protein 8

452. Tomatoes and Basil Mix

Preparation time: 10 minutes

Cooking time: 14 minutes

Servings: 2

Ingredients:

- 1 bunch basil, chopped
- 3 garlic clove, minced
- A drizzle of olive oil
- Salt and black pepper to the taste
- 2 cups cherry tomatoes, halved

Directions:

1. In a pan that fits your air fryer, combine tomatoes with garlic, salt, pepper, basil and oil, toss, introduce in your air fryer and cook at 320 degrees F for 12 minutes.
2. Divide between plates and serve as a side dish.
3. Enjoy!

Nutrition information:calories 140, fat 1, fiber 1, carbs 2, protein 10

453. Tomatoes and Bell Peppers Mix

Preparation time: 10 minutes

Cooking time: 15 minutes

Servings: 4

Ingredients:

- 2 red bell peppers, chopped
- 2 garlic cloves, minced
- 1 pound cherry tomatoes, halved
- 1 teaspoon rosemary, dried
- 3 bay leaves
- 2 tablespoons olive oil
- 1 tablespoon balsamic vinegar
- Salt and black pepper to the taste

Directions:

1. In a bowl mix tomatoes with garlic, salt, black pepper, rosemary, bay leaves, half of the oil and half of the vinegar, toss to coat, introduce in your air fryer and roast them at 320 degrees F for 15 minutes.
2. In your food processor, mix bell peppers with salt, black pepper, the rest of the oil and the rest of the vinegar and blend very well.
3. Divide roasted tomatoes between plates, drizzle the bell peppers sauce over them and serve them as a side dish.
4. Enjoy!

Nutrition information:calories 123, fat 1, fiber 1, carbs 8, protein 10

454. Mexican Peppers Mix

Preparation time: 10 minutes

Cooking time: 16 minutes

Servings: 4

Ingredients:

- 4 bell peppers, cut into medium chunks
- ½ cup tomato juice
- 2 tablespoons jarred jalapenos, chopped
- 1 cup tomatoes, chopped
- ¼ cup yellow onion, chopped
- ¼ cup green peppers, chopped
- 2 cups tomato sauce
- Salt and black pepper to the taste
- 2 teaspoons onion powder
- ½ teaspoon red pepper, crushed
- 1 teaspoon chili powder
- ½ teaspoons garlic powder
- 1 teaspoon cumin, ground

Directions:

1. In a pan that fits your air fryer, mix tomato juice, jalapenos, tomatoes, onion, green peppers, salt, pepper, onion powder, red pepper, chili powder, garlic powder, oregano and cumin, stir well, introduce in your air fryer and cook at 350 degrees F for 6 minutes
2. Add bell peppers and cook at 320 degrees F for 10 minutes more.
3. Divide peppers mix between plates and serve them as a side dish.
4. Enjoy!

Nutrition information:calories 180, fat 4, fiber 3, carbs 7, protein 14

455. Garlic Eggplants

Preparation time: 10 minutes

Cooking time: 10 minutes

Servings: 4

Ingredients:

- 2 tablespoons olive oil
- 2 garlic cloves, minced

- 3 eggplants, halved and sliced
- 1 red chili pepper, chopped
- 1 green onion stalk, chopped
- 1 tablespoon ginger, grated
- 1 tablespoon coconut aminos
- 1 tablespoon balsamic vinegar

Directions:

1. Heat up a pan that fits your air fryer with the oil over medium-high heat, add eggplant slices and cook for 2 minutes.
2. Add chili pepper, garlic, green onions, ginger, coconut aminos and vinegar, introduce in your air fryer and cook at 320 degrees F for 7 minutes.
3. Divide between plates and serve as a side dish.
4. Enjoy!

Nutrition information:calories 130, fat 2, fiber 4, carbs 7, protein 9

456. Broccoli and Mushrooms Mix

Preparation time: 30 minutes

Cooking time: 8 minutes

Servings: 2

Ingredients:

- 10 ounces mushrooms, halved
- 1 broccoli head, florets separated
- 1 garlic clove, minced
- 1 tablespoon balsamic vinegar
- 1 yellow onion, chopped
- 1 tablespoon olive oil
- Salt and black pepper
- 1 teaspoon basil, dried
- 1 avocado, peeled, pitted and roughly cubed
- A pinch of red pepper flakes

Directions:

1. In a bowl, mix mushrooms with broccoli, onion, garlic and avocado.
2. In another bowl, mix vinegar, oil, salt, pepper and basil and whisk well.
3. Pour this over veggies, toss to coat, leave aside for 30 minutes, transfer to your air fryer's basket and cook at 350 degrees F for 8 minutes,
4. Divide between plates and serve with pepper flakes on top as a side dish.
5. Enjoy!

Nutrition information:calories 182, fat 3, fiber 3, carbs 5, protein 8

457. Green Beans Side Salad

Preparation time: 10 minutes

Cooking time: 15 minutes

Servings: 4

Ingredients:

- 1-pint cherry tomatoes
- 1 pound green beans
- 2 tablespoons olive oil
- Salt and black pepper to the taste

Directions:

1. In a bowl, mix cherry tomatoes with green beans, olive oil, salt and pepper, toss, transfer to a pan that fits your air fryer and cook at 400 degrees F for 15 minutes.
2. Divide between plates and serve as a side dish.

3. Enjoy!

Nutrition information:calories 142, fat 6, fiber 5, carbs 8, protein 9

458. Red Potatoes and Green Beans

Preparation time: 10 minutes

Cooking time: 15 minutes

Servings: 4

Ingredients:

- 1 pound red potatoes, cut into wedges
- 1 pound green beans
- 2 garlic cloves, minced
- 2 tablespoons olive oil
- Salt and black pepper to the taste
- ½ teaspoon oregano, dried

Directions:

1. In a pan that fits your air fryer, combine potatoes with green beans, garlic, oil, salt, pepper and oregano, toss, introduce in your air fryer and cook at 380 degrees F for 15 minutes.
2. Divide between plates and serve as a side dish.
3. Enjoy!

Nutrition information:calories 201, fat 6, fiber 4, carbs 8, protein 5

459. Baby Potatoes Salad

Preparation time: 10 minutes

Cooking time: 20 minutes

Servings: 4

Ingredients:

- 1 and ½ pounds baby potatoes, halved
- 2 garlic cloves, chopped
- 2 red onions, chopped
- 9 ounces cherry tomatoes
- 3 tablespoons olive oil
- 1 and ½ tablespoons balsamic vinegar
- 2 thyme springs, chopped
- Salt and black pepper to the taste

Directions:

1. In your food processor, mix garlic with onions, oil, vinegar, thyme, salt and pepper and pulse really well.
2. In a bowl, mix potatoes with tomatoes and balsamic mix, toss, transfer to your air fryer and cook at 380 degrees F for 20 minutes.
3. Divide between plates and serve cold as a side dish.
4. Enjoy!

Nutrition information:calories 201, fat 6, fiber 3, carbs 14, protein 6

460. Arabic Plums Mix

Preparation time: 10 minutes

Cooking time: 12 minutes

Servings: 4

Ingredients:

- 3 tablespoons stevia
- 3 ounces almonds, peeled and chopped
- 12 ounces plumps, pitted

- 2 tablespoons veggie stock
- 2 yellow onions, chopped
- 2 garlic cloves, minced
- Salt and black pepper to the tastes
- 1 teaspoon cumin powder
- 1 teaspoon turmeric powder
- 1 teaspoon ginger powder
- 1 teaspoon cinnamon powder
- 3 tablespoons olive oil

Directions:

1. In a pan that fits your air fryer, combine almonds with plums, stevia, stock, onions, garlic, salt, pepper, cumin, turmeric, ginger, cinnamon and oil, toss, introduce in your air fryer and cook at 350 degrees F for 12 minutes.
2. Divide plums mix between plates and serve as a side dish
3. Enjoy!

Nutrition information:calories 152, fat 3, fiber 6, carbs 12, protein 4

461. Lemony Baby Potatoes

Preparation time: 10 minutes

Cooking time: 25 minutes

Servings: 6

Ingredients:

- 2 tablespoons olive oil
- 2 springs rosemary, chopped
- 2 tablespoons parsley, chopped
- 2 tablespoons oregano, chopped
- Salt and black pepper to the taste
- 1 tablespoon lemon rind, grated
- 3 garlic cloves, minced
- 2 tablespoons lemon juice
- 2 pounds baby potatoes

Directions:

1. In a bowl, mix baby potatoes with oil, rosemary, parsley, oregano, salt, pepper, lemon rind, garlic and lemon juice, toss, transfer potatoes to your air fryer's basket and cook at 356 degrees F for 25 minutes.
2. Divide potatoes between plates and serve as a side dish.
3. Enjoy!

Nutrition information:calories 204, fat 4, fiber 5, carbs 17, protein 6

462. White Mushrooms Mix

Preparation time: 10 minutes

Cooking time: 15 minutes

Servings: 2

Ingredients:

- Salt and black pepper to the taste
- 7 ounces snow peas
- 8 ounces white mushrooms, halved
- 1 yellow onion, cut into rings
- 2 tablespoons coconut aminos
- 1 teaspoon olive oil

Directions:

1. In a bowl, snow peas with mushrooms, onion, aminos, oil, salt and pepper, toss well, transfer to a pan that fits your air fryer, introduce in the fryer and cook at 350 degrees F for 15 minutes.

2. Divide between plates and serve as a side dish
3. Enjoy!

Nutrition information:calories 175, fat 4, fiber 2, carbs 12, protein 7

463. Gold Potatoes and Bell Pepper Mix

Preparation time: 10 minutes

Cooking time: 25 minutes

Servings: 4

Ingredients:

- 4 gold potatoes, cubed
- 1 yellow onion, chopped
- 2 teaspoons olive oil
- 1 green bell pepper, chopped
- Salt and black pepper to the taste
- ½ teaspoon thyme, dried

Directions:

1. Heat up your air fryer at 350 degrees F, add oil, heat it up, add onion, bell pepper, salt and pepper, stir and cook for 5 minutes.
2. Add potatoes and thyme, stir, cover and cook at 360 degrees F for 20 minutes.
3. Divide between plates and serve as a side dish.
4. Enjoy!

Nutrition information:calories 201, fat 4, fiber 4, carbs 12, protein 7

464. Delicious Potato Mix

Preparation time: 10 minutes

Cooking time: 25 minutes

Servings: 6

Ingredients:

- 6 ounces jarred roasted red bell peppers, chopped
- 3 garlic cloves, minced
- 2 tablespoons parsley, chopped
- Salt and black pepper to the taste
- 2 tablespoons chives, chopped
- 4 potatoes, peeled and cut into wedges
- Cooking spray

Directions:

1. In a pan that fits your air fryer, combine roasted bell peppers with garlic, parsley, salt, pepper, chives, potato wedges and the oil, toss, transfer to your air fryer and cook at 350 degrees F for 25 minutes.
2. Divide between plates and serve as a side dish.
3. Enjoy!

Nutrition information:calories 212, fat 6, fiber 4, carbs 11, protein 5

465. Chinese Long Beans Mix

Preparation time: 10 minutes

Cooking time: 10 minutes

Servings: 3

Ingredients:

- ½ teaspoon coconut aminos
- 1 tablespoon olive oil
- A pinch of salt and black pepper

- 4 garlic cloves, minced
- 4 long beans, trimmed and sliced

Directions:

1. In a pan that fits your air fryer, combine long beans with oil, aminos, salt, pepper and garlic, toss, introduce in your air fryer and cook at 350 degrees F for 10 minutes.
2. Divide between plates and serve as a side dish.
3. Enjoy!

Nutrition information:calories 170, fat 3, fiber 3, carbs 7, protein 3

466. Easy Portobello Mushrooms

Preparation time: 10 minutes

Cooking time: 12 minutes

Servings: 4

Ingredients:

- 4 big Portobello mushroom caps
- 1 tablespoon olive oil
- 1 cup spinach, torn
- 1/3 cup vegan breadcrumbs
- ¼ teaspoon rosemary, chopped

Directions:

1. Rub mushrooms caps with the oil, place them in your air fryer's basket and cook them at 350 degrees F for 2 minutes.
2. Meanwhile, in a bowl, mix spinach, rosemary and breadcrumbs and stir well.
3. Stuff mushrooms with this mix, place them in your air fryer's basket again and cook at 350 degrees F for 10 minutes.
4. Divide them between plates and serve as a side dish.
5. Enjoy!

Nutrition information:calories 152, fat 4, fiber 7, carbs 9, protein 5

467. Summer Squash Mix

Preparation time: 10 minutes

Cooking time: 10

Servings: 4

Ingredients:

- 3 ounces coconut cream
- ½ teaspoon oregano, dried
- Salt and black pepper
- 1 big yellow summer squash, peeled and cubed
- 1/3 cup carrot, cubed
- 2 tablespoons olive oil

Directions:

1. In a pan that fits your air fryer, combine squash with carrot, oil, oregano, salt, pepper and coconut cream, toss, transfer to your air fryer and cook at 400 degrees F for 10 minutes.
2. Divide between plates and serve as a side dish.
3. Enjoy!

Nutrition information:calories 170, fat 4, fiber 7, carbs 8, protein 6

VEGETABLES

468. Mustard Brussels Sprouts

Preparation time: 5 minutes

Cooking time: 15 minutes

Servings: 4

Ingredients:

- 1 pound Brussels sprouts, trimmed
- Salt and black pepper to taste
- 1 tablespoon mustard
- 1 tablespoon olive oil
- 2 tablespoons cilantro, chopped

Directions:

1. In a bowl, mix the sprouts with the salt, pepper, mustard, and the oil; toss well.
2. Transfer the sprouts to your air fryer's basket and cook at 380 degrees F for 15 minutes.
3. Divide the sprouts between plates, sprinkle the cilantro on top, and serve.

Nutrition information:calories 122, fat 2, fiber 2, carbs 9, protein 4

469. Parmesan Broccoli

Preparation time: 5 minutes

Cooking time: 8 minutes

Servings: 4

Ingredients:

- 1 broccoli head, florets separated
- Juice of 1 lime
- Salt and black pepper to taste
- 2 tablespoons olive oil
- 3 tablespoons parmesan cheese, grated

Directions:

1. Put the broccoli in your air fryer's basket; add the salt, pepper, and the oil, and toss.
2. Cook at 400 degrees F for 8 minutes.
3. Transfer the broccoli to a bowl, add the lime juice and parmesan, toss, and serve.

Nutrition information:calories 122, fat 3, fiber 6, carbs 8, protein 9

470. Red Cabbage and Carrots

Preparation time: 5 minutes

Cooking time: 8 minutes

Servings: 4

Ingredients:

- 1 red cabbage head, shredded
- 1 tablespoon olive oil
- 1 carrot, grated
- ¼ cup balsamic vinegar
- Salt and black pepper to taste

Directions:

1. Place all ingredients in a pan that fits your air fryer, and mix well.
2. Put the pan in the fryer and cook at 380 degrees F for 8 minutes.
3. Divide between plates and serve.

Nutrition information:calories 100, fat 4, fiber 2, carbs 7, protein 2

471. Butter Carrots

Preparation time: 5 minutes

Cooking time: 15 minutes

Servings: 4

Ingredients:

- 1 pound carrots, cut into wedges
- A pinch of salt and black pepper
- 1 teaspoon sweet paprika
- ½ tablespoon butter, melted

Directions:

1. In a bowl, combine all of the ingredients and toss well.
2. Put the carrots in your air fryer and cook at 350 degrees F for 15 minutes.
3. Divide between plates and serve.

Nutrition information:calories 90, fat 2, fiber 3, carbs 4, protein 4

472. Green Beans Mix

Preparation time: 5 minutes

Cooking time: 6 minutes

Servings: 4

Ingredients:

- 1 pound green beans, trimmed
- 2 tablespoons olive oil
- 3 garlic cloves, minced
- Salt and black pepper to taste
- 1 tablespoon balsamic vinegar

Directions:

1. Place all of the ingredients in a bowl, except the vinegar, and mix well.
2. Put the beans in your air fryer and cook at 400 degrees F for 6 minutes.
3. Divide the green beans between plates, drizzle the vinegar all over, and serve.

Nutrition information:calories 101, fat 3, fiber 3, carbs 4, protein 2

473. Spicy Kale Mix

Preparation time: 5 minutes

Cooking time: 12 minutes

Servings: 6

Ingredients:

- 2 tablespoons olive oil
- 3 garlic cloves, minced
- 2½ pounds kale leaves
- Salt and black pepper to taste
- 2 tablespoons balsamic vinegar
- 1 tablespoon chili powder
- ½ teaspoon crushed red pepper

Directions:

1. In a bowl, mix the kale with salt, pepper, oil, red pepper, and chili powder; toss well.
2. Transfer the kale to your air fryer and cook at 250 degrees F for 12 minutes.
3. Put the kale leaves in a bowl, add the garlic and the vinegar, and toss.
4. Serve, and enjoy!

Nutrition information:calories 102, fat 4,

fiber 8, carbs 4, protein 2

474. Eggplant Mix

Preparation time: 5 minutes

Cooking time: 15 minutes

Servings: 4

Ingredients:

- 4 eggplants, roughly cubed
- 2 tablespoons lime juice
- Salt and black pepper to taste
- 1 teaspoon oregano, dried
- 2 tablespoons olive oil

Directions:

1. Place all of the ingredients in a pan that fits your air fryer and mix / toss well.
2. Put the pan into the fryer and cook at 400 degrees F for 15 minutes.
3. Divide the eggplants between plates and serve.

Nutrition information:calories 125, fat 5, fiber 2, carbs 11, protein 5

475. Hot Greek Potatoes

Preparation time: 5 minutes

Cooking time: 15 minutes

Servings: 4

Ingredients:

- 1½ pounds potatoes, peeled and cubed
- 1 tablespoon olive oil
- Salt and black pepper to taste
- 1 tablespoon hot paprika
- 2 tablespoons black olives, pitted and sliced
- 1 cup Greek yogurt

Directions:

1. In a bowl, mix the potatoes with the oil, salt, pepper, and paprika; toss well.
2. Put the potatoes in your air fryer's basket and cook at 400 degrees F for 15 minutes.
3. Place the potatoes in a serving dish, and add the yogurt and the black olives.
4. Toss, serve, and enjoy.

Nutrition information:calories 140, fat 3, fiber 4, carbs 10, protein 4

476. Coconut Mushroom Mix

Preparation time: 5 minutes

Cooking time: 8 minutes

Servings: 8

Ingredients:

- 1 pound brown mushrooms, halved
- 1 small yellow onion, chopped
- Salt and black pepper to taste
- 2 tablespoons olive oil
- 14 ounces coconut milk

Directions:

1. Add all ingredients to a pan that fits your air fryer and mix well.
2. Place the pan in the fryer and cook at 400 degrees F for 8 minutes.
3. Divide between plates and serve.

Nutrition information:calories 202, fat 4, fiber 1, carbs 13, protein 4

477. Oregano Pearl Onions

Preparation time: 5 minutes

Cooking time: 10 minutes

Servings: 8

Ingredients:

- 1 pound pearl onions, trimmed
- 3 ounces feta cheese, crumbled
- 1 tablespoon olive oil
- A pinch of salt and black pepper
- 2 tablespoons oregano, chopped

Directions:

1. In a bowl, mix the onions with the salt, pepper, and oil.
2. Transfer the contents to your air fryer and cook at 400 degrees F for 10 minutes.
3. Transfer the onions to a bowl, add the oregano and the cheese, toss, and serve.

Nutrition information:calories 140, fat 4, fiber 2, carbs 9, protein 5

478. Goat Cheese Brussels Sprouts

Preparation time: 5 minutes

Cooking time: 15 minutes

Servings: 8

Ingredients:

- 1 pound Brussels sprouts, trimmed
- 1 tablespoon olive oil
- Salt and black pepper to taste
- 3 ounces goat cheese, crumbled

Directions:

1. In a bowl, mix the sprouts with the oil, salt, and pepper; toss well.
2. Put the sprouts in your air fryer's basket and cook at 380 degrees F for 15 minutes.
3. Divide between plates, sprinkle the cheese on top, and serve.

Nutrition information:calories 150, fat 3, fiber 4, carbs 4, protein 6

479. Tarragon Green Beans

Preparation time: 5 minutes

Cooking time: 7 minutes

Servings: 4

Ingredients:

- 1 pound green beans, trimmed
- 1 tablespoon tarragon, chopped
- Zest of 2 lemons
- 1 tablespoon olive oil
- Salt and black pepper to taste

Directions:

1. In a bowl, mix the green beans with the lemon zest, oil, salt, and pepper; toss well.
2. Put the beans in your air fryer and cook at 400 degrees F for 7 minutes.
3. Divide the beans between plates, sprinkle the tarragon on top, and serve.

Nutrition information:calories 181, fat 7, fiber 4, carbs 9, protein 3

480. Balsamic Zucchini Mix

Preparation time: 5 minutes

Cooking time: 12 minutes

Servings: 4

Ingredients:

- 4 zucchinis, sliced
- Salt and black pepper to taste
- 2 tablespoons lime juice
- 2 tablespoons olive oil
- 2 teaspoons balsamic vinegar
- 1 teaspoon oregano, dried

Directions:

1. In a pan that fits your air fryer, mix all the ingredients well.
2. Place the pan in the fryer and cook at 400 degrees F for 12 minutes.
3. Divide the mix between plates and serve.

Nutrition information:calories 100, fat 1, fiber 3, carbs 8, protein 4

481. Artichokes and Mayonnaise

Preparation time: 5 minutes

Cooking time: 15 minutes

Servings: 6

Ingredients:

- 14 ounces canned artichoke hearts
- A drizzle of olive oil
- 16 ounces parmesan cheese, grated
- 3 garlic cloves, minced
- ½ cup mayonnaise
- 1 teaspoon garlic powder

Directions:

1. In a pan that fits your air fryer, mix the artichokes with the oil, garlic, and garlic powder, and then toss well.
2. Place the pan in the fryer and cook at 350 degrees F for 15 minutes.
3. Cool the mix down, add the mayo, and toss.
4. Divide between plates, sprinkle the parmesan on top, and serve.

Nutrition information:calories 200, fat 11, fiber 3, carbs 9, protein 4

482. Coconut Artichokes

Preparation time: 5 minutes

Cooking time: 15 minutes

Servings: 2

Ingredients:

- 2 artichokes, washed, trimmed and halved
- 2 garlic cloves, minced
- ¼ cup coconut, shredded
- Juice of 1 lemon
- 1 tablespoon coconut oil, melted

Directions:

1. In a bowl, mix the artichokes with the garlic, oil, and lemon juice; toss well.
2. Put the artichokes into your air fryer and cook at 360 degrees F for 15 minutes.
3. Divide the artichokes between plates, sprinkle the coconut on top, and serve.
4. Enjoy!

Nutrition information:calories 213, fat 8, fiber 6, carbs 13, protein 6

483. Wrapped Asparagus

Preparation time: 5 minutes

Cooking time: 5 minutes

Servings: 4

Ingredients:

- 8 asparagus spears, trimmed
- 8 ounces prosciutto slices
- A pinch of salt and black pepper

Directions:

1. Wrap the asparagus in prosciutto slices and then season with salt and pepper.
2. Put all in your air fryer's basket and cook at 400 degrees F for 5 minutes.
3. Divide between plates and serve.

Nutrition information:calories 100, fat 2, fiber 5, carbs 8, protein 4

484. Simple Grilled Vegetables

Servings: 4

Preparation Time: 20 minutes

Ingredients:

- 1 tablespoon rosemary, chopped
- 1 clove of garlic, minced
- 1 tablespoon fresh basil, chopped
- 1 tablespoon fresh parsley
- 1 medium eggplant, sliced
- 1 zucchini, sliced
- 1 yellow squash, seeded and sliced
- 1 red onion, sliced
- Salt and pepper to taste
- 3 tablespoons nutritional yeast

Directions:

1. Preheat the air fryer at 3900F.
2. Place the grill pan accessory in the air fryer.
3. Place all ingredients: in a bowl and toss the vegetables until all vegetables are seasoned well.
4. Dump the vegetables on to the grill pan and cook for 15 to 20 minutes.
5. Make sure to give the vegetables a shake to grill evenly on all sides.

Nutrition information:

Calories:68; Carbs: 12.6g; Protein: 5.1g; Fat: 0.5g

485. Italian Grilled Vegetables

Servings: 4

Preparation Time:15 minutes

Ingredients:

- 8-ounce baby bella mushrooms, sliced
- 12 ounces baby potatoes, scrubbed and halved
- 12 ounces cherry tomatoes, halved
- 2 zucchinis, sliced
- 12 garlic cloves, peeled and grated
- 2 tablespoon extra-virgin olive oil
- ½ tablespoon dried oregano
- 1 teaspoon dried thyme
- Salt and pepper to taste
- 3 tablespoons grated parmesan

cheese

- A pinch of crushed red pepper flakes

Directions:

1. Preheat the air fryer at 3900F.
2. Place the grill pan accessory in the air fryer.
3. Place all Ingredients: in a bowl and toss the vegetables until all vegetables are seasoned well.
4. Dump the seasoned vegetables on the grill pan and cook for 15 minutes.
5. Give a good shake every 5 minutes to evenly grill the vegetables.

Nutrition information:

Calories: 353; Carbs: 77g; Protein: 10.3g; Fat: 4.9g

486. Balsamic Grilled Vegetables

Servings: 6

Preparation Time: 20 minutes

Ingredients:

- 2 small zucchinis, sliced
- 1 yellow squash, seeded and sliced
- 1 large yellow onion, cut into rings
- 1 small head broccoli, cut into florets
- ½ head cauliflower, cut into florets
- 1 carrot, peeled and sliced
- Salt and pepper to taste
- ½ cup balsamic vinegar
- 2 tablespoons olive oil

Directions:

1. Preheat the air fryer at 3500F.
2. Place the grill pan accessory in the air fryer.
3. Put all vegetables in a Ziploc bag and season with salt, pepper, balsamic vinegar, and olive oil.
4. Shake to season all vegetables.
5. Dump on to the grill pan and cook for 15 to 20 minutes.
6. Make sure to give the vegetables a good shake every 5 minutes.

Nutrition information:

Calories: 124; Carbs: 24g; Protein: 6g; Fat: 1g

487. Lemon Herb Vinaigrette

Servings: 4

Preparation Time: 15 minutes

Ingredients:

- 1 cup sliced carrots
- 1 zucchini, sliced
- 1 red bell pepper, seeded and julienned
- 1 cup snow peas
- Salt and pepper to taste
- 1 tablespoon olive oil
- 2 tablespoons nutritional yeast
- 1/8 cup red wine vinegar
- 1 teaspoon Dijon mustard
- 2 cloves of garlic, minced
- 1 tablespoon lemon juice
- 2 tablespoons honey

Directions:

1. Preheat the air fryer at 3500F.
2. Place the grill pan accessory in the

air fryer.

3. In a Ziploc bag, combine the carrots, zucchini, bell pepper, and snow peas. Season with salt, pepper, olive oil, and nutritional yeast. Give a good shake to combine everything.
4. Dump on to the grill pan and cook for 15 minutes.
5. Meanwhile, combine the red wine vinegar, Dijon mustard, garlic, lemon juice, and honey. Season with salt and pepper to taste.
6. Drizzle the grilled vegetables with the sauce.

Nutrition information:

Calories: 93; Carbs: 13.5g; Protein: 2.8g; Fat: 2.5g

488. Grilled Vegetables with Garlic

Servings: 4

Preparation Time: 15 minutes

Ingredients:

- 1 package frozen chopped vegetables
- 1 red onion, sliced
- 1 cup baby Portobello mushrooms, chopped
- Salt and pepper to taste
- 4 cloves of garlic, minced
- 3 tablespoon red wine vinegar
- ¼ cup chopped fresh basil
- 1 ½ tablespoons honey1 teaspoon Dijon mustard
- 1/3 cup olive oil

Directions:

1. Preheat the air fryer at 3500F.
2. Place the grill pan accessory in the air fryer.
3. In a Ziploc bag, combine the vegetables and season with salt, pepper, and garlic. Give a good shake to combine everything.
4. Dump on to the grill pan and cook for 15 minutes.
5. Meanwhile, combine the rest of the Ingredients in a bowl and season with more salt and pepper.
6. Drizzle the grilled vegetables with the sauce. Serve and enjoy.

Nutrition information:

Calories: 200; Carbs: 8.3g; Protein: 2.1g; Fat: 18.2g

489. Grilled Asparagus with Sauce

Servings: 6

Preparation Time: 15 minutes

Ingredients:

- 3 pounds asparagus spears, trimmed
- 2 tablespoons olive oil
- ½ teaspoon salt
- ¼ teaspoon black pepper
- 3 egg yolks
- ½ lemon juice
- ½ teaspoon salt
- A pinch of mustard powder
- A punch of ground white pepper
- ½ cup butter, melted
- 1 teaspoon chopped tarragon leaves

Directions:

1. Preheat the air fryer at 3500F.
2. Place the grill pan accessory in the air fryer.
3. In a Ziploc bag, combine the asparagus, olive oil, salt and pepper. Give a good shake to combine everything.
4. Dump on to the grill pan and cook for 15 minutes.
5. Meanwhile, on a double boiler over medium flame, whisk the egg yolks, lemon juice, and salt until silky. Add in the mustard powder, white pepper and melted butter. Keep whisking until the sauce is smooth. Garnish with tarragon leaves.
6. Drizzle the sauce over asparagus spears.

Nutrition information:

Calories: 253; Carbs: 10.2g; Protein: 6.7g; Fat: 22.4g

490. Zucchini with Mozzarella

Servings: 6

Preparation Time: 20 minutes

Ingredients:

- 3 medium zucchinis, sliced lengthwise
- 3 tablespoons extra virgin olive oil
- Salt and ground black pepper
- 18-ounce mozzarella ball, pulled into large pieces
- 2 tablespoons fresh dill
- ¼ crushed red pepper
- 1 tablespoon lemon juice

Directions:

1. Preheat the air fryer at 3500F.
2. Place the grill pan accessory in the air fryer.
3. Drizzle the zucchini with olive oil and season with salt and pepper to taste.
4. Place on the grill pan and cook for 15 to 20 minutes.
5. Serve the zucchini with mozzarella, dill, red pepper and lemon juice.

Nutrition information:

Calories:182; Carbs: 18.3g; Protein: 11.4g; Fat: 7.1g

491. Grilled Tomato Melts

Servings: 3

Preparation Time: 20 minutes

Ingredients:

- 3 large tomatoes
- 4 ounces Monterey Jack cheese
- 1 yellow red bell pepper, chopped
- ¼ cup toasted almonds
- Salt and pepper to taste

Directions:

1. Preheat the air fryer at 3500F.
2. Place the grill pan accessory in the air fryer.
3. Slice the tops of the tomatoes and remove the seeds to create hollow "cups."
4. In a mixing bowl, combine the cheese, bell pepper, and almonds. Season with salt and pepper to taste.
5. Stuff the tomatoes with the cheese filling.
6. Place the stuffed tomatoes on the

grill pan and cook for 15 to 20 minutes.

Nutrition information:

Calories: 125; Carbs: 13g; Protein: 10g; Fat: 14g

492. Asparagus and Arugula Salad

Servings: 4

Preparation Time: 15 minutes

Ingredients:

- 1-pound fresh asparagus, trimmed
- 2 tablespoons olive oil
- Salt and pepper to taste
- ¼ cup olive oil
- 2 teaspoons lemon zest
- 3 tablespoons lemon juice
- 3 tablespoons balsamic vinegar
- 4 cups arugula leaves
- 1 cup parmesan cheese, grated

Directions:

1. Preheat the air fryer at 3500F.
2. Place the grill pan accessory in the air fryer.
3. In a Ziploc bag, combine the asparagus, olive oil, salt and pepper. Give a good shake to combine everything. Dump on to the grill pan and cook for 15 minutes.
4. Meanwhile, prepare the sauce by mixing together the olive oil, lemon, zest, lemon juice, and balsamic vinegar. Season with salt and pepper to taste. Set aside.
5. Assemble the salad by mixing the asparagus, arugula, and parmesan cheese. Drizzle with sauce on top.

Nutrition information:

Calories: 231; Carbs: 14g; Protein: 10g; Fat: 29g

493. Grilled Mushrooms

Servings: 2

Preparation Time: 20 minutes

Ingredients:

- 6 large Portobello mushrooms, sliced
- ½ cup Italian vinaigrette
- ½ teaspoon black pepper
- 4 eggplants, sliced
- 4 onion, sliced
- 2 yellow bell peppers, seeded and sliced
- 5 ounces shredded mozzarella cheese

Directions:

1. Preheat the air fryer at 3500F.
2. Place the grill pan accessory in the air fryer.
3. In a Ziploc bag, put all Ingredients, except for the cheese. Shake to combine.
4. Dump on the grill pan and cook for 20 minutes.
5. While still hot, garnish with mozzarella cheese.

Nutrition information:

Calories: 212; Carbs: 23g; Protein: 13g; Fat: 14g

494. Spicy Thai –Style Veggies

Servings: 4

Preparation Time: 15 minutes

Ingredients:

- 1 ½ cups packed cilantro leaves
- 8 cloves of garlic, minced
- 2 tablespoons fish sauce
- 1 tablespoon black pepper
- 1 tablespoon chili garlic sauce
- 1/3 cup vegetable oil
- 2 pounds vegetable of your choice, sliced into cubes

Directions:

1. Preheat the air fryer at 3500F.
2. Place the grill pan accessory in the air fryer.
3. Place all ingredients: in a mixing bowl and toss to coat all ingredients.
4. Put in the grill pan and cook for 15 minutes.

Nutrition information:

Calories: 340; Carbs: 34.44g; Protein:8.8 g; Fat: 19.5g

495. Smokey Mustard Sauce

Servings: 5

Preparation Time: 15 minutes

Ingredients:

- 2 medium zucchinis, cut into ½ inch thick slices
- 2 large yellow squash, cut into ½ inch thick slices
- 1 large red bell pepper, sliced
- 3 tablespoons olive oil
- 1 teaspoon salt
- 1 teaspoon black pepper
- ¼ cup yellow mustard
- ¼ cup honey
- 2 teaspoons smoked paprika
- 2 teaspoons creole seasoning

Directions:

1. Preheat the air fryer at 3500F.
2. Place the grill pan accessory in the air fryer.
3. In a Ziploc bag, put the zucchini, squash, red bell pepper, olive oil, salt and pepper. Give a shake to season all vegetables.
4. Place on the grill pan and cook for 15 minutes.
5. Meanwhile, prepare the sauce by combining the mustard, honey, paprika, and creole seasoning. Season with salt to taste.
6. Serve the vegetables with the sauce.

Nutrition information:

Calories: 164; Carbs: 21.5g; Protein: 2.6g; Fat: 8.9g

496. Indian Grilled Vegetables

Servings: 6

Preparation Time: 20 minutes

Ingredients:

- ½ cup yogurt
- 6 cloves of garlic, minced
- 2-inch fresh ginger, minced

- 3 tablespoons Tandoori spice blend
- 2 tablespoons canola oil
- 2 small onions, cut into wedges
- 1 small zucchini, cut into thick slices
- 1 carrot, peeled and shaved to 1/8-inch thick
- 1 yellow sweet pepper, seeded and chopped
- ½ head cauliflower, cut into florets
- 1 handful sugar snap peas
- 1 cup young ears of corn

Directions:

1. Preheat the air fryer at 3500F.
2. Place the grill pan accessory in the air fryer.
3. In a Ziploc bag, put all ingredients: and give a shake to season all vegetables.
4. Dump all Ingredients: on the grill pan and cook for 20 minutes.
5. Make sure to give the vegetables a shake halfway through the cooking time.

Nutrition information:

Calories:126; Carbs: 17.9g; Protein: 2.9g; Fat: 6.1g

497. Grilled Sweet Potato Wedges

Servings: 3

Preparation Time: 20 minutes

Ingredients:

- 3 medium sweet potatoes, peeled and sliced
- 2 tablespoons olive oil
- Salt and pepper to taste
- ½ cup sour cream
- ½ cup mayonnaise
- 2 tablespoons fresh chives, chopped
- 3 tablespoons Asiago cheese, grated
- 2 tablespoons parmesan cheese

Directions:

1. Preheat the air fryer at 3500F.
2. Place the grill pan accessory in the air fryer.
3. Brush the potatoes with olive oil and drizzle with salt and pepper to taste.
4. Place on the grill pan and cook for 20 minutes.
5. Meanwhile, mix the sour cream, mayonnaise, fresh chives, Asiago cheese, and parmesan cheese in a bowl. Season with salt and pepper to taste.
6. Serve the potatoes with the sauce.

Nutrition information:

Calories: 625; Carbs: 50.5g; Protein: 12.7g; Fat: 42.3g

498. Grilled Green Beans with Shallots

Servings: 6

Preparation Time: 25 minutes

Ingredients:

- 1-pound fresh green beans, trimmed
- 2 large shallots, sliced
- 1 tablespoon vegetable oil
- 1 teaspoon soy sauce
- 2 tablespoons fresh basil, chopped

- 1 tablespoon fresh mint, chopped
- 1 tablespoon sesame seeds, toasted
- 2 tablespoons pine nuts

Directions:

1. Preheat the air fryer at 3500F.
2. Place the grill pan accessory in the air fryer.
3. In a mixing bowl, combine the green beans, shallots, vegetable oil, and soy sauce.
4. Dump in the air fryer and cook for 25 minutes.
5. Once cooked, garnish with basil, mints, sesame seeds, and pine nuts.

Nutrition information:

Calories:307; Carbs: 11.2g; Protein: 23.7g; Fat: 19.7g

499. Grille Tomatoes with Herb Salad

Servings: 4

Preparation Time: 20 minutes

Ingredients:

- 3 large green tomatoes
- 1 clove of garlic, minced
- 5 tablespoons olive oil
- Salt and pepper to taste
- ¾ cup fresh parsley, chopped
- ¾ cup cilantro leaves, chopped
- ½ cup chopped chives
- 4 leaves iceberg lettuce
- ¼ cup hazelnuts, toasted and chopped
- ¼ cup pistachios, toasted and chopped
- ¼ cup golden raisins
- 2 tablespoons white balsamic vinegar

Directions:

1. Preheat the air fryer at 3500F.
2. Place the grill pan accessory in the air fryer.
3. In a mixing bowl, season the tomatoes with garlic, oil, salt and pepper to taste.
4. Place on the grill pan and grill for 20 minutes.
5. Once the tomatoes are done, toss in a salad bowl together with the rest of the ingredients.

Nutrition information:

Calories: 287; Carbs: 12.2g; Protein: 4.8g; Fat: 25.9g

SNACKS

500. Easy Broccoli Patties

Preparation Time: 20 Minutes

Servings: 12

Ingredients:

- 4 cups broccoli florets
- 1 ½ cup almond flour
- 1 tsp. paprika
- 2 eggs
- 1/4 cup olive oil
- 2 cups cheddar cheese; grated
- 1 tsp. garlic powder
- 1/2 tsp. apple cider vinegar
- 1/2 tsp. baking soda
- Salt and black pepper to the taste

Directions:

1. Put broccoli florets in your food processor; add salt and pepper, blend well and transfer to a bowl.
2. Add almond flour, salt, pepper, paprika, garlic powder, baking soda, cheese, oil, eggs and vinegar; stir well and shape 12 patties out of this mix.
3. Place them in your preheated air fryer's basket and cook at 350 °F, for 10 minutes. Arrange patties on a platter and serve as an appetizer.

Nutrition information:Calories: 203; Fat: 12; Fiber: 2; Carbs: 14; Protein: 2

501. Tasty Stuffed Peppers

Preparation Time: 18 Minutes

Servings: 8

Ingredients:

- 8 small bell peppers; tops cut off and seeds removed
- oz. goat cheese; cut into 8 pieces
- 1 tbsp. olive oil
- Salt and black pepper to the taste

Directions:

1. In a bowl; mix cheese with oil with salt and pepper and toss to coat. Stuff each pepper with goat cheese, place them in your air fryer's basket, cook at 400 °F, for 8 minutes; arrange on a platter and serve as an appetizer.

Nutrition information:Calories: 120; Fat: 1; Fiber: 1; Carbs: 12; Protein: 8

502. Mouthwatering Beef Rolls

Preparation Time: 24 Minutes

Servings: 4

Ingredients:

- 2 lbs. beef steak; opened and flattened with a meat tenderizer
- 3 oz. red bell pepper; roasted and chopped.
- 6 slices provolone cheese
- Salt and black pepper to the taste
- 1 cup baby spinach
- 3 tbsp. pesto

Directions:

1. Arrange flattened beef steak on a cutting board, spread pesto all over,

add cheese in a single layer, add bell peppers, spinach, salt and pepper to the taste.

2. Roll your steak, secure with toothpicks, season again with salt and pepper; place roll in your air fryer's basket and cook at 400 °F, for 14 minutes; rotating roll halfway. Leave aside to cool down, cut into 2-inch smaller rolls, arrange on a platter and serve them as an appetizer.

Nutrition information:Calories: 230; Fat: 1; Fiber: 3; Carbs: 12; Protein: 10

503. White Mushrooms Appetizer

Preparation Time: 20 Minutes

Servings: 4

Ingredients:

- 1/2 cup Mexican cheese; shredded
- 4 oz. cream cheese; soft
- 1/4 cup sour cream
- 1 cup shrimp; cooked, peeled, deveined and chopped.
- 1/4 cup mayonnaise
- 1 tsp. garlic powder
- 1 small yellow onion; chopped.
- 24 oz. white mushroom caps
- Salt and black pepper to the taste
- 1 tsp. curry powder

Directions:

1. In a bowl; mix mayo with garlic powder, onion, curry powder, cream cheese, sour cream, Mexican cheese, shrimp, salt and pepper to the taste and whisk well.
2. Stuff mushrooms with this mix; place them in your air fryer's basket and cook at 300 °F, for 10 minutes. Arrange on a platter and serve as an appetizer.

Nutrition information:Calories: 200; Fat: 20; Fiber: 3; Carbs: 16; Protein: 14

504. Party Pork Rolls

Preparation Time:50 Minutes

Servings: 4

Ingredients:

- 1 (15 oz.) pork fillet
- 1/2 tsp. chili powder
- 1 tsp. cinnamon powder
- 1 red onion; chopped
- 3 tbsp. parsley; chopped
- 1 garlic clove; minced
- 2 tbsp. olive oil
- 1 ½ tsp. cumin; ground
- Salt and black pepper to the taste

Directions:

1. In a bowl; mix cinnamon with garlic, salt, pepper, chili powder, oil, onion, parsley and cumin and stir well
2. Put pork fillet on a cutting board, flatten it using a meat tenderizer. And use a meat tenderizer to flatten it.
3. Spread onion mix on pork, roll tight, cut into medium rolls, place them in your preheated air fryer at 360 °F and cook them for 35 minutes. Arrange them on a platter and serve as an appetizer

Nutrition information:Calories: 304; Fat: 12; Fiber: 1; Carbs: 15; Protein: 23

505. Delicious Wrapped Shrimp

Preparation Time: 18 Minutes

Servings: 16

Ingredients:

- 10 oz. already cooked shrimp; peeled and deveined
- 2 tbsp. olive oil
- 1/3 cup blackberries; ground
- 11 prosciutto sliced
- 1/3 cup red wine
- 1 tbsp. mint; chopped.

Directions:

1. Wrap each shrimp in a prosciutto slices, drizzle the oil over them, rub well, place in your preheated air fryer at 390 °F and fry them for 8 minutes.
2. Meanwhile; heat up a pan with ground blackberries over medium heat, add mint and wine; stir, cook for 3 minutes and take off heat. Arrange shrimp on a platter, drizzle blackberries sauce over them and serve as an appetizer.

Nutrition information:Calories: 224; Fat: 12; Fiber: 2; Carbs: 12; Protein: 14

506. Shrimp and Calamari Snack

Preparation Time: 30 Minutes

Servings: 1

Ingredients:

- 8 oz. calamari; cut into medium rings
- 1/2 tsp. turmeric powder
- 2 tbsp. avocado; chopped
- 7 oz. shrimp; peeled and deveined
- 1 eggs
- 3 tbsp. white flour
- 1 tbsp. olive oil
- 1 tsp. tomato paste
- 1 tbsp. mayonnaise
- 1 tsp. lemon juice
- A splash of Worcestershire sauce
- Salt and black pepper to the taste

Directions:

1. In a bowl; whisk egg with oil, add calamari rings and shrimp and toss to coat.
2. In another bowl; mix flour with salt, pepper and turmeric and stir.
3. Dredge calamari and shrimp in this mix, place them in your air fryer's basket and cook at 350 °F, for 9 minutes; flipping them once.
4. Meanwhile; in a bowl, mix avocado with mayo and tomato paste and mash using a fork.
5. Add Worcestershire sauce, lemon juice, salt and pepper and stir well. Arrange calamari and shrimp on a platter and serve with the sauce on the side.

Nutrition information:Calories: 288; Fat: 23; Fiber: 3; Carbs: 10; Protein: 15

507. Egg White Chips Snack

Preparation Time: 13 Minutes

Servings: 2

Ingredients:

- 1/2 tbsp. water
- 4 eggs whites
- 2 tbsp. parmesan; shredded
- Salt and black pepper to the taste

Directions:

1. In a bowl; mix egg whites with salt, pepper and water and whisk well.
2. Spoon this into a muffin pan that fits your air fryer, sprinkle cheese on top; introduce in your air fryer and cook at 350 °F, for 8 minutes. Arrange egg white chips on a platter and serve as a snack.

Nutrition information:Calories: 180; Fat: 2; Fiber: 1; Carbs: 12; Protein: 7

508. Delicious Tuna Cakes

Preparation Time: 20 Minutes

Servings: 12

Ingredients:

- 15 oz. canned tuna; drain and flaked
- 1 tsp. parsley; dried
- 1/2 cup red onion; chopped.
- 1 tsp. garlic powder
- 3 eggs
- 1/2 tsp. dill; dried
- Salt and black pepper to the taste
- Cooking spray

Directions:

1. In a bowl; mix tuna with salt, pepper, dill, parsley, onion, garlic powder and eggs; stir well and shape medium cakes out of this mix.
2. Place tuna cakes in your air fryer's basket, spray them with cooking oil and cook at 350 °F, for 10 minutes; flipping them halfway. Arrange them on a platter and serve as an appetizer.

Nutrition information:Calories: 140; Fat: 2; Fiber: 1; Carbs: 8; Protein: 6

509. Holyday Beef Patties

Preparation Time: 18 Minutes

Servings: 4

Ingredients:

- 14 oz. beef; minced
- 1/2 tsp. nutmeg; ground
- 2 tbsp. ham; cut into strips
- 1 leek; chopped
- 3 tbsp. bread crumbs
- Salt and black pepper to the taste

Directions:

1. In a bowl; mix beef with leek, salt, pepper, ham, breadcrumbs and nutmeg; stir well and shape small patties out of this mix. Place them in your air fryer's basket, cook at 400 °F, for 8 minutes; arrange on a platter and serve as an appetizer.

Nutrition information:Calories: 260; Fat: 12; Fiber: 3; Carbs: 12; Protein: 21

510. Cheesy Chicken Rolls

Preparation Time: 30 Minutes

Servings: 12

Ingredients:

- 4 oz. blue cheese; crumbled
- 2 celery stalks; finely chopped.
- 1/2 cup tomato sauce
- 12 egg roll wrappers
- 2 cups chicken; cooked and chopped.
- 2 green onions; chopped
- Salt and black pepper to the taste
- Cooking spray

Directions:

2. In a bowl; mix chicken meat with blue cheese, salt, pepper, green onions, celery and tomato sauce; stir well and keep in the fridge for 2 hours.
3. Place egg wrappers on a working surface, divide chicken mix on them, roll and seal edges. Place rolls in your air fryer's basket, spray them with cooking oil and cook at 350 °F, for 10 minutes; flipping them halfway.

Nutrition information:Calories: 220; Fat: 7; Fiber: 2; Carbs: 14; Protein: 10

511. Kale and Celery Crackers

Preparation Time: 30 Minutes

Servings: 6

Ingredients:

- 2 cups flax seed; ground
- 1 bunch basil; chopped
- 1/2 bunch celery; chopped.
- 2 cups flax seed; soaked overnight and drained
- 4 bunches kale; chopped
- 4 garlic cloves; minced
- 1/3 cup olive oil

Directions:

1. In your food processor mix ground flaxseed with celery, kale, basil and garlic and blend well.
2. Add oil and soaked flaxseed and blend again, spread in your air fryer's pan; cut into medium crackers and cook them at 380 °F, for 20 minutes. Divide into bowls and serve as an appetizer.

Nutrition information:Calories: 143; Fat: 1; Fiber: 2; Carbs: 8; Protein: 4

512. Cheesy Chicken Wings

Preparation Time: 22 Minutes

Servings: 6

Ingredients:

- 6 lb. chicken wings; halved
- 1/2 tsp. Italian seasoning
- 1 tsp. garlic powder
- 1 egg
- 2 tbsp. butter
- 1/2 cup parmesan cheese; grated
- A pinch of red pepper flakes; crushed
- Salt and black pepper to the taste

Directions:

1. Arrange chicken wings in your air fryer's basket and cook at 390 °F and cook for 9 minutes.
2. Meanwhile; in your blender, mix butter with cheese, egg, salt, pepper,

pepper flakes, garlic powder and Italian seasoning and blend very well.

3. Take chicken wings out; pour cheese sauce over them, toss to coat well and cook in your air fryer's basket at 390 °F, for 3 minutes. Serve them as an appetizer.

Nutrition information:Calories: 204; Fat: 8; Fiber: 1; Carbs: 18; Protein: 14

513. Traditional Sweet Bacon Snack

Preparation Time: 40 Minutes

Servings: 16

Ingredients:

- 1/2 tsp. cinnamon powder
- 16 bacon slices
- 1 tbsp. avocado oil
- 3 oz. dark chocolate
- 1 tsp. maple extract

Directions:

1. Arrange bacon slices in your air fryer's basket; sprinkle cinnamon mix over them and cook them at 300 °F, for 30 minutes.
2. Heat up a pot with the oil over medium heat, add chocolate and stir until it melts.
3. Add maple extract; stir, take off heat and leave aside to cool down a bit.
4. Take bacon strips out of the oven; leave them to cool down, dip each in chocolate mix; place them on a parchment paper and leave them to cool down completely. Serve cold as a snack.

Nutrition information:Calories: 200; Fat: 4; Fiber: 5; Carbs: 12; Protein: 3

514. Fast Mango Dip

Preparation time: 5 minutes

Cooking time: 20 minutes

Servings: 4

Ingredients:

- 1 shallot, chopped
- 1 tablespoon avocado oil
- 2 tablespoons ginger, minced
- ½ teaspoon cinnamon powder
- 2 mangos, chopped
- 2 red hot chilies, chopped
- 1¼ cups sugar
- 1¼ cups apple cider vinegar

Directions:

1. In a pan that fits your air fryer, mix all the ingredients well.
2. Place the pan in the fryer and cook at 350 degrees F for 20 minutes.
3. Transfer the contents to a blender and pulse.
4. Divide into bowls and serve as a party dip.

Nutrition information:calories 100, fat 1, fiber 0, carbs 6, protein 2

515. Hot Dip

Preparation time: 5 minutes

Cooking time: 5 minutes

Servings: 6

Ingredients:

- 12 ounces hot peppers, chopped
- Salt and black pepper to taste
- 1¼ cups apple cider vinegar

Directions:

1. Add the ingredients to a pan that fits your air fryer and mix.
2. Place the pan in the fryer and cook at 380 degrees F for 5 minutes.
3. Blend using an immersion blender, divide into bowls, and serve.

Nutrition information:calories 20, fat 0, fiber 2, carbs 3, protein 1

516. Spiced Tomato Party Mix

Preparation time: 5 minutes

Cooking time: 13 minutes

Servings: 6

Ingredients:

- 3 pounds tomatoes, roughly cubed
- 1 cup balsamic vinegar
- 1 tablespoon ginger, grated
- 3 garlic cloves, minced
- 2 onions, chopped
- ¼ cup raisins
- ¾ teaspoon cinnamon powder
- ½ teaspoon coriander, ground
- ¼ teaspoon nutmeg powder
- 1 teaspoon sweet paprika
- 1 teaspoon chili powder

Directions:

1. Add all the ingredients to a pan that fits your air fryer and toss.
2. Place the pan in the air fryer and cook at 360 degrees F for 13 minutes.
3. Remove, place in a bowl, and chill.
4. Serve cold as an appetizer or snack.

Nutrition information:calories 151, fat 8, fiber 4, carbs 11, protein 5

517. Tomatoes and Dates Salsa

Preparation time: 5 minutes

Cooking time: 15 minutes

Servings: 12

Ingredients:

- 1½ pounds tomatoes, peeled and cubed
- 1 apple, cored and cubed
- 1 yellow onion, chopped
- 6 ounces sultanas, chopped
- 3 ounces dates, roughly chopped
- Salt and black pepper to taste
- 1 tablespoon balsamic vinegar
- 1 teaspoon whole spice
- ½ tablespoon brown sugar

Directions:

1. In a pan that fits your air fryer, add and toss all the ingredients.
2. Place the pan in the fryer and cook at 370 degrees F for 15 minutes.
3. Remove the salsa, place in a bowl, and chill.
4. Serve the salsa cold as a snack or appetizer.

Nutrition information:calories 131, fat 7, fiber 4, carbs 9, protein 3

518. Chili Tomato Salsa

Preparation time: 5 minutes

Cooking time: 10 minutes

Servings: 12

Ingredients:

- 1½ pounds green tomatoes, cubed
- 1 white onion, chopped
- ¼ cup currants
- 4 red chili peppers, chopped
- 2 tablespoons ginger, grated
- 1 tablespoon brown sugar
- 1 tablespoon balsamic vinegar

Directions:

1. Mix all the ingredients in a pan that fits your air fryer and toss.
2. Place the pan in the fryer and cook at 370 degrees F for 10 minutes.
3. Put the salsa into a bowl and chill.
4. Serve cold as a party salsa or as an appetizer.

Nutrition information:calories 100, fat 1, fiber 3, carbs 7, protein 4

519. Buttery Onion Dip

Preparation time: 10 minutes

Cooking time: 30 minutes

Servings: 8

Ingredients:

- 6 tablespoons butter, softened
- 2½ pounds red onions, chopped
- Salt and black pepper to taste
- ½ teaspoon baking soda

Directions:

1. Place the butter into a pan that fits your air fryer and heat over medium heat.
2. Add the onions and the baking soda, stir, and sauté for 5 minutes.
3. Transfer the pan to your air fryer and cook at 370 degrees F for 25 minutes.
4. Serve warm as a party dip.

Nutrition information:calories 151, fat 2, fiber 4, carbs 9, protein 4

520. Cranberry Dip

Preparation time: 10 minutes

Cooking time: 30 minutes

Servings: 10

- **Ingredients:**

- 4 garlic cloves, minced
- 2 red onions, chopped
- 4 red chili peppers, seeded and chopped
- 17 ounces cranberries
- 4 ounces sugar
- 1 teaspoon olive oil
- Black pepper to taste
- 2 tablespoons balsamic vinegar

Directions:

1. In a pan that fits your air fryer, place all the ingredients and mix well.
2. Place the pan in the air fryer and cook at 370 degrees F for 30 minutes.
3. Blend using an immersion blender and cool.
4. Serve cold as a party dip or appetizer.

Nutrition information:calories 121, fat 1, fiber 3, carbs 7, protein 3

521. Onion and Chili Dip

You must try this sauce soon!

Preparation time: 5 minutes

Cooking time: 20 minutes

Servings: 6

Ingredients:

- 5 ounces red chilies, seeded and chopped
- 4 ounces red onion, chopped
- 3 tablespoons sugar
- 12 garlic cloves, minced
- 2 ounces distilled vinegar
- 2 ounces water

Directions:

1. Place all the ingredients into a pan that fits your air fryer and mix well.
2. Put the pan into the air fryer and cook at 370 degrees F for 20 minutes.
3. Blend using an immersion blender, divide into bowls, and serve as a party dip.

Nutrition information:calories 100, fat 1, fiber 2, carbs 7, protein 4

522. Easy Eggplant Spread

Preparation time: 10 minutes

Cooking time: 25 minutes

Servings: 6

Ingredients:

- 15 ounces canned tomatoes, chopped
- 5 garlic cloves, minced
- 3 ounces canned tomato paste
- 1 sweet onion, chopped
- 3 small eggplants, chopped
- ½ cup olive oil
- ½ teaspoon turmeric powder
- 1 cup beef stock
- 1 tablespoon apple cider vinegar
- Salt and black pepper to taste
- ¼ cup parsley, chopped

Directions:

1. In a pan that fits your air fryer, place all the ingredients except the parsley; stir well.
2. Put the pan in the fryer and cook at 380 degrees F for 25 minutes.
3. Blend a bit using an immersion blender, add the parsley, and stir.
4. Put into a bowl, chill, and serve cold.

Nutrition information:calories 151, fat 8, fiber 6, carbs 11, protein 5

523. Broccoli Spread

Preparation time: 10 minutes

Cooking time: 15 minutes

Servings: 4

Ingredients:

- 1½ cups veggie stock
- 3 cups broccoli florets
- 2 garlic cloves, minced
- Salt and black pepper to taste
- ⅓ cup coconut milk
- 1 tablespoon white wine vinegar

- 1 tablespoon olive oil

Directions:

1. In a pan that fits your air fryer, mix all the ingredients except the coconut milk.
2. Place the pan in the fryer and cook at 390 degrees F for 15 minutes.
3. Add the coconut milk and blend using an immersion blender.
4. Put the spread into a bowl and chill.
5. Serve cold as an appetizer.

Nutrition information:calories 151, fat 4, fiber 7, carbs 12, protein 5

524. Buttery Carrot Dip

Preparation time: 10 minutes

Cooking time: 15 minutes

Servings: 6

Ingredients:

- 4 tablespoons butter, melted
- 2 cups carrots, grated
- Salt and black pepper to taste
- A pinch of cayenne pepper
- 1 tablespoon chives

Directions:

1. Add all ingredients to a pan that fits your air fryer and mix.
2. Place the pan in the fryer and cook at 380 degrees F for 15 minutes.
3. Blend a bit using an immersion blender, and then divide into bowls.
4. Serve as a dip.

Nutrition information:calories 151, fat 4, fiber 5, carbs 13, protein 5

525. Apple and Dates Dip

Preparation time: 5 minutes

Cooking time: 19 minutes

Servings: 6

Ingredients:

- 2 cups apples, cored, peeled and grated
- ¼ cup apple juice
- 2 cups dates, dried
- 1 tablespoon lemon juice

Directions:

1. In a pan that fits your air fryer, mix all the ingredients.
2. Place the pan in the fryer and cook at 380 degrees F for 19 minutes.
3. Blend a bit using an immersion blender, then place in a bowl and chill.
4. Serve cold as a dip.

Nutrition information:calories 100, fat 1, fiber 3, carbs 9, protein 3

526. Simple Fennel and Tomato Spread

Preparation time: 10 minutes

Cooking time: 16 minutes

Servings: 6

Ingredients:

- 1 fennel bulb, chopped
- 2 pints grape tomatoes, chopped

- ¼ cup dry white wine
- 3 tablespoons olive oil
- Salt and black pepper to taste

Directions:

1. In a pan that fits your air fryer, mix all the ingredients.
2. Place the pan in the fryer and cook at 390 degrees F for 16 minutes.
3. Stir well, divide into bowls, and serve as a dip.

Nutrition information:calories 100, fat 2, fiber 2, carbs 11, protein 4

527. Creamy Leek Spread

Preparation time: 5 minutes

Cooking time: 15 minutes

Servings: 6

Ingredients:

- 3 leeks, roughly chopped
- 2 tablespoons butter, melted
- ½ cup whipping cream
- 3 tablespoons lemon juice
- Salt and pepper to taste

Directions:

1. In a pan that fits your air fryer, mix the leeks, butter, lemon juice, salt, and pepper; stir well.
2. Put the pan into the fryer and cook at 380 degrees F for 15 minutes.
3. Transfer the mixture to a blender, add the cream, and pulse.
4. Divide into bowls and serve cold.

Nutrition information:calories 161, fat 8, fiber 2, carbs 14, protein 6

528. Fast Parsley Dip

Preparation time: 5 minutes

Cooking time: 8 minutes

Servings: 6

Ingredients:

- ¼ cup chicken stock
- 1 yellow onion, chopped
- 2 tablespoons butter, melted
- 3 tablespoons whole milk
- 6 tablespoons parsley, chopped
- ¼ cup heavy cream
- Salt and white pepper to taste

Directions:

1. Place all of the ingredients—except the cream—into a pan that fits your air fryer; mix well.
2. Put the pan into the fryer and cook at 370 degrees F for 8 minutes.
3. Transfer to a blender, add the cream, and pulse.
4. Put the mixture into a bowl and chill.
5. Serve cold.

Nutrition information:calories 100, fat 2, fiber 5, carbs 11, protein 3

529. Scallions and Shallots Dip

Preparation time: 5 minutes

Cooking time: 15 minutes

Servings: 6

Ingredients:

- 3 garlic cloves, minced
- 1 tablespoon olive oil
- 2 red chilies, minced
- 3 shallots, minced
- 3 scallions, chopped
- 1 tomato, chopped
- Salt and black pepper to taste
- 2 tablespoons cilantro, chopped
- 3½ tablespoons veggie stock

Directions:

1. In a pan that fits your air fryer, add all the ingredients and toss.
2. Place the pan in the fryer and cook at 390 degrees F for 15 minutes.
3. Blend a bit using an immersion blender, then put in a bowl and chill.
4. Serve cold as a snack or appetizer; enjoy!

Nutrition information:calories 131, fat 5, fiber 4, carbs 14, protein 3

530. Corn Dip

Preparation time: 5 minutes

Cooking time: 18 minutes

Servings: 4

Ingredients:

- 1 yellow onion, chopped
- 1 tablespoon olive oil
- 1 cup chicken stock
- 2 tablespoons white wine
- 2 cups corn kernels
- Salt and black pepper to taste
- 2 teaspoons butter, melted
- 1 teaspoon thyme, chopped

Directions:

1. Put a pan that fits your air fryer over medium heat and add the oil and the butter; heat up.
2. Add the onion; stir, and sauté for 3 minutes.
3. Add the corn, stock, wine, salt, pepper, and thyme; stir.
4. Place the pan in the fryer and cook at 390 degrees F for 15 minutes.
5. Blend a bit using an immersion blender, divide into bowls, and serve as a party dip or appetizer.

Nutrition information:calories 151, fat 2, fiber 5, carbs 14, protein 4

531. Polenta Biscuits

Preparation time: 10 minutes

Cooking time: 25 minutes

Servings: 4

Ingredients:

- 18 ounces cooked polenta roll, cold
- 1 tablespoon olive oil

Directions:

1. Cut polenta in medium slices and brush them with the olive oil.
2. Place polenta biscuits into your air fryer and cook at 400 degrees F for 25 minutes, flipping them after 10 minutes.
3. Serve biscuits as a snack.

Nutrition information:calories 120, fat 0, fiber 3, carbs 7, protein 3

532. Potato and Beans Dip

Preparation time: 10 minutes

Cooking time: 10 minutes

Servings: 10

Ingredients:

- 19 ounces canned garbanzo beans, drained
- 1 cup sweet potatoes, peeled and chopped
- ¼ cup sesame paste
- 2 tablespoons lemon juice
- 1 tablespoon olive oil
- 5 garlic cloves, minced
- ½ teaspoon cumin, ground
- 2 tablespoons water
- Salt and white pepper to the taste

Directions:

1. Put potatoes in your air fryer's basket, cook them at 360 degrees F for 10 minutes, cool them down, peel, put them in your food processor and pulse well.
2. Add sesame paste, garlic, beans, lemon juice, cumin, water, oil, salt and pepper, pulse again, divide into bowls and serve cold.
3. Enjoy!

Nutrition information:calories 170, fat 3, fiber 10, carbs 12, protein 11

533. Squash Party Muffins

Preparation time: 10 minutes

Cooking time: 26 minutes

Servings: 6

- **Ingredients:**

- 1 spaghetti squash, peeled and halved
- 2 tablespoons avocado mayonnaise
- 1 cup cashew cheese, shredded
- 1 and ½ cups vegan breadcrumbs
- 1 teaspoon parsley, dried
- 1 garlic clove, minced
- Salt and black pepper to the taste
- Cooking spray

Directions:

1. Put squash halves in your air fryer, cook at 350 degrees F for 16 minutes, leave aside to cool down, scrape flesh into a bowl, add salt, pepper, parsley, breadcrumbs, mayo and cashew cheese and stir well.
2. Spray a muffin tray that fits your air fryer with cooking spray and divide squash mix in each cup, introduce in the fryer and cook at 360 degrees F for 10 minutes.
3. Arrange muffins on a platter and serve as a snack.
4. Enjoy!

Nutrition information:calories 120, fat 2, fiber 3, carbs 7, protein 4

534. Cauliflower Crackers

Preparation time: 10 minutes

Cooking time: 25 minutes

Servings: 12

Ingredients:

- 1 big cauliflower head, florets separated and riced

- ½ cup cashew cheese, shredded
- 1 tablespoon flax meal mixed with 1 tablespoon water
- 1 teaspoon Italian seasoning
- Salt and black pepper to the taste

Directions:

1. Spread cauliflower rice on a lined baking sheet that fits your air fryer, introduce in the fryer and cook at 360 degrees F for 10 minutes.
2. Transfer cauliflower to a bowl, add salt, pepper, cashew cheese, flax meal and Italian seasoning, stir really well, spread this into a rectangle pan that fits your air fryer, press well, introduce in the fryer and cook at 360 degrees F for 15 minutes more.
3. Cut into medium crackers and serve as a snack.
4. Enjoy!

Nutrition information:calories 120, fat 1, fiber 2, carbs 7, protein 3

535. Basil Crackers

Preparation time: 10 minutes

Cooking time: 17 minutes

Servings: 6

Ingredients:

- ½ teaspoon baking powder
- Salt and black pepper to the taste
- 1 and ¼ cups whole wheat flour
- ¼ teaspoon basil, dried
- 1 garlic clove, minced
- 2 tablespoons vegan basil pesto
- 2 tablespoons olive oil

Directions:

1. In a bowl, mix flour with salt, pepper, baking powder, garlic, cayenne, basil, pesto and oil, stir until you obtain a dough, spread this on a lined baking sheet that fits your air fryer, introduce in the fryer at 325 degrees F and bake for 17 minutes.
2. Leave aside to cool down, cut crackers and serve them as a snack.
3. Enjoy!

Nutrition information:calories 170, fat 20, fiber 1, carbs 6, protein 7

536. Potato Party Patties

Preparation time: 10 minutes

Cooking time: 12 minutes

Servings: 4

Ingredients:

- 3 big potatoes, boiled, drained and mashed
- 2 tablespoons parsley, chopped
- 2 tablespoon dill, chopped
- Salt and black pepper to the taste
- 1 tablespoon flax meal combined with 1 tablespoon water
- 2 tablespoons vegan breadcrumbs
- Cooking spray

Directions:

1. In a bawl, mix potatoes, salt, pepper, dill, parsley, flax meal and breadcrumbs, stir well and shape 8 patties out of this mix.
2. Place patties in your air fryer's basket, spray them with cooking oil, cook at 360 degrees F for 12 minutes,

flipping them halfway, transfer them to a platter and serve as an appetizer.

3. Enjoy!

Nutrition information:calories 201, fat 3, fiber 7, carbs 14, protein 4

537. Mini Peppers Appetizer

Preparation time: 10 minutes

Cooking time: 6 minutes

Servings: 6

Ingredients:

- 1 pound mini bell peppers, halved
- Salt and black pepper to the taste
- 1 teaspoon garlic powder
- 1 teaspoon sweet paprika
- ½ teaspoon oregano, dried
- ¼ teaspoon red pepper flakes
- 2 cups soft tofu, crumbled
- 1 tablespoons chili powder
- 1 teaspoon cumin, ground

Directions:

1. In a bowl, mix chili powder with paprika, salt, pepper, cumin, oregano, pepper flakes, tofu and garlic powder and stir.
2. Stuff pepper halves with this mix, place them in your air fryer's basket and cook them at 350 degrees F for 6 minutes.
3. Arrange peppers on a platter and serve them as an appetizer.
4. Enjoy!

Nutrition information:calories 170, fat 22, fiber 3, carbs 6, protein 6

538. Kale Crackers

Preparation time: 10 minutes

Cooking time: 20 minutes

Servings: 6

Ingredients:

- 2 cups flaxseed, ground
- 2 cups flaxseed, soaked overnight and drained
- 4 bunches kale, chopped
- 1 bunch basil, chopped
- 4 garlic cloves, minced
- 1/3 cup olive oil

Directions:

1. In your food processor mix ground flaxseed with kale, basil and garlic and blend well.
2. Add oil and soaked flaxseed, blend again, spread in your air fryer's pan, cut into medium crackers and cook them at 380 degrees F for 20 minutes.
3. Divide into bowls and serve as a snack.
4. Enjoy!

Nutrition information:calories 173, fat 1, fiber 2, carbs 8, protein 4

539. Squash Pate

Preparation time: 10 minutes

Cooking time: 25 minutes

Servings: 4

Ingredients:

- 2 cups butternut squash, peeled and

cubed

- 3 tablespoons coconut milk
- A pinch of rosemary, dried
- A pinch of sage, dried
- A pinch of salt and black pepper

Directions:

1. In your air fryer's pan, mix squash, coconut milk, sage, rosemary, salt and pepper, toss, introduce in your air fryer and cook at 375 degrees F for 25 minutes.
2. Blend using an immersion blender, divide into bowls and serve cold.
3. Enjoy!

Nutrition information:calories 182, fat 5, fiber 7, carbs 12, protein 5

540. Eggplant Appetizer Salad

Preparation time: 10 minutes

Cooking time: 20 minutes

Servings: 4

Ingredients:

- 1 and ½ cups tomatoes, chopped
- 3 cups eggplant, cubed
- 6 ounces black olives, pitted and sliced
- 2 teaspoons balsamic vinegar
- 1 tablespoon oregano, chopped
- Salt and black pepper to the taste

Directions:

1. In a pan that fits your air fryer, mix tomatoes with eggplant, olives, vinegar, oregano, salt and pepper, toss, introduce in your fryer and cook at 370 degrees F for 20 minutes
2. Divide between small appetizer plates and serve as an appetizer.
3. Enjoy!

Nutrition information:calories 170, fat 6, fiber 5, carbs 9, protein 2

541. Vegan Veggie Dip

Preparation time: 10 minutes

Cooking time: 25 minutes

Servings: 4

Ingredients:

- 1 cup carrots, sliced
- 1 and ½ cups cauliflower florets
- 1/3 cup cashews
- ½ cup turnips, chopped
- 2 and ½ cups water
- 1 cup almond milk
- 1 teaspoon garlic powder
- ¼ cup nutritional yeast
- ¼ teaspoon smoked paprika
- ¼ teaspoon mustard powder
- A pinch of salt

Directions:

1. In a pan that fits your air fryer, mix carrots with cauliflower, cashews, turnips and water, stir, put in your air fryer and cook at 365 degrees F for 25 minutes
2. Transfer to a blender, add almond milk, garlic powder, yeast, paprika, mustard powder and salt, blend well and serve.
3. Enjoy!

Nutrition information:calories 261, fat 7, fiber 4, carbs 14, protein 3

542. Cauliflower and Mushroom Dip

Preparation time: 10 minutes

Cooking time: 25 minutes

Servings: 7

Ingredients:

- ½ cauliflower head, riced
- 54 ounces canned tomatoes, crushed
- 10 ounces white mushrooms, chopped
- 2 cups carrots, shredded
- 2 cups eggplant, cubed
- 6 garlic cloves, minced
- 2 tablespoons agave nectar
- 2 tablespoons balsamic vinegar
- 2 tablespoons tomato paste
- 1 tablespoon basil, chopped
- 1 and ½ tablespoons oregano, chopped
- 1 and ½ teaspoons rosemary, dried
- A pinch of salt and black pepper

Directions:

1. In a pan that fits your air fryer, mix cauliflower with tomatoes, mushrooms, carrots, eggplant cubes, garlic, agave nectar, balsamic vinegar, tomato paste, rosemary, salt and pepper, stir, transfer to your air fryer and cook at 365 degrees F for 25 minutes
2. Add basil and oregano, stir, divide into bowls and serve as an appetizer.
3. Enjoy!

Nutrition information:calories 241, fat 7, fiber 6, carbs 10, protein 6

543. Chickpeas Dip

Preparation time: 10 minutes

Cooking time: 20 minutes

Servings: 10

Ingredients:

- 1 cup canned chickpeas, drained and some of the liquid reserved
- 2 tablespoons olive oil
- 1 tablespoon sesame paste
- A pinch of salt and black pepper
- 1 garlic clove, minced
- 1 tablespoon lemon juice

Directions:

1. In a pan that fits your air fryer mix chickpeas with salt, pepper, lemon juice and oil, stir, transfer to your air fryer and cook at 365 degrees F for 20 minutes.
2. Transfer chickpeas to a blender, add sesame paste, reserved liquid and garlic, blend well, divide into bowls and serve as a dip
3. Enjoy!

Nutrition information:calories 241, fat 6, fiber 7, carbs 8, protein 4

544. Spinach Spread

Preparation time: 10 minutes

Cooking time: 10 minutes

Servings: 4

Ingredients:

- ½ cup coconut cream
- ¾ cup coconut yogurt
- 10 ounces spinach
- 8 ounces water chestnuts, chopped
- 1 garlic clove, minced

Directions:

1. In a pan that fits your air fryer, mix coconut cream with spinach, coconut yogurt, chestnuts and garlic, stir, transfer to your air fryer, cook at 365 degrees F for 10 minutes, blend using an immersion blender, divide into bowls and serve as an appetizer.
2. Enjoy!

Nutrition information:calories 201, fat 5, fiber 7, carbs 12, protein 5

545. Italian Veggie Appetizer Salad

Preparation time: 10 minutes

Cooking time: 15 minutes

Servings: 4

Ingredients:

- 2 red bell peppers, cut into medium wedges
- 1 sweet potato, cut into medium wedges
- 3 zucchinis, sliced
- ½ cup garlic, minced
- 2 tablespoons olive oil
- Salt and black pepper to the taste
- 1 teaspoon Italian seasoning

Directions:

1. In your air fryer's pan, mix bell peppers with sweet potato, zucchinis, garlic, oil, salt, pepper and seasoning, toss, transfer to your air fryer and cook at 365 degrees F for 15 minutes
2. Divide into small bowls and serve cold as an appetizer.
3. Enjoy!

Nutrition information:calories 132, fat 3, fiber 3, carbs 4, protein 4

DESSERT

546. Cinnamon Rolls

Preparation time: 2 hours

Cooking time: 10 minutes

Servings: 8

Ingredients:

- 1 pound bread dough
- ¾ cup brown sugar
- 1½ tablespoons cinnamon, ground
- ¼ cup butter, melted

Directions:

1. Roll the dough on a floured working surface, shape a rectangle, and brush with the butter.
2. In a bowl, combine the cinnamon and sugar, and then sprinkle this over the dough.
3. Roll the dough into a log, seal, cut into 8 pieces, and leave the rolls to rise for 2 hours.
4. Place the rolls in your air fryer's basket and cook at 350 degrees F for 5 minutes on each side.
5. Serve warm, and enjoy!

Nutrition information:calories 200, fat 11, fiber 2, carbs 15, protein 4

547. Simple Nutmeg Pumpkin Pie

Preparation time: 10 minutes

Cooking time: 35 minutes

Servings: 8

Ingredients:

- 1 pie crust
- 3½ ounces pumpkin flesh, chopped
- 1 teaspoon nutmeg, ground
- 3 ounces water
- 1 egg, whisked
- 1 tablespoon sugar

Directions:

1. Put the water in a pot and bring to a boil over medium-high heat.
2. Add the pumpkin, egg, sugar, and the nutmeg; stir, and allow to boil for 20 minutes.
3. Remove the mixture from the heat and blend using an immersion blender.
4. Put the pie crust in a lined pan that fits your air fryer and spread the pumpkin mix all over.
5. Place the pan in the fryer and cook at 360 degrees F for 15 minutes.
6. Slice and serve warm.

Nutrition information:calories 212, fat 5, fiber 2, carbs 15, protein 7

548. Cinnamon Pears

Preparation time: 5 minutes

Cooking time: 15 minutes

Servings: 4

Ingredients:

- 2 pears, halved
- ½ teaspoon cinnamon powder

- 2 tablespoons sugar

Directions:

1. Put the pears in your air fryer, and sprinkle the cinnamon and the sugar all over.
2. Cook at 320 degrees F for 15 minutes.
3. Serve these pears warm, and enjoy!

Nutrition information:calories 210, fat 2, fiber 1, carbs 12, protein 3

549. Butter Donuts

Preparation time: 10 minutes

Cooking time: 15 minutes

Servings: 4

Ingredients:

- 8 ounces flour
- 1 tablespoon brown sugar
- 1 tablespoon white sugar
- 1 egg
- 2½ tablespoons butter
- 4 ounces whole milk
- 1 teaspoon baking powder

Directions:

1. Place all of the ingredients in a bowl and mix well.
2. Shape donuts from this mix and place them in your air fryer's basket.
3. Cook at 360 degrees F for 15 minutes.
4. Arrange the donuts on a platter and serve them warm.

Nutrition information:calories 190, fat 8, fiber 1, carbs 14, protein 3

550. Cinnamon Apples

Preparation time: 5 minutes

Cooking time: 15 minutes

Servings: 4

Ingredients:

- 3 tablespoons butter, melted
- 4 apples, peeled, cored and cut into wedges
- 3 tablespoons cinnamon sugar

Directions:

1. In a pan that fits your air fryer, mix the apples with the sugar and the butter; toss.
2. Place the pan in the fryer and cook at 370 degrees F for 15 minutes.
3. Serve warm.

Nutrition information:calories 204, fat 3, fiber 4, carbs 12, protein 4

551. Lemon Cake

Preparation time: 5 minutes

Cooking time: 17 minutes

Servings: 6

Ingredients:

- 3½ ounces butter, melted
- 3 eggs
- 3 ounces brown sugar
- 3 ounces flour
- 1 teaspoon dark chocolate, grated
- ½ teaspoon lemon juice

Directions:

1. Mix all of the ingredients in a bowl.
2. Pour the mixture into a greased cake pan, and place in the fryer.
3. Cook at 360 degrees F for 17 minutes.
4. Let cake cool before serving.

Nutrition information:calories 220, fat 11, fiber 3, carbs 15, protein 7

552. Yogurt Cake

Preparation time: 5 minutes

Cooking time: 30 minutes

Servings: 8

Ingredients:

- 1½ cups white flour
- 1 teaspoon baking soda
- ¾ cup sugar
- 1 banana, mashed
- ½ teaspoon baking powder
- 2 tablespoons vegetable oil
- 1 cup Greek yogurt
- 8 ounces canned pumpkin puree
- Cooking spray
- 1 egg
- ½ teaspoon vanilla extract

Directions:

1. In a bowl, combine all ingredients (except the cooking spray) and stir well.
2. Pour the mixture into a cake pan greased with cooking spray and put it in your air fryer's basket.
3. Cook at 330 degrees F for 30 minutes.
4. Cool down, slice, and serve.

Nutrition information:calories 192, fat 7, fiber 7, carbs 12, protein 4

553. Zucchini Bread

Preparation time: 10 minutes

Cooking time: 40 minutes

Servings: 6

Ingredients:

- 3 cups zucchinis, grated
- 1 cup sugar
- 1 tablespoon vanilla extract
- 2 eggs, whisked
- 2 cups white flour
- 1 tablespoon baking powder
- 1 stick butter, melted

Directions:

1. Add all of the ingredients to a bowl and mix well.
2. Pour the mixture into a lined loaf pan and place in the fryer. and cook at 320 degrees F for 40 minutes.
3. Slice and serve warm.

Nutrition information:calories 132, fat 6, fiber 7, carbs 11, protein 7

554. Cream of Tartar Bread

Preparation time: 10 minutes

Cooking time: 40 minutes

Servings: 6

Ingredients:

- ¾ cup sugar
- ⅓ cup butter
- 1 teaspoon vanilla extract
- 1 egg
- 2 zucchinis, grated
- 1 teaspoon baking powder
- 1½ cups flour
- ½ teaspoon baking soda
- ⅓ cup milk
- 1½ teaspoons cream of tartar

Directions:

1. Place all ingredients in a bowl and mix well.
2. Pour the mixture into a lined loaf pan and place the pan in the air fryer.
3. Cook at 320 degrees F for 40 minutes
4. Cool down, slice, and serve.

Nutrition information:calories 222, fat 7, fiber 8, carbs 14, protein 4

555. Orange Cake

Preparation time: 10 minutes

Cooking time: 20 minutes

Servings: 3

Ingredients:

- 1 egg
- 4 tablespoons sugar
- 2 tablespoons vegetable oil
- 4 tablespoons milk
- 2 tablespoons orange juice
- 4 tablespoons flour
- 1 tablespoon cocoa powder
- ½ teaspoon baking powder
- ½ teaspoon orange zest

Directions:

1. Place all of the ingredients in a bowl and mix well.
2. Divide the mixture between 3 ramekins and place them in your air fryer.
3. Cook at 320 degrees F for 20 minutes.
4. Serve the cakes warm, and enjoy!

Nutrition information:calories 191, fat 7, fiber 3, carbs 14, protein 4

556. Maple Apples

Preparation time: 10 minutes

Cooking time: 10 minutes

Servings: 4

Ingredients:

- 2 teaspoons cinnamon powder
- 5 apples, cored and cut into wedges
- ½ teaspoon nutmeg powder
- 1 tablespoon maple syrup
- 4 tablespoons butter
- ¼ cup brown sugar

Directions:

1. In a pan that fits your air fryer, mix the apples with the other ingredients and toss.
2. Place the pan in the fryer and cook at 360 degrees F for 10 minutes.
3. Divide into cups and serve.

Nutrition information:calories 180, fat 6, fiber 8, carbs 19, protein 12

557. Pineapple and Carrot Cake

Preparation time: 10 minutes

Cooking time: 45 minutes

Servings: 6

Ingredients:

- 5 ounces flour
- ¾ teaspoon baking powder
- ½ teaspoon baking soda
- ½ teaspoon cinnamon powder
- 1 egg, whisked
- 3 tablespoons yogurt
- ½ cup sugar
- ¼ cup pineapple juice
- 4 tablespoons vegetable oil
- ⅓ cup carrots, grated
- ⅓ cup coconut flakes, shredded
- Cooking spray

Directions:

1. Place all of the ingredients (except the cooking spray) in a bowl, and mix well.
2. Pour the mixture into a spring form pan, greased with cooking spray, that fits your air fryer.
3. Place the pan in your air fryer and cook at 320 degrees F for 45 minutes.
4. Allow the cake to cool before cutting and serving.

Nutrition information:calories 200, fat 6, fiber 7, carbs 12, protein 4

558. Rum Cheesecake

Preparation time:10 minutes

Cooking time: 20 minutes

Servings: 6

Ingredients:

- 2 teaspoons butter, melted
- ½ cup graham cookies, crumbled
- 16 ounces cream cheese, softened
- 2 eggs
- ½ cup sugar
- 1 teaspoon rum
- ½ teaspoon vanilla extract

Directions:

1. Grease a pan with the butter and spread the cookie crumbs on the bottom.
2. In a bowl, mix all the remaining ingredients and whisk well; then spread this mixture over the cookie crumbs.
3. Place the pan in your air fryer and cook at 340 degrees F for 20 minutes.
4. Let the cheesecake cool down, refrigerate, and serve cold.

Nutrition information:calories 212, fat 12, fiber 6, carbs 12, protein 7

559. Strawberry Cream

Preparation time: 5 minutes

Cooking time: 15 minutes

Servings: 6

Ingredients:

- 1 teaspoon gelatin
- 8 ounces cream cheese
- 4 ounces strawberries

- 2 tablespoons water
- ½ tablespoon lemon juice
- ¼ teaspoon sugar
- ½ cup heavy cream

Directions:

1. Place all ingredients in your blender and pulse.
2. Divide the mixture into 6 ramekins and place them in your air fryer.
3. Cook at 330 degrees F for 15 minutes.
4. Refrigerate (or place briefly in freezer) and serve the cream really cold.

Nutrition information:calories 202, fat 8, fiber 2, carbs 6, protein 7

560. Coffee Cream

Preparation time: 5 minutes

Cooking time: 10 minutes

Servings: 6

Ingredients:

- 2 tablespoons butter
- 8 ounces cream cheese
- 3 tablespoons coffee
- 3 eggs
- ⅓ cup sugar
- 1 tablespoon caramel syrup

Directions:

1. Place all ingredients in your blender and pulse.
2. Divide the mixture between 6 ramekins, and place in the fryer.
3. Cook at 320 degrees F; bake for 10 minutes.
4. Let cool down and then place in the freezer before serving.

Nutrition information:calories 234, fat 13, fiber 4, carbs 11, protein 5

561. Cream Cheese Cookies

Preparation time: 10 minutes

Cooking time: 14 minutes

Servings: 12

Ingredients:

- 6 ounces vegetable oil
- 6 eggs
- 3 ounces cocoa powder
- 2 teaspoons vanilla extract
- ½ teaspoon baking powder
- 4 ounces cream cheese
- 5 tablespoons sugar

Directions:

1. Add all the ingredients to a blender and pulse a bit.
2. Pour this mixture into a baking dish lined with parchment paper that fits your air fryer.
3. Place the pan in the fryer at 320 degrees F, and bake for 14 minutes.
4. Slice into rectangles and serve.

Nutrition information:calories 178, fat 11, fiber 3, carbs 3, protein 5

562. Tangerine Cake

Preparation time: 10 minutes
Cooking time: 20 minutes
Servings: 8

Ingredients:

- ¾ cup sugar
- 2 cups flour
- ¼ cup olive oil
- ½ cup milk
- 1 teaspoon cider vinegar
- ½ teaspoon vanilla extract
- Juice and zest from 2 lemons
- Juice and zest from 1 tangerine
- Tangerine segments, for serving

Directions:

1. In a bowl, mix flour with sugar and stir.
2. In another bowl, mix oil with milk, vinegar, vanilla extract, lemon juice and zest and tangerine zest and whisk very well.
3. Add flour, stir well, pour this into a cake pan that fits your air fryer, introduce in the fryer and cook at 360 degrees F for 20 minutes.
4. Serve right away with tangerine segments on top.
5. Enjoy!

Nutrition information: calories 190, fat 1, fiber 1, carbs 4, protein 4

563. Blueberry Pudding

Preparation time: 10 minutes
Cooking time: 25 minutes
Servings: 6

Ingredients:

- 2 cups flour
- 2 cups rolled oats
- 8 cups blueberries
- 1 stick butter, melted
- 1 cup walnuts, chopped
- 3 tablespoons maple syrup
- 2 tablespoons rosemary, chopped

Directions:

1. Spread blueberries in a greased baking pan and leave aside.
2. In your food processor, mix rolled oats with flour, walnuts, butter, maple syrup and rosemary, blend well, layer this over blueberries, introduce everything in your air fryer and cook at 350 degrees for 25 minutes.
3. Leave dessert to cool down, cut and serve.
4. Enjoy!

Nutrition information: calories 150, fat 3, fiber 2, carbs 7, protein 4

564. Cocoa and Almond Bars

Preparation time: 30 minutes
Cooking time: 4 minutes
Servings: 6

Ingredients:

- ¼ cup cocoa nibs
- 1 cup almonds, soaked and drained
- 2 tablespoons cocoa powder
- ¼ cup hemp seeds

- ¼ cup goji berries
- ¼ cup coconut, shredded
- 8 dates, pitted and soaked

Directions:

1. Put almonds in your food processor, blend, add hemp seeds, cocoa nibs, cocoa powder, goji, coconut and blend very well.
2. Add dates, blend well again, spread on a lined baking sheet that fits your air fryer and cook at 320 degrees F for 4 minutes.
3. Cut into equal parts and keep in the fridge for 30 minutes before serving.
4. Enjoy!

Nutrition information: calories 140, fat 6, fiber 3, carbs 7, protein 19

565.Turkey Wontons with Garlic-Parmesan Sauce

Preparation time:15 minutes

Servings 8

Nutrition Information:362 Calories; 13.5g Fat; 40.4g Carbs; 18.5g Protein; 1.2g Sugars

Ingredients

- 8 ounces cooked turkey breasts, shredded
- 16 wonton wrappers
- 1 ½ tablespoons butter, melted
- 1/3 cup cream cheese, room temperature
- 8 ounces Asiago cheese, shredded
- 3 tablespoons Parmesan cheese,grated
- 1 teaspoon garlic powder
- Fine sea salt and freshly ground black pepper, to taste

Directions

1. In a small-sized bowl, mix the butter, Parmesan, garlic powder, salt, and black pepper; give it a good stir.
2. Lightly grease a mini muffin pan; lay 1 wonton wrapper in each mini muffin cup. Fill each cup with the cream cheese and turkey mixture.
3. Air-fry for 8 minutes at 335 degrees F. Immediately top with Asiago cheese and serve warm.Bon appétit!

566. Cajun Turkey Meatloaf

Preparation time: 45 minutes

Servings 6

Nutrition Information:429 Calories; 31.6g Fat; 8.3g Carbs; 25.3g Protein; 2.2g Sugars

Ingredients

- 1 1/3 pounds turkey breasts, ground
- ½ cup vegetable stock
- 2 eggs, lightly beaten
- 1/2 sprig thyme, chopped
- 1/2 teaspoon Cajun seasonings
- 1/2 sprig coriander, chopped
- ½ cup seasoned breadcrumbs
- 2 tablespoons butter, room temperature
- 1/2 cup scallions,chopped
- 1/3 teaspoon ground nutmeg
- 1/3 cup tomato ketchup
- 1/2 teaspoon table salt

- 2 teaspoons whole grain mustard
- 1/3 teaspoon mixed peppercorns, freshly cracked

Directions

1. Firstly, warm the butter in a medium-sized saucepan that is placed over a moderate heat; sauté the scallions together with the chopped thyme and coriander leaves until just tender.
2. While the scallions are sautéing, set your air fryer to cook at 365 degrees F.
3. Combine all the ingredients, minus the ketchup, in a mixing dish; fold in the sautéed mixture and mix again.
4. Shape into a meatloaf and top with the tomato ketchup. Air-fry for 50 minutes. Bon appétit!

567. Wine-Braised Turkey Breasts

Preparation time: 30 minutes + marinating time

Servings 4

Nutrition Information:230 Calories; 11.6g Fat; 15.2g Carbs; 16.1g Protein; 2.2g Sugars

Ingredients

- 1/3 cup dry white wine
- 1½ tablespoon sesame oil
- 1/2 pound turkey breasts, boneless, skinless and sliced
- 1/2 tablespoon honey
- 1/2 cup plain flour
- 2 tablespoons oyster sauce
- Sea salt flakes and cracked black peppercorns, to taste

Directions

1. Set the air fryer to cook at 385 degrees. Pat the turkey slices dry and season with the sea salt flakes and the cracked peppercorns.
2. In a bowl, mix the other ingredients together, minus the flour; rub your turkey with this mixture. Set aside to marinate for at least 55 minutes.
3. Coat each turkey slice with the plain flour. Cook for 27 minutes; make sure to flip once or twice and work in batches. Bon appétit!

568. Peppery Roasted Potatoes with Smoked Bacon

Preparation time: 15 minutes

Servings 2

Nutrition Information:242 Calories; 11.6g Fat; 15,4g Carbs; 14.9g Protein; 5.7g Sugars

Ingredients

- 5 small rashers smoked bacon
- 1/3 teaspoon garlic powder
- 1 teaspoon sea salt
- 2 teaspoons paprika
- 1/3 teaspoon ground black pepper
- 1 bell pepper, seeded and sliced
- 1 teaspoon mustard
- 2 habanero peppers, halved

Directions

1. Simply toss all the ingredients in a mixing dish; then, transfer them to

your air fryer's basket.

2. Air-fry at 375 degrees F for 10 minutes. Serve warm.

569. Cornbread with Pulled Pork

Preparation time: 24 minutes

Servings 2

Nutrition Information:239 Calories; 7.6g Fat; 6.3g Carbs; 34.6g Protein; 4g Sugars

Ingredients

- 2 ½ cups pulled pork, leftover works well too
- 1 teaspoon dried rosemary
- 1/2 teaspoon chili powder
- 3 cloves garlic, peeled and pressed
- 1/2 recipe cornbread
- 1/2 tablespoon brown sugar
- 1/3 cup scallions, thinly sliced
- 1 teaspoon sea salt

Directions

1. Preheat a large-sized nonstick skillet over medium heat; now, cook the scallions together with the garlic and pulled pork.
2. Next, add the sugar, chili powder, rosemary, and salt. Cook, stirring occasionally, until the mixture is thickened.
3. Preheat your air fryer to 335 degrees F. Now, coat two mini loaf pans with a cooking spray. Add the pulled pork mixture and spread over the bottom using a spatula.
4. Spread the previously prepared cornbread batter over top of the spiced pulled pork mixture.
5. Bake this cornbread in the preheated air fryer until a tester inserted into the center of it comes out clean, or for 18 minutes. Bon appétit!

570. Famous Cheese and Bacon Rolls

Preparation time: 10 minutes

Servings 6

Nutrition Information:386 Calories; 16.2g Fat; 29.7g Carbs; 14.7g Protein; 4g Sugars

Ingredients

- 1/3 cup Swiss cheese, shredded
- 10 slices of bacon
- 10 ounces canned crescent rolls
- 2 tablespoons yellow mustard 6

Directions

1. Start by preheating your air fryer to 325 degrees F.
2. Then, form the crescent rolls into "sheets". Spread mustard over the sheets. Place the chopped Swiss cheese and bacon in the middle of each dough sheet.
3. Create the rolls and bake them for about 9 minutes.
4. Then, set the machine to 385 degrees F; bake for an additional 4 minutes in the preheated air fryer. Eat warm with some extra yellow mustard.

571. Baked Eggs with Kale and Ham

Preparation time: 15 minutes

Servings 2

Nutrition Information:417 Calories; 17.8g Fat; 3g Carbs; 61g Protein; 0.9g Sugars

Ingredients

- 2 eggs
- 1/4 teaspoon dried or fresh marjoram
- 2 teaspoons chili powder
- 1/3 teaspoon kosher salt
- ½ cup steamed kale
- 1/4 teaspoon dried or fresh rosemary
- 4 pork ham slices
- 1/3 teaspoon ground black pepper, or more to taste

Directions

- Divide the kale and ham among 2 ramekins; crack an egg into each ramekin. Sprinkle with seasonings.
- Cook for 15 minutes at 335 degrees F or until your eggs reach desired texture.
- Serve warm with spicy tomato ketchup and pickles. Bon appétit!

572. Easiest Pork Chops Ever

Preparation time: 22 minutes

Servings 6

Nutrition Information:398 Calories; 21g Fat; 4.7g Carbs; 44.2g Protein; 0.5g Sugars

Ingredients

- 1/3 cup Italian breadcrumbs
- Roughly chopped fresh cilantro, to taste
- 2 teaspoons Cajun seasonings
- Nonstick cooking spray
- 2 eggs, beaten
- 3 tablespoons white flour
- 1 teaspoon seasoned salt
- Garlic & onion spice blend, to taste
- 6 pork chops
- 1/3 teaspoon freshly cracked black pepper

Directions

1. Coat the pork chops with Cajun seasonings, salt, pepper, and the spice blend on all sides.
2. Then, add the flour to a plate. In a shallow dish, whisk the egg until pale and smooth. Place the Italian breadcrumbs in the third bowl.
3. Dredge each pork piece in the flour; then, coat them with the egg; finally, coat them with the breadcrumbs. Spritz them with cooking spray on both sides.
4. Now, air-fry pork chops for about 18 minutes at 345 degrees F; make sure to taste for doneness after first 12 minutes of cooking. Lastly, garnish with fresh cilantro. Bon appétit!

573. Onion Rings Wrapped in Bacon

Preparation time: 25 minutes

Servings 4

Nutrition Information:317 Calories; 16.8g Fat; 22.7g Carbs; 20.2g Protein; 2.7g Sugars

Ingredients

- 12 rashers back bacon
- 1/2 teaspoon ground black pepper
- Chopped fresh parsley, to taste
- 1/2 teaspoon paprika
- 1/2 teaspoon chili powder
- 1/2 tablespoon soy sauce
- ½ teaspoon salt

Directions

- Start by preheating your air fryer to 355 degrees F.
- Season the onion rings with paprika, salt, black pepper, and chili powder. Simply wrap the bacon around the onion rings; drizzle with soy sauce.
- Bake for 17 minutes, garnish with fresh parsley and serve. Bon appétit!

574. Easy Pork Burgers with Blue Cheese

Preparation time: 44 minutes

Servings 6

Nutrition Information:383 Calories; 19.5g Fat; 24.7g Carbs; 25.7g Protein; 4g Sugars

Ingredients

- 1/3 cup blue cheese, crumbled
- 6 hamburger buns, toasted
- 2 teaspoons dried basil
- 1/3 teaspoon smoked paprika
- 1 pound ground pork
- 2 tablespoons tomato puree
- 2 small-sized onions, peeled and chopped
- 1/2 teaspoon ground black pepper
- 3 garlic cloves, minced
- 1 teaspoon fine sea salt

Directions

1. Start by preheating your air fryer to 385 degrees F.
2. In a mixing dish, combine the pork, onion, garlic, tomato puree, and seasonings; mix to combine well.
3. Form the pork mixture into six patties; cook the burgers for 23 minutes. Pause the machine, turn the temperature to 365 degrees F and cook for 18 more minutes.
4. Place the prepared burger on the bottom bun; top with blue cheese; assemble the burgers and serve warm.

575. Sausage, Pepper and Fontina Frittata

Preparation time: 14 minutes

Servings 5

Nutrition Information:420 Calories; 19.6g Fat; 3.7g Carbs; 41g Protein; 2g Sugars

Ingredients

- 3 pork sausages, chopped
- 5 well-beaten eggs
- 1 ½ bell peppers, seeded and chopped
- 1 teaspoon smoked cayenne pepper
- 2 tablespoons Fontina cheese
- 1/2 teaspoon tarragon
- 1/2 teaspoon ground black pepper
- 1 teaspoon salt

Directions

1. In a cast-iron skillet, sweat the bell peppers together with the chopped pork sausages until the peppers are fragrant and the sausage begins to release liquid.
2. Lightly grease the inside of a baking dish with pan spray.
3. Throw all of the above ingredients into the prepared baking dish, including the sautéed mixture; stir to combine.
4. Bake at 345 degrees F approximately 9 minutes. Serve right away with the salad of choice.

576. Country-Style Pork Meatloaf

Preparation time: 25 minutes

Servings 4

Nutrition Information:460 Calories; 26.6g Fat; 3.9g Carbs; 48.9g Protein; 2g Sugars

Ingredients

- 1/2 pound lean minced pork
- 1/3 cup breadcrumbs
- 1/2 tablespoons minced green garlic
- 1½ tablespoon fresh cilantro, minced
- 1/2 tablespoon fish sauce
- 1/3 teaspoon dried basil
- 2 leeks, chopped
- 2 tablespoons tomato puree
- 1/2 teaspoons dried thyme
- Salt and ground black pepper, to taste

Directions

1. Add all ingredients, except forbreadcrumbs, to a large-sized mixing dish and combine everything using your hands.
2. Lastly, add the breadcrumbs to form a meatloaf.
3. Bake for 23 minutes at 365 degrees F.Afterward, allow your meatloaf to rest for 10 minutes before slicing and serving. Bon appétit!

577. Grilled Lemony Pork Chops

Preparation time: 34 minutes

Servings 5

Nutrition Information:400 Calories; 23g Fat; 4.1g Carbs; 40.5g Protein; 1.5g Sugars

Ingredients

- 5 pork chops
- 1/3 cup vermouth
- 1/2 teaspoon paprika
- 2 sprigs thyme, only leaves, crushed
- 1/2 teaspoon dried oregano
- Fresh parsley, to serve
- 1 teaspoon garlic salt½ lemon, cut into wedges
- 1 teaspoon freshly cracked black pepper
- 3 tablespoons lemon juice
- 3 cloves garlic, minced
- 2 tablespoons canola oil

Directions

1. Firstly, heat the canola oil in a sauté pan over a moderate heat. Now, sweat the garlic until just fragrant.

2. Remove the pan from the heat and pour in the lemon juice and vermouth. Now, throw in the seasonings. Dump the sauce into a baking dish, along with the pork chops.
3. Tuck the lemon wedges among the pork chops and air-fry for 27 minutes at 345 degrees F. Bon appétit!

578. Herbed Crumbed Filet Mignon

Preparation time: 20 minutes

Servings 4

Nutrition Information:268 Calories; 14.5g Fat; 1.0g Carbs; 32.0g Protein; 0.0g Sugars

Ingredients

- 1/2 pound filet mignon
- Sea salt and ground black pepper, to your liking
- 1/2 teaspoon cayenne pepper
- 1 teaspoon dried basil
- 1 teaspoon dried rosemary
- 1 teaspoon dried thyme
- 1 tablespoon sesame oil
- 1 small-sized egg, well-whisked
- 1/2 cup seasoned breadcrumbs

Directions

1. Season the filet mignon with salt, black pepper, cayenne pepper, basil, rosemary, and thyme. Brush with sesame oil.
2. Put the egg in a shallow plate. Now, place the breadcrumbs in another plate.
3. Coat the filet mignon with the egg; then, lay it into the crumbs. Set your Air Fryer to cook at 360 degrees F.
4. Cook for 10 to 13 minutes or until golden. Serve with mixed salad leaves and enjoy!

579. The Best London Broil Ever

Preparation time: 30 minutes + marinating time

Servings 8

Nutrition Information:257 Calories; 9.2g Fat; 0.1g Carbs; 41.0g Protein; 0.4g Sugars

Ingredients

- 2 pounds London broil
- 3 large garlic cloves, minced
- 3 tablespoons balsamic vinegar
- 3 tablespoons whole-grain mustard
- 2 tablespoons olive oil
- Sea salt and ground black pepper, to taste
- 1/2 teaspoon dried hot red pepper flakes

Directions

1. Score both sides of the cleaned London broil.
2. Thoroughly combine the remaining ingredients; massage this mixture into the meat to coat it on all sides. Let it marinate for at least 3 hours.
3. Set the Air Fryer to cook at 400 degrees F; Then cook the London broil for 15 minutes. Flip it over and cook another 10 to 12 minutes.Bon appétit!

580. Old-Fashioned Beef Stroganoff

Preparation time: 20 minutes

Servings 4

Nutrition Information:352 Calories; 20.8g Fat; 10.0g Carbs; 29.8g Protein; 1.4g Sugars

Ingredients

- 3/4 pound beef sirloin steak, cut into small-sized strips
- 1/4 cup balsamic vinegar
- 1 tablespoon brown mustard
- 2 tablespoons all-purpose flour
- 1 tablespoon butter
- 1 cup beef broth
- 1 cup leek, chopped
- 2 cloves garlic, crushed
- 1 teaspoon cayenne pepper
- Sea salt flakes and crushed red pepper, to taste
- 1 cup sour cream
- 2 ½ tablespoons tomato paste

Directions

1. Place the beef along with the balsamic vinegar and the mustard in a mixing dish; cover and marinate in your refrigerator for about 1 hour.
2. Then, coat the beef strips with the flour; butter the inside of a baking dish and put the beef into the dish.
3. Add the broth, leeks and garlic. Cook at 380 degrees for 8 minutes. Pause the machine and add the cayenne pepper, salt, red pepper, sour cream and tomato paste; cook for additional 7 minutes.
4. Check for doneness and serve with warm egg noodles, if desired. Bon appétit!

581. Tender Beef Chuck with Brussels Sprouts

Preparation time: 25 minutes + marinating time

Servings 4

Nutrition Information:302 Calories; 14.2g Fat; 6.5g Carbs; 36.6g Protein; 1.6g Sugars

Ingredients

- 1 pound beef chuck shoulder steak
- 2 tablespoons vegetable oil
- 1 tablespoon red wine vinegar
- 1 teaspoon fine sea salt
- 1/2 teaspoon ground black pepper
- 1 teaspoon smoked paprika
- 1 teaspoon onion powder
- 1/2 teaspoon garlic powder
- 1/2 pound Brussels sprouts, cleaned and halved
- 1/2 teaspoon fennel seeds
- 1 teaspoon dried basil
- 1 teaspoon dried sage

Directions

1. Firstly, marinate the beef with vegetable oil, wine vinegar, salt, black pepper, paprika, onion powder, and garlic powder. Rub the marinade into the meat and let it stay at least for 3 hours.
2. Air fry at 390 degrees F for 10 minutes. Pause the machine and add the prepared Brussels sprouts;

sprinkle them with fennel seeds, basil, and sage.

3. Turn the machine to 380 degrees F; press the power button and cook for 5 more minutes. Pause the machine, stir and cook for further 10 minutes.
4. Next, remove the meat from the cooking basket and cook the vegetables a few minutes more if needed and according to your taste. Serve with your favorite mayo sauce.

582. All-In-One Spicy Spaghetti with Beef

Preparation time: 30 minutes

Servings 4

Nutrition Information:359 Calories; 5.5g Fat; 59.9g Carbs; 16.9g Protein; 2.7g Sugars

Ingredients

- 3/4 pound ground chuck
- 1 onion, peeled and finely chopped
- 1 teaspoon garlic paste
- 1 bell pepper, chopped
- 1 small-sized habanero pepper, deveined and finely minced
- 1/2 teaspoon dried rosemary
- 1/2 teaspoon dried marjoram
- 1 ¼ cups crushed tomatoes, fresh or canned
- 1/2 teaspoon sea salt flakes
- 1/4 teaspoon ground black pepper, or more to taste
- 1 package cooked spaghetti, to serve

Directions

1. In the Air Fryer baking dish, place the ground meat, onion, garlic paste, bell pepper, habanero pepper, rosemary, and the marjoram.
2. Air-fry, uncovered, for 10 to 11 minutes. Next step, stir in the tomatoes along with salt and pepper; cook 17 to 20 minutes. Serve over cooked spaghetti. Bon appétit!

583. Beer-Braised Short Loin

Preparation time: 15 minutes

Servings 4

Nutrition Information:379 Calories; 16.4g Fat; 3.7g Carbs; 46.0g Protein; 0.0g Sugars

Ingredients

- 1 ½ pounds short loin
- 2 tablespoons olive oil
- 1 bottle beer
- 2-3 cloves garlic, finely minced
- 2 Turkish bay leaves

Directions

1. Pat the beef dry; then, tenderize the beef with a meat mallet to soften the fibers. Place it in a large-sized mixing dish.
2. Add the remaining ingredients; toss to coat well and let it marinate for at least 1 hour.
3. Cook about 7 minutes at 395 degrees F; after that, pause the Air Fryer. Flip the meat over and cook for another 8 minutes, or until it's done.

584. Leftover Beef and Kale Omelet

Preparation time: 20 minutes

Servings 4

Nutrition Information:236 Calories; 13.7g Fat; 4.0g Carbs; 23.8g Protein; 1.0g Sugars

Ingredients

- Non-stick cooking spray
- 1/2 pound leftover beef, coarsely chopped
- 2 garlic cloves, pressed
- 1 cup kale, torn into pieces and wilted
- 1 tomato, chopped
- 1/4 teaspoon brown sugar
- 4 eggs, beaten
- 4 tablespoons heavy cream
- 1/2 teaspoon turmeric powder
- Salt and ground black pepper, to your liking
- 1/8 teaspoon ground allspice

Directions

1. Spritz the inside of four ramekins with a cooking spray.
2. Divide all of the above ingredients among the prepared ramekins. Stir until everything is well combined.
3. Air-fry at 360 degrees F for 16 minutes; check with a wooden stick and return the eggs to the Air Fryer for a few more minutes as needed. Serve immediately.

585. Chocolate and Pomegranate Bars

Preparation time: 2 hours

Cooking time: 10 minutes

Servings: 6

Ingredients:

- ½ cup milk
- 1 teaspoon vanilla extract
- 1 and ½ cups dark chocolate, chopped
- ½ cup almonds, chopped
- ½ cup pomegranate seeds

Directions:

1. Heat up a pan with the milk over medium low heat, add chocolate, stir for 5 minutes, take off heat add vanilla extract, half of the pomegranate seeds and half of the nuts and stir.
2. Pour this into a lined baking pan, spread, sprinkle a pinch of salt, the rest of the pomegranate arils and nuts, introduce in your air fryer and cook at 300 degrees F for 4 minutes.
3. Keep in the fridge for 2 hours before serving.
4. Enjoy!

Nutrition information: calories 68, fat 1, fiber 4, carbs 6, protein 1

586. Tomato Cake

Preparation time: 10 minutes

Cooking time: 30 minutes

Servings: 4

Ingredients:

- 1 and ½ cups flour
- 1 teaspoon cinnamon powder

- 1 teaspoon baking powder
- 1 teaspoon baking soda
- ¾ cup maple syrup
- 1 cup tomatoes chopped
- ½ cup olive oil
- 2 tablespoon apple cider vinegar

Directions:

1. In a bowl, mix flour with baking powder, baking soda, cinnamon and maple syrup and stir well.
2. In another bowl, mix tomatoes with olive oil and vinegar and stir well.
3. Combine the 2 mixtures, stir well, pour into a greased round pan that fits your air fryer, introduce in the fryer and cook at 360 degrees F for 30 minutes.
4. Leave cake to cool down, slice and serve.
5. Enjoy!

Nutrition information: calories 153, fat 2, fiber 1, carbs 25, protein 4

587. Berries Mix

Preparation time: 5 minutes

Cooking time: 6 minutes

Servings: 4

Ingredients:

- 2 tablespoons lemon juice
- 1 and ½ tablespoons maple syrup
- 1 and ½ tablespoons champagne vinegar
- 1 tablespoon olive oil
- 1 pound strawberries, halved
- 1 and ½ cups blueberries
- ¼ cup basil leaves, torn

Directions:

1. In a pan that fits your air fryer, mix lemon juice with maple syrup and vinegar, bring to a boil over medium high heat, add oil, blueberries and strawberries, stir, introduce in your air fryer and cook at 310 degrees F for 6 minutes.
2. Sprinkle basil on top and serve!
3. Enjoy!

Nutrition information: calories 163, fat 4, fiber 4, carbs 10, protein 2.1

588. Passion Fruit Pudding

Preparation time: 10 minutes

Cooking time: 40 minutes

Servings: 6

Ingredients:

- 1 cup Paleo passion fruit curd
- 4 passion fruits, pulp and seeds
- 3 and ½ ounces maple syrup
- 3 eggs
- 2 ounces ghee, melted
- 3 and ½ ounces almond milk
- ½ cup almond flour
- ½ teaspoon baking powder

Directions:

1. In a bowl, mix the half of the fruit curd with passion fruit seeds and pulp, stir and divide into 6 heat proof ramekins.
2. In a bowl, whisked eggs with maple syrup, ghee, the rest of the curd,

baking powder, milk and flour and stir well.
3. Divide this into the ramekins as well, introduce in the fryer and cook at 200 degrees F for 40 minutes.
4. Leave puddings to cool down and serve!
5. Enjoy!

Nutrition information: calories 430, fat 22, fiber 3, carbs 7, protein 8

589. Air Fried Apples

Preparation time: 10 minutes

Cooking time: 17 minutes

Servings: 4

Ingredients:

- 4 big apples, cored
- A handful raisins
- 1 tablespoon cinnamon, ground
- Raw honey to the taste

Directions:

1. Fill each apple with raisins, sprinkle cinnamon, drizzle honey, put them in your air fryer and cook at 367 degrees F for 17 minutes.
2. Leave them to cool down and serve.
3. Enjoy!

Nutrition information:calories 220, fat 3, fiber 4, carbs 6, protein 10

590. Pumpkin Cookies

Preparation time: 10 minutes

Cooking time: 15 minutes

Servings: 24

Ingredients:

- 2 and ½ cups flour
- ½ teaspoon baking soda
- 1 tablespoon flax seed, ground
- 3 tablespoons water
- ½ cup pumpkin flesh, mashed
- ¼ cup honey
- 2 tablespoons butter
- 1 teaspoon vanilla extract
- ½ cup dark chocolate chips

Directions:

1. In a bowl, mix flax seed with water, stir and leave aside for a few minutes.
2. In another bowl, mix flour with salt and baking soda.
3. In a third bowl, mix honey with pumpkin puree, butter, vanilla extract and flaxseed.
4. Combine flour with honey mix and chocolate chips and stir.
5. Scoop 1 tablespoon of cookie dough on a lined baking sheet that fits your air fryer, repeat with the rest of the dough, introduce them in your air fryer and cook at 350 degrees F for 15 minutes.
6. Leave cookies to cool down and serve.
7. Enjoy!

Nutrition information:calories 140, fat 2, fiber 2, carbs 7, protein 10

591. Figs and Coconut Butter Mix

Preparation time: 6 minutes

Cooking time: 4 minutes

Servings: 3

Ingredients:

- 2 tablespoons coconut butter
- 12 figs, halved
- ¼ cup sugar
- 1 cup almonds, toasted and chopped

Directions:

1. Put butter in a pan that fits your air fryer and melt over medium high heat.
2. Add figs, sugar and almonds, toss, introduce in your air fryer and cook at 300 degrees F for 4 minutes.
3. Divide into bowls and serve cold.
4. Enjoy!

Nutrition information: calories 170, fat 4, fiber 5, carbs 7, protein 9

592. Lemon Bars

Preparation time: 10 minutes

Cooking time: 25 minutes

Servings: 6

Ingredients:

- 4 eggs
- 2 and ¼ cups flour
- Juice from 2 lemons
- 1 cup butter, soft
- 2 cups sugar

Directions:

1. In a bowl, mix butter with ½ cup sugar and 2 cups flour, stir well, press on the bottom of a pan that fits your air fryer, introduce in the fryer and cook at 350 degrees F for 10 minutes.
2. In another bowl, mix the rest of the sugar with the rest of the flour, eggs and lemon juice, whisk well and spread over crust.
3. Introduce in the fryer at 350 degrees F for 15 minutes more, leave aside to cool down, cut bars and serve them.
4. Enjoy!

Nutrition information:calories 125, fat 4, fiber 4, carbs 16, protein 2

593. Pears and Espresso Cream

Preparation time: 10 minutes

Cooking time: 30 minutes

Servings: 4

Ingredients:

1. 4 pears, halved and cored
2. 2 tablespoons lemon juice
3. 1 tablespoon sugar
4. 2 tablespoons water
5. 2 tablespoons butter
6. For the cream:
7. 1 cup whipping cream
8. 1 cup mascarpone
9. 1/3 cup sugar
10. 2 tablespoons espresso, cold

Directions:

1. In a bowl, mix pears halves with lemon juice, 1 tablespoons sugar, butter and water, toss well, transfer

them to your air fryer and cook at 360 degrees F for 30 minutes.

2. Meanwhile, in a bowl, mix whipping cream with mascarpone, 1/3 cup sugar and espresso, whisk really well and keep in the fridge until pears are done.
3. Divide pears on plates, top with espresso cream and serve them.
4. Enjoy!

Nutrition information:calories 211, fat 5, fiber 7, carbs 8, protein 7

594. Poppyseed Cake

Preparation time: 10 minutes

Cooking time: 30 minutes

Servings: 6

Ingredients:

- 1 and ¼ cups flour
- 1 teaspoon baking powder
- ¾ cup sugar
- 1 tablespoon orange zest, grated
- 2 teaspoons lime zest, grated
- ½ cup butter, soft
- 2 eggs, whisked
- ½ teaspoon vanilla extract
- 2 tablespoons poppy seeds
- 1 cup milk
- For the cream:
- 1 cup sugar
- ½ cup passion fruit puree
- 3 tablespoons butter, melted
- 4 egg yolks

Directions:

1. In a bowl, mix flour with baking powder, ¾ cup sugar, orange zest and lime zest and stir.
2. Add ½ cup butter, eggs, poppy seeds, vanilla and milk, stir using your mixer, pour into a cake pan that fits your air fryer and cook at 350 degrees F for about 30 minutes.
3. Meanwhile, heat up a pan with 3 tablespoons butter over medium heat, add sugar and stir until it dissolves.
4. Take off heat, add passion fruit puree and egg yolks gradually and whisk really well.
5. Take cake out of the fryer, cool it down a bit and cut into halves horizontally.
6. Spread ¼ of passion fruit cream over one half, top with the other cake half and spread ¼ of the cream on top.
7. Serve cold.
8. Enjoy!

Nutrition information:calories 211, fat 6, fiber 7, carbs 12, protein 6

595. Sweet Squares

Preparation time: 10 minutes

Cooking time: 30 minutes

Servings: 6

Ingredients:

- 1 cup flour
- ½ cup butter, soft
- 1 cup sugar
- ¼ cup powdered sugar
- 2 teaspoons lemon peel, grated
- 2 tablespoons lemon juice

- 2 eggs, whisked
- ½ teaspoon baking powder

Directions:

1. In a bowl, mix flour with powdered sugar and butter, stir well, press on the bottom of a pan that fits your air fryer, introduce in the fryer and bake at 350 degrees F for 14 minutes.
2. In another bowl, mix sugar with lemon juice, lemon peel, eggs and baking powder, stir using your mixer and spread over baked crust.
3. Bake for 15 minutes more, leave aside to cool down, cut into medium squares and serve cold.
4. Enjoy!

Nutrition information:calories 100, fat 4, fiber 1, carbs 12, protein 1

596. Plum Bars

Preparation time: 10 minutes

Cooking time: 16 minutes

Servings: 8

Ingredients:

- 2 cups dried plums
- 6 tablespoons water
- 2 cup rolled oats
- 1 cup brown sugar
- ½ teaspoon baking soda
- 1 teaspoon cinnamon powder
- 2 tablespoons butter, melted
- 1 egg, whisked
- Cooking spray

Directions:

1. In your food processor, mix plums with water and blend until you obtain a sticky spread.
2. In a bowl, mix oats with cinnamon, baking soda, sugar, egg and butter and whisk really well.
3. Press half of the oats mix in a baking pan that fits your air fryer sprayed with cooking oil, spread plums mix and top with the other half of the oats mix.
4. Introduce in your air fryer and cook at 350 degrees F for 16 minutes.
5. Leave mix aside to cool down, cut into medium bars and serve.
6. Enjoy!

Nutrition information:calories 111, fat 5, fiber 6, carbs 12, protein 6

597. Plum and Currant Tart

Preparation time: 30 minutes

Cooking time: 35 minutes

Servings: 6

Ingredients:

- For the crumble:
- ¼ cup almond flour
- ¼ cup millet flour
- 1 cup brown rice flour
- ½ cup cane sugar
- 10 tablespoons butter, soft
- 3 tablespoons milk
- For the filling:
- 1 pound small plums, pitted and halved
- 1 cup white currants
- 2 tablespoons cornstarch

- 3 tablespoons sugar
- ½ teaspoon vanilla extract
- ½ teaspoon cinnamon powder
- ¼ teaspoon ginger powder
- 1 teaspoon lime juice

Directions:

1. In a bowl, mix brown rice flour with ½ cup sugar, millet flour, almond flour, butter and milk and stir until you obtain a sand like dough.
2. Reserve ¼ of the dough, press the rest of the dough into a tart pan that fits your air fryer and keep in the fridge for 30 minutes.
3. Meanwhile, in a bowl, mix plums with currants, 3 tablespoons sugar, cornstarch, vanilla extract, cinnamon, ginger and lime juice and stir well.
4. Pour this over tart crust, crumble reserved dough on top, introduce in your air fryer and cook at 350 degrees F for 35 minutes.
5. Leave tart to cool down, slice and serve.
6. Enjoy!

Nutrition information:calories 200, fat 5, fiber 4, carbs 8, protein 6

598. Tasty Orange Cookies

Preparation time: 10 minutes

Cooking time: 12 minutes

Servings: 8

Ingredients:

- 2 cups flour
- 1 teaspoon baking powder
- ½ cup butter, soft
- ¾ cup sugar
- 1 egg, whisked
- 1 teaspoon vanilla extract
- 1 tablespoon orange zest, grated
- For the filling:
- 4 ounces cream cheese, soft
- ½ cup butter
- 2 cups powdered sugar

Directions:

1. In a bowl, mix cream cheese with ½ cup butter and 2 cups powdered sugar, stir well using your mixer and leave aside for now.
2. In another bowl, mix flour with baking powder.
3. In a third bowl, mix ½ cup butter with ¾ cup sugar, egg, vanilla extract and orange zest and whisk well.
4. Combine flour with orange mix, stir well and scoop 1 tablespoon of the mix on a lined baking sheet that fits your air fryer.
5. Repeat with the rest of the orange batter, introduce in the fryer and cook at 340 degrees F for 12 minutes.
6. Leave cookies to cool down, spread cream filling on half of them top with the other cookies and serve.
7. Enjoy!

Nutrition information:calories 124, fat 5, fiber 6, carbs 8, protein 4

599. Cashew Bars

Preparation time: 10 minutes

Cooking time: 15 minutes

Servings: 6

Ingredients:

- 1/3 cup honey
- ¼ cup almond meal
- 1 tablespoon almond butter
- 1 and ½ cups cashews, chopped
- 4 dates, chopped
- ¾ cup coconut, shredded
- 1 tablespoon chia seeds

Directions:

1. In a bowl, mix honey with almond meal and almond butter and stir well.
2. Add cashews, coconut, dates and chia seeds and stir well again.
3. Spread this on a lined baking sheet that fits your air fryer and press well.
4. Introduce in the fryer and cook at 300 degrees F for 15 minutes.
5. Leave mix to cool down, cut into medium bars and serve.
6. Enjoy!

Nutrition information:calories 121, fat 4, fiber 7, carbs 5, protein 6

600. Brown Butter Cookies

Preparation time: 10 minutes

Cooking time: 10 minutes

Servings: 6

Ingredients:

- 1 and ½ cups butter
- 2 cups brown sugar
- 2 eggs, whisked
- 3 cups flour
- 2/3 cup pecans, chopped
- 2 teaspoons vanilla extract
- 1 teaspoon baking soda
- ½ teaspoon baking powder

Directions:

1. Heat up a pan with the butter over medium heat, stir until it melts, add brown sugar and stir until this dissolves.
2. In a bowl, mix flour with pecans, vanilla extract, baking soda, baking powder and eggs and stir well.
3. Add brown butter, stir well and arrange spoonfuls of this mix on a lined baking sheet that fits your air fryer.
4. Introduce in the fryer and cook at 340 degrees F for 10 minutes.
5. Leave cookies to cool down and serve.
6. Enjoy!

Nutrition information:calories 144, fat 5, fiber 6, carbs 19, protein 2

601. Sweet Potato Cheesecake

Preparation time: 10 minutes

Cooking time: 5 minutes

Servings: 4

Ingredients:

- 4 tablespoons butter, melted
- 6 ounces mascarpone, soft
- 8 ounces cream cheese, soft
- 2/3 cup graham crackers, crumbled
- ¾ cup milk
- 1 teaspoon vanilla extract
- 2/3 cup sweet potato puree
- ¼ teaspoons cinnamon powder

Directions:

1. In a bowl, mix butter with crumbled crackers, stir well, press on the bottom of a cake pan that fits your air fryer and keep in the fridge for now.
2. In another bowl, mix cream cheese with mascarpone, sweet potato puree, milk, cinnamon and vanilla and whisk really well.
3. Spread this over crust, introduce in your air fryer, cook at 300 degrees F for 4 minutes and keep in the fridge for a few hours before serving.
4. Enjoy!

Nutrition information:calories 172, fat 4, fiber 6, carbs 8, protein 3

602. Peach Pie

Preparation time: 10 minutes

Cooking time: 35 minutes

Servings: 4

Ingredients:

- 1 pie dough
- 2 and ¼ pounds peaches, pitted and chopped
- 2 tablespoons cornstarch
- ½ cup sugar
- 2 tablespoons flour
- A pinch of nutmeg, ground
- 1 tablespoon dark rum
- 1 tablespoon lemon juice
- 2 tablespoons butter, melted

Directions:

1. Roll pie dough into a pie pan that fits your air fryer and press well.
2. In a bowl, mix peaches with cornstarch, sugar, flour, nutmeg, rum, lemon juice and butter and stir well.
3. Pour and spread this into pie pan, introduce in your air fryer and cook at 350 degrees F for 35 minutes.
4. Serve warm or cold.
5. Enjoy!

Nutrition information:calories 231, fat 6, fiber 7, carbs 9, protein 5

603. Cranberry Pudding

Preparation time: 10 minutes

Cooking time: 30 minutes

Servings: 4

Ingredients:

- 4 ounces dried cranberries, chopped
- A drizzle of olive oil
- 4 ounces dried apricots, chopped
- 1 cup white flour
- 3 teaspoons baking powder
- 1 cup coconut sugar
- 1 teaspoon ginger powder
- A pinch of cinnamon powder
- 15 tablespoons coconut butter
- 3 tablespoons maple syrup
- 3 tablespoons flax meal mixed with 3 tablespoons water
- 1 carrot, grated

Directions:

Grease a heatproof pudding pan with a drizzle of oil.

1. In a blender, mix flour with baking powder, sugar, cinnamon, ginger, butter, maple syrup and flax meal

and pulse well.

2. Add dried fruits and carrot, fold them into the batter and spread this mix into the pudding mold.
3. Put the pudding in your air fryer and cook at 365 degrees F for 30 minutes.
4. Leave the pudding aside to cool down, slice and serve.
5. Enjoy!

Nutrition information:calories 262, fat 7, fiber 4, carbs 12, protein 4

604. Chocolate and Coconut Bars

Preparation time: 10 minutes

Cooking time: 7 minutes

Servings: 12

Ingredients:

- 1 cup sugar free and vegan chocolate chips
- 2 tablespoons coconut butter
- 2/3 cup coconut cream
- 2 tablespoons stevia
- ¼ teaspoon vanilla extract

Directions:

1. Put the cream in a bowl, add stevia, butter and chocolate chips and stir
2. Leave aside for 5 minutes, stir well and mix the vanilla.
3. Transfer the mix into a lined baking sheet, introduce in your air fryer and cook at 356 degrees F for 7 minutes.
4. Leave the mix aside to cool down, slice and serve.
5. Enjoy!

Nutrition information:calories 120, fat 5, fiber 4, carbs 6, protein 1

605. Raspberry Bars

Preparation time: 10 minutes

Cooking time: 6 minutes

Servings: 12

Ingredients:

- ½ cup coconut butter, melted
- ½ cup coconut oil
- ½ cup raspberries, dried
- ¼ cup swerve
- ½ cup coconut, shredded

Directions:

1. In your food processor, blend dried berries very well.
2. In a bowl that fits your air fryer, mix oil with butter, swerve, coconut and raspberries, toss well, introduce in the fryer and cook at 320 degrees F for 6 minutes.
3. Spread this on a lined baking sheet, keep in the fridge for an hour, slice and serve.
4. Enjoy!

Nutrition information:calories 164, fat 22, fiber 2, carbs 4, protein 2

606. Vanilla and Blueberry Squares

Preparation time: 10 minutes

Cooking time: 20 minutes

Servings: 8

Ingredients:

- 5 ounces coconut oil, melted
- ½ teaspoon baking powder
- 4 tablespoons stevia
- 1 teaspoon vanilla
- 4 ounces coconut cream
- 3 tablespoons flax meal combined with 3 tablespoons water
- ½ cup blueberries

Directions:

1. In a bowl, mix coconut oil with flax meal, coconut cream, vanilla, stevia and baking powder and blend using an immersion blender.
2. Fold blueberries, pour everything into a square baking dish that fits your air fryer, introduce in the fryer and cook at 320 degrees F for 20 minutes.
3. Slice into squares and serve cold.
4. Enjoy!

Nutrition information:calories 150, fat 2, fiber 3, carbs 6, protein 4

607. Cocoa Brownies

Preparation time: 10 minutes

Cooking time: 20 minutes

Servings: 12

Ingredients:

- 6 ounces coconut oil, melted
- 3 tablespoons flax meal combined with 3 tablespoons water
- 3 ounces cocoa powder
- 2 teaspoons vanilla
- ½ teaspoon baking powder
- 4 ounces coconut cream
- 5 tablespoons stevia

Directions:

- In a blender, mix flax meal with oil, cocoa powder, baking powder, vanilla, cream and stevia and stir using a mixer.
- Pour this into a lined baking dish that fits your air fryer, introduce in the fryer and cook at 350 degrees F for 20 minutes.
- Slice into rectangles and serve cold
- Enjoy!

Nutrition information:calories 208, fat 14, fiber 2, carbs 13, protein 5

608. Easy Blackberries Scones

Preparation time: 10 minutes

Cooking time: 10 minutes

Servings: 10

Ingredients:

- ½ cup coconut flour
- 1 cup blackberries
- 2 tablespoons flax meal combined with 2 tablespoons water
- ½ cup coconut cream
- ½ cup coconut butter
- ½ cup almond flour
- 5 tablespoons stevia
- 2 teaspoons vanilla extract
- 2 teaspoons baking powder

Directions:

1. In a bowl, mix almond flour with coconut flour, baking powder and blackberries and stir well.
2. In another bowl, mix cream with butter, vanilla extract, stevia and flax meal and stir well.
3. Combine the 2 mixtures, stir until you obtain your dough, shape 10 triangles from this mix, place them on a lined baking sheet, introduce in the air fryer and cook at 350 degrees F for 10 minutes.
4. Serve them cold.
5. Enjoy!

Nutrition information:calories 170, fat 2, fiber 2, carbs 4, protein 3

609. Easy Buns

Preparation time: 10 minutes

Cooking time: 30 minutes

Servings: 8

Ingredients:

- ½ cup coconut flour
- 1/3 cup psyllium husks
- 2 tablespoons stevia
- 1 teaspoon baking powder
- ½ teaspoon cinnamon powder
- ½ teaspoon cloves, ground
- 3 tablespoons flax meal combined with 3 tablespoons water
- Some chocolate chips, unsweetened

Directions:

- In a bowl, mix flour with psyllium husks, swerve, baking powder, salt, cinnamon, cloves and chocolate chips and stir well.
- Add water and flax meal, stir well until you obtain a dough, shape 8 buns and arrange them on a lined baking sheet.
- Introduce in the air fryer and cook at 350 degrees for 30 minutes.
- Serve these buns warm.

Nutrition information:calories 140, fat 3, fiber 3, carbs 7, protein 6

610. Lemon Cream

Preparation time: 10 minutes

Cooking time: 30 minutes

Servings: 6

Ingredients:

- 1 and 1/3 pint almond milk
- 1 medium banana
- 4 tablespoons lemon zest, grated
- 3 tablespoons flax meal combined with 3 tablespoons water
- 5 tablespoons stevia
- 2 tablespoons lemon juice

Directions:

1. In a bowl, mix mashed banana with milk and swerve and stir very well.
2. Add lemon zest and lemon juice, whisk well, pour into ramekins, place them in your air fryer, cook at 360 degrees F for 30 minutes and serve cold.
3. Enjoy!

Nutrition information:calories 180, fat 6, fiber 2, carbs 5, protein 7

611. Cocoa Berries Cream

Preparation time: 10 minutes

Cooking time: 10 minutes

Servings: 4

Ingredients:

- 3 tablespoons cocoa powder
- 14 ounces coconut cream
- 1 cup blackberries
- 1 cup raspberries
- 2 tablespoons stevia

Directions:

1. In a bowl, whisk cocoa powder with stevia and cream and stir.
2. Add raspberries and blackberries, toss gently, transfer to a pan that fits your air fryer, introduce in the fryer and cook at 350 degrees F for 10 minutes.
3. Divide into bowls and serve cold.
4. Enjoy!

Nutrition information:calories 205, fat 34, fiber 2, carbs 6, protein 2

612. Easy Cocoa Pudding

Preparation time: 10 minutes

Cooking time: 20 minutes

Servings: 2

Ingredients:

- 2 tablespoons water
- ½ tablespoon agar
- 4 tablespoons stevia
- 4 tablespoons cocoa powder
- 2 cups coconut milk, hot

Directions:

1. In a bowl, mix milk with stevia and cocoa powder and stir well.
2. In a bowl, mix agar with water, stir well, add to the cocoa mix, stir and transfer to a pudding pan that fits your air fryer.
3. Introduce in the fryer and cook at 356 degrees F for 20 minutes.
4. Serve the pudding cold.
5. Enjoy!

Nutrition information:calories 170, fat 2, fiber 1, carbs 4, protein 3

613. Blueberry Crackers

Preparation time: 10 minutes

Cooking time: 30 minutes

Servings: 12

Ingredients:

- ½ cup coconut butter
- ½ cup coconut oil, melted
- 1 cup blueberries
- 3 tablespoons coconut sugar

Directions:

1. In a pan that fits your air fryer, mix coconut butter with coconut oil, raspberries and sugar, toss, introduce in the fryer and cook at 367 degrees F for 30 minutes
2. Spread on a lined baking sheet, keep in the fridge for a few hours, slice crackers and serve.
3. Enjoy!

Nutrition information:calories 174, fat 5, fiber 2, carbs 4, protein 7

614. Zucchini Bread

Preparation time: 10 minutes
Cooking time: 35 minutes
Servings: 6

Ingredients:

- 1 cup natural applesauce
- 1 ½ banana, mashed
- 1 tablespoon vanilla extract
- 4 tablespoons coconut sugar
- 2 cups zucchini, grated
- 2 and ½ cups coconut flour
- ½ cup baking cocoa powder
- 1 teaspoon baking soda
- ¼ teaspoon baking powder
- 1 teaspoon cinnamon powder
- ½ cup walnuts, chopped
- Cooking spray

Directions:

1. Grease a loaf pan with cooking spray, add zucchini, sugar, vanilla, banana, applesauce, flour, cocoa powder, baking soda, baking powder, cinnamon and walnuts, whisk well, introduce in the fryer and cook at 365 degrees F for 35 minutes.
2. Leave the bread to cool down, slice and serve.
3. Enjoy!

Nutrition information:calories 192, fat 3, fiber 6, carbs 8, protein 3

615. Pear Pudding

Preparation time: 5 minutes
Cooking time: 30 minutes
Servings: 4

Ingredients:

- 2 cups pears, chopped
- 2 cups coconut milk
- 1 tablespoon coconut butter, melted
- 3 tablespoons stevia
- ½ teaspoon cinnamon powder
- 1 cup coconut flakes
- ½ cup walnuts, chopped

Directions:

1. In a pudding pan, mix milk with stevia, butter, coconut, cinnamon, pears and walnuts, stir, introduce in your air fryer and cook at 365 degrees F for 30 minutes
2. Divide into bowls and serve cold.
3. Enjoy!

Nutrition information:calories 202, fat 3, fiber 4, carbs 8, protein 7

616. Cauliflower Pudding

Preparation time: 10 minutes
Cooking time: 30 minutes
Servings: 4

Ingredients:

- 2 and ½ cups water
- 1 cup coconut sugar
- 2 cups cauliflower rice
- 2 cinnamon sticks

- ½ cup coconut, shredded

Directions:

1. In a pan that fits your air fryer, mix water with coconut sugar, cauliflower rice, cinnamon and coconut, stir, introduce in the fryer and cook at 365 degrees F for 30 minutes
2. Divide pudding into cups and serve cold.
3. Enjoy!

Nutrition information:calories 203, fat 4, fiber 6, carbs 9, protein 4

617. Sweet Cauliflower Rice

Preparation time: 10 minutes

Cooking time: 30 minutes

Servings: 4

Ingredients:

- 1 and ½ cups cauliflower rice
- 1 and ½ teaspoons cinnamon powder
- 1/3 cup stevia
- 2 tablespoons coconut butter, melted
- 2 apples, peeled, cored and sliced
- 1 cup natural apple juice
- 3 cups almond milk
- ½ cup cherries, dried

Directions:

1. In a pan that fits your air fryer, combine rice with cinnamon, stevia, butter, apples, apple juice, almond milk and cherries, toss, introduce in your air fryer and cook at 365 degrees F for 30 minutes.
2. Divide between bowls and serve.
3. Enjoy!

Nutrition information:calories 160,fat 3, fiber 3, carbs 7, protein 5

618. Espresso Vanilla Dessert

Preparation time: 10 minutes

Cooking time: 20 minutes

Servings: 4

Ingredients:

- 1 cup almond milk
- 4 tablespoons flax meal
- 2 tablespoons coconut flour
- 2 and ½ cups water
- 2 tablespoons stevia
- 1 teaspoon espresso powder
- 2 teaspoons vanilla extract
- Coconut cream for serving

Directions:

1. In a pan that fits your air fryer, mix flax meal with flour, water, stevia, milk, vanilla and espresso powder, stir, introduce in the fryer and cook at 365 degrees F for 20 minutes.
2. Divide into bowls and serve with coconut cream on top.
3. Enjoy!

Nutrition information:calories 202, fat 2, fiber 1, carbs 6, protein 4

619. Sweet Rhubarb

Preparation time: 10 minutes

Cooking time: 10 minutes

Servings: 4

Ingredients:

- 5 cups rhubarb, chopped
- 2 tablespoons coconut butter, melted
- 1/3 cup water
- 1 tablespoon stevia
- 1 teaspoon vanilla extract

Directions:

1. Put rhubarb, ghee, water, stevia and vanilla extract in a pan that fits your air fryer, introduce in the fryer and cook at 365 degrees F for 10 minutes
2. Divide into small bowls and serve cold.
3. Enjoy!

Nutrition information:calories 103, fat 2, fiber 1, carbs 6, protein 2

620. Pineapple and Apricots Delight

Preparation time: 10 minutes

Cooking time: 12 minutes

Servings: 10

Ingredients:

- 6 cups canned pineapple chunks, drained
- 4 cups canned apricots, halved and drained
- 3 cups natural applesauce
- 2 cups canned mandarin oranges, drained
- 2 tablespoons stevia
- 1 teaspoon cinnamon powder

Directions:

1. Put pineapples, apricots, applesauce, oranges, cinnamon and stevia in a pan that fits your air fryer, introduce in the fryer and cook at 360 degrees F for 12 minutes.
2. Divide into small bowls and serve cold.
3. Enjoy!

Nutrition information:calories 130, fat 1, fiber 2, carbs 7, protein 2

30-day meal plan

Day	Breakfast	Lunch/dinner	Snack	Dessert
1	Potato Frittata	Italian Eggplant Sandwich	Easy Broccoli Patties	Cinnamon Rolls
2	Healthy Asparagus Frittata	Tasty Hash Brown toasts	Basil Crackers	Cocoa and Almond Bars
3	Yummy Creamy Eggs	Special Lunch Seafood Stew	Cauliflower Crackers	Blueberry Pudding
4	Peppers Frittata	Bacon Pudding	Squash Party Muffins	Tangerine Cake
5	Browns Mixed Bell	Meatballs Sandwich	Potato and Beans Dip	Cream Cheese Cookies
6	Special Hash	Beef Stew	Polenta Biscuits	Coffee Cream
7	Eggs, Sausage and Cheese Mix	Cheese Ravioli and Marinara Sauce	Corn Dip	Strawberry Cream
8	Baked Eggs	Turkey Cakes	Scallions and Shallots Dip	Rum Cheesecake
9	Casserole Delight	Lunch Pork and Potatoes	Fast Parsley Dip	Pineapple and Carrot Cake
10	Simple Breakfast Biscuits	Creamy Chicken Stew	Cranberry Dip	Maple Apples
11	Quick Turkey Burrito	Sweet Potato Lunch Casserole	Creamy Leek Spread	Simple Nutmeg Pumpkin Pie
12	Yummy Hash	Air Fried Thai Salad	Simple Fennel and Tomato Spread	Orange Cake
13	Bacon and Tomato	Turkey Burgers	Apple and Dates Dip	Cream of Tartar Bread
14	Smoked Sausage Breakfast	Coconut and Chicken Casserole	Buttery Carrot Dip	Zucchini Bread
15	Veggie Burritos	Special Gnocchi	Broccoli Spread	Yogurt Cake
16	Creamy Breakfast Tofu	Succulent Turkey Breast	Easy Eggplant Spread	Lemon Cake
17	Breakfast Doughnuts	Awesome Buttermilk Chicken	Onion and Chili Dip	Cinnamon Apples
18	Breakfast Mix	Fried Thai Salad	Cheesy Chicken Rolls	Butter Donuts
19	French Beans and Egg	Delicious Fajitas	Chili Tomato alsa	Cinnamon Pears

20	Long Beans Omelet	Mouth-watering Chicken Kabobs	Tomatoes and Dates Salsa	Turkey Wontons with Garlic-Parmesan Sauce
21	Corn Pudding	Stuffed Portobello Mushrooms	Spiced Tomato Party Mix	The Best London Broil Ever
22	Italian Eggplant Sandwich	Delicious Lentils Fritters	Hot Dip	Herbed Crumbed Filet Mignon
23	Tomato and Eggs Mix	Tasty Hot Dogs	Fast Mango Dip	Grilled Lemony Pork Chops
24	Parmesan Breakfast Muffins	Shrimp Croquettes	Traditional Sweet Bacon Snack	Country-Style Pork Meatloaf
25	Vanilla Toast	Tasty Turkey Burgers	Cheesy Chicken Wings	Sausage, Pepper and Fontina Frittata
26	Breakfast Yummy Tofu Scramble	Different Pasta Salad	Holyday Beef Patties	Easy Pork Burgers with Blue Cheese
27	Rice, Almonds Pudding	Chicken Salad	Kale and Celery Crackers	Onion Rings Wrapped in Bacon
28	Pesto Breakfast Toast	Beef Cubes	Eggplant Appetizer Salad	Easiest Pork Chops Ever
29	Sausage Omelet	Japanese Style Chicken	Italian Veggie Appetizer Salad	Baked Eggs with Kale and Ham
30	Polenta Cakes	Asian Chicken	Chickpeas Dip	Famous Cheese and Bacon Rolls

CONCLUSION

A healthy means of replicating the things that you miss most about fried foods; air frying is a perfect way to add variety to everyday meals. A must have fixture in any kitchen, the air fryer is easy to use, fast to cook with, and ideal for adding a healthier touch to previously unhealthy foods.

I hope that through reading through this book, you have come to understand the idea of air frying a little more. With this knowledge, I also hope that you dare to invest in your own air fryer and give air frying a try! While it may seem a little overwhelming at first, after reading your machine's manual, you will be frying your own food in no time. So, what are you waiting for? Grab your air fryer and start trying these delicious 5 ingredient or less low budget recipes today!

67342937R00152

Made in the USA
Columbia, SC
25 July 2019